More Praise for *The 7 Hidden Reasons Employees Leave:*

"If you are a business leader who recognizes that maximizing your company's human capital will be the key for competitive success in the 21st century, this book offers a practical guide to retaining that valuable asset. Backed by a mixture of research, data, and common sense, Branham provides the business rationale and specific steps that any manager can implement to combat the issues that are driving their employees to leave."

—Wayne M. Keegan, Chief Human Resources Officer,
Ingram Book Group, Inc.

"Leigh Branham has written a concise and engaging book. Several key factors make this a valuable read: He has included insights that underscore the mutuality between employer and employee in retention efforts. He has used evidence of various levels to support his framework. And, he provides case examples to illustrate his points. This is definitely a book any new manager would want to read."

—Karen Haase-Herrick, RN, MN, 2004 President,
American Organization of Nurse Executives

"If you truly understand that your people are your most important asset, this is must reading for all of your management team! A clear roadmap for positioning your company as an employer of choice!"

—Melanie Ways, PHR, Human Resources Manager,
EEO/Affirmative Action Officer, Duncan Aviation, Inc.

"The book provides a great 'roadmap' for successful hiring and retention, with many common (and not-so-common) sense ideas. I found especially instructive the real-world examples from companies that have experienced success retaining top talent."

Keith Wiedenkeller, Senior Vice President,
Human Resources, AMC Entertainment, Inc.

The 7 Hidden Reasons Employees Leave

How to Recognize the Subtle Signs and Act Before It's Too Late

Leigh Branham

American Management Association

New York • Atlanta • Brussels • Chicago • Mexico City • San Francisco
Shanghai • Tokyo • Toronto • Washington, D.C.

Library of Congress Cataloging-in-Publication Data

Branham, Leigh.
      The 7 hidden reasons employees leave : how to recognize the subtle signs and act before it's too late / Leigh Branham.
            p.   cm.
      Includes index.
      ISBN 0-8144-0851-6
      1. Labor turnover.   2. Employee retention.   3. Job satisfaction.
I. Title: Seven hidden reasons employees leave.   II. Title.

HF5549.5.T8B7   2005
658.3'14—dc22

                                        2004013353

Printing Number

10   9   8   7   6   5   4

THIS BOOK IS DEDICATED TO THE LOVING MEMORY OF MY PARENTS, FRANK LEIGH BRANHAM, SR. AND BETTY GUILD BRANHAM, AND MY BROTHER, LEWIS GUILD BRANHAM.

PREFACE   xi
ACKNOWLEDGMENTS   xiii

Chapter One

WHY CARE ABOUT WHY THEY LEAVE?   1
  Managers Will Not Hear What Workers Will Not Speak   2
  Turnover: Just a "Cost of Doing Business?"   5
  When the Tide Turns, Mindsets Must Change   7
  What About HR's Role in Exit Interviewing?   8

Chapter Two

HOW THEY DISENGAGE AND QUIT   11
  The Disengagement Process   11
  The Deliberation Process   15

Chapter Three

WHY THEY LEAVE: WHAT THE RESEARCH REVEALS   17
  Why Employees Say They Leave   20
  What Caused Their Initial Dissatisfaction?   24
  A Few Words About Pay   24
  Respecting the Differences   26
  Who Has the Power to Meet These Needs?   27
  The Next Seven Chapters: Hidden Reasons and Practical Actions   28

Chapter Four

REASON #1: THE JOB OR WORKPLACE WAS NOT AS EXPECTED   31
  Hidden Mutual Expectations: The Psychological Contract   34

How to Recognize the Warning Signs of Unmet Expectations   37
Obstacles to Meeting Mutual Expectations   38
Engagement Practices for Matching Mutual Expectations   39
How Prospective Employees Can Do Their Part   44
The Beginning or Ending of Trust   45
Employer-of-Choice Engagement Practices Review and
    Checklist   45

Chapter Five

REASON #2: THE MISMATCH BETWEEN JOB AND PERSON   **47**

What's Missing: A Passion for Matching   49
Common Misconceptions and Truths About Talent   50
Recognizing the Signs of Job-Person Mismatch   52
Obstacles to Preventing and Correcting Job-Person Mismatch   53
Best-Fit Selection Practices   54
Best Practices for Engaging and Re-Engaging Through Job Task
    Assignment   62
The Employee's Role in the Matching Process   67
Employer-of-Choice Engagement Practices Review and
    Checklist   68

Chapter Six

REASON #3: TOO LITTLE COACHING AND FEEDBACK   **70**

Why Coaching and Feedback Are Important to Engagement and
    Retention   72
Why Don't Managers Provide Coaching and Feedback?   73
Recognizing the Signs   75
More Than an Event: It's About the Relationship   75
Engagement Practices for Coaching and Giving Feedback   77
A Five-Step Coaching Process   82
What the Employee Can Do to Get More Feedback and
    Coaching   89
Employer-of-Choice Engagement Practices Review and
    Checklist   90

Chapter Seven

REASON #4: TOO FEW GROWTH AND ADVANCEMENT
OPPORTUNITIES   **93**

What They Are Really Saying   95

Employers of Choice Start by Understanding the New Career
Realities 97
Recognizing the Signs of Blocked Growth and Career
Frustration 99
Best Practices for Creating Growth and Advancement
Opportunities 100
What Employees Can Do to Create Their Own Growth and
Advancement Opportunities 114
Employer-of-Choice Engagement Practices Review and
Checklist 115

Chapter Eight

REASON #5: FEELING DEVALUED AND UNRECOGNIZED **118**
Why Managers Are Reluctant to Recognize 122
Recognizing the Signs That Employees Feel Devalued and
Unrecognized 123
Pay: The Most Emotional Issue of All 124
Pay Practices That Engage and Retain 125
Three Types of Variable Pay 129
The Total Rewards Approach to Scarce Talent 132
Nonpay Best Practices for Valuing and Recognizing People 133
Focus on the People, Not Just the Numbers 136
What Employees Can Do to Be More Valued and Better
Recognized 144
Employer-of-Choice Engagement Practice Review and
Checklist 145

Chapter Nine

**REASON #6: STRESS FROM OVERWORK AND WORK-LIFE
IMBALANCE** **147**
How Big a Problem Is Stress? 150
Causes of Increased Stress 151
Signs that Your Workers May Be Stressed-Out or Overworked 151
Healthy vs. Toxic Cultures 152
More Than Just the Right Thing to Do 154
The Best Places in America to Work 156
It's Not Just the "Big Boys" You're Competing With 158
A Big Menu of Benefits and Services 160
What the Employee Can Do to Relieve Stress and Overwork 175
Employer-of-Choice Engagement Practices Review and
Checklist 176

Chapter Ten

**REASON #7: LOSS OF TRUST AND CONFIDENCE IN SENIOR
LEADERS**   **179**
A Crisis of Trust and Confidence   182
Reading the Signs of Distrust and Doubt   183
The Three Questions Employees Need Answered   183
Criteria for Evaluating Whether to Trust and Have Confidence   184
What the Employee Can Do to Build Reciprocal Trust and
   Confidence   193
Employer-of-Choice Engagement Practices Review and
   Checklist   194

Chapter 11

PLANNING TO BECOME AN EMPLOYER OF CHOICE   **196**
Talent Engagement Strategies in Action   198
What Do We Learn from These Success Stories?   205
Linking Talent and Business Objectives   205
Linking the Right Measures to Business Results   206
Creating an Employer-of-Choice Scorecard   207
The Plan Works . . . If You Work the Plan   211
Partners in Working the Plan   211

Appendix A

**SUMMARY CHECKLIST OF EMPLOYER-OF-CHOICE ENGAGEMENT
   PRACTICES**   **215**

Appendix B

**GUIDELINES AND CONSIDERATIONS FOR EXIT INTERVIEWING/
   SURVEYING AND TURNOVER ANALYSIS**   **218**

BIBLIOGRAPHY   **225**

INDEX   **231**

This book is about the hidden, elusive motivations that cause capable employees to start questioning their decision to join your company, start thinking of leaving, eventually disengage, and finally, leave.

The true root causes of voluntary employee turnover are hiding in plain sight. If we really think about it, we already know what they are: lack of recognition (including low pay), unfulfilling jobs, limited career advancement, poor management practices, untrustworthy leadership, and dysfunctional work cultures.

So, in what way are these root causes hidden, and from whom? Surveys tell us they are hidden from the very people who need to be most aware of them—the line managers who are charged with engaging and keeping valued employees in every organization. The vast majority of line managers, in fact, believe that most employees leave because they are "pulled" away by better offers. Of course most do leave for better offers, but it is simplistic and superficial to accept "pull factors" as root causes.

What these managers fail to perceive is that "push factors," mostly within their own power, are the initial stimuli—the first causes—that open the door to the "pull" of outside opportunities. The important question that remains unasked in so many exit interviews is not "Why are you *leaving?*" but "Why are you not *staying?*"

Over the years, I have listened to hundreds of departing employees emotionally describe the sources of their dissatisfaction with, and disengagement from, their former employers. And, I have been intrigued by the fact that so many managers see things so differently. Eventually, in an effort to authoritatively document the root causes of voluntarily employee turnover, I contacted the Saratoga Institute in Santa Clara, California, now a division of PriceWaterhouseCoopers, and considered by many to be the world leader in third-party exit interviewing and employee commitment surveying. Saratoga was founded in 1977 by Dr. Jac Fitz-enz, a pioneer in human resource practices benchmarking and human capital return on investment.

Saratoga Institute maintained a database of 19,700 exit and current employee surveys it had conducted from 1999 through 2003, a five-year period that started during a war for talent and ended during the buyer's market that followed. Saratoga's survey data included companies in a wide range of industries—financial, industrial medical, technology, manufacturing, distribution, insurance, health care, telecommunications, transportation, computer services, electronics, consumer products, consumer services, business services, consulting, and "other services."

I was pleased that the Saratoga Institute was interested in the premise of this book and willing to let me analyze the data and verbatim comments from these surveys. The "seven hidden reasons" I identified through this analysis are remarkably similar to the turnover causes I described in my earlier book, *Keeping the People Who Keep You in Business*. When you read about them, you will probably not be surprised to see any of them among the top seven. The real surprise is that even when companies know what the root causes are, they aren't doing nearly as much as they could be doing to eradicate them.

Too many companies are still relying on the tangible, easy-to-implement solutions that revolve around pay, benefits, and trendy perks, when we know the most powerful solutions revolve around the more challenging intangibles, such as good management and a healthy corporate culture. This book is ultimately more about solutions than it is about the reasons employees disengage and leave. You will find in these pages 54 practices for engaging workers and bonding them to your organization. You will find that some of these practices fit your current needs and situation better than others.

The good news is that you don't have to implement all of the 54 engagement practices. All you have to do is implement the right ones—the ones that will best engage and retain the employees you need most to achieve your business objectives. So please feel free to skip from chapter to chapter, picking and choosing among the practices that best fit the needs of your company and your key talent.

I also invite you to visit the Web site of Keeping the People, Inc.—*www.keepingthepeople.com*—and anonymously complete one or both of the confidential surveys you will find there. Your response to these surveys will serve to support my ongoing research into employee engagement and what managers believe about the real causes of turnover.

ACKNOWLEDGMENTS

For his initial interest in the idea for this book and his ongoing cooperation and contributions during the writing process, I offer my sincere thanks to Michael Kelly, director of research at Saratoga Institute in Santa Clara, California. Michael responded to each chapter as it was written with long, thoughtful missives and phone conversations that provided a valuable perspective.

For her supportive encouragement and ongoing technical assistance, I am deeply grateful to my wife, Cheryl.

For their inspiration and support, I thank my sons, Christopher Reed and Jonathan Spencer.

For taking the time to bring his expertise to bear on an important section of the book, special appreciation goes to Don Feltham.

Thanks to all the workers who responded to the thousands of Saratoga surveys with honesty, candor, and the faith that maybe their comments would help to make things better.

Thanks to all the kindred authors, executives, human resource professionals, colleagues, fellow consultants, and clients whose thoughts and actions have inspired and contributed to the continuing quest for human capital management practices that produce business success. Their names, ideas, and wisdom enrich this book.

For his expert and professional editing, I acknowledge the conscientious assistance of Niels Buessem.

And last but not least, for her guiding hand and constructive suggestions, I thank Adrienne Hickey, editorial director at AMACOM.

The 7 Hidden Reasons
Employees Leave

CHAPTER ONE

Why Care About Why They Leave?

The greatest obstacle
to discovery is not
ignorance—it is the
illusion of knowledge.

—DANIEL J. BOORSTIN

It was almost six weeks since Anna had resigned her position with her former employer, but it was obvious that strong feelings were still stirring inside her:

"I was thrown into the job with no training. I asked for some one-on-one time with my manager to go over the project inside out, but he never had the time. I sensed he didn't really know enough to be able to thoroughly brief me anyway.

"When I got feedback that certain work wasn't acceptable, he wouldn't be specific about how to correct it in the future. . . . He actually enjoyed intimidating people and he had a terrible temper—he would ask me a question and if I didn't know the answer, he would make fun of me in front of my coworkers. As it turns out, he wasn't following the right work procedures himself.

"Later, when I was working way below my skill set, I was told they weren't ready to give me a promotion, even though I had mastered everything.

"Finally, when I resigned, they didn't seem interested in why I was leaving. There was no exit interview. They never listened to me when I was there, and they certainly didn't care to listen when I left."

Anna went on to say that she loved her management position with her new employer: "I'm still doing what I love to do, but in a much more

1

professional environment. There's open communication and no game-playing. I know where I stand with them at all times."

One more thing—Anna went on to mention that she had hired away a talented colleague from her former company.

In the post-exit interviews I conduct for client companies with employees they regretted losing, these are the kinds of stories I hear. I know there are two sides to every story, and that Anna's former manager might tell it differently. But I also know that there is truth in Anna's story, and in all the stories I hear—more truth than they were willing to tell their former employers when they checked out on their last day of employment.

The good news is that some companies do wake up and realize it's not too late to start listening to former, and current, employees. Some grow alarmed when several highly valued workers leave over the course of a few weeks, and others become concerned about protecting their reputation as a good place to work. Most companies, however, simply want to make sure they have the talent they need to achieve their business objectives.

But the fact remains that many managers and senior executives don't care about why valued employees are leaving. Their attitude seems to be "If you don't like it, don't let the door hit you in the backside on your way out!"

You care, or you wouldn't have picked up this book. So why *do* you care? Why even take the time and effort to uncover the real reasons employees leave? It would be much easier just to accept what most employees say in exit interviews. You know the usual answers: "more money" or "better opportunity."

Who has time to stop and wonder why they left, anyway? They're gone. They didn't want to be here, so why worry about what they think? We can't expect to retain everybody we hire. Let's just get on with finding a replacement.

If this sounds familiar, it should, because it describes the prevailing mindset of most managers in American companies today. Most are over-worked and many are frustrated with their inability to meet the demands of the workforce, much less have time to do exit interviews. And increasingly, human resource departments are so understaffed that they can do little more than ask departing employees to quickly fill out exit surveys on their last day.

Managers Will Not Hear What Workers Will Not Speak

As we know, when exiting employees are asked, "Why are you leaving?" most are not inclined to tell the whole truth. Rather than risk burning a bridge with the former manager whose references they might need, they'll just write down "better opportunity" or "higher pay." Why would they want to go into the unpleasant truth about how they never got any feedback or recognition from the boss, or how they were passed over for promotion?

So, it is no wonder that, according to one survey, 89 percent of managers said they believe that employees leave and stay mostly for the money.[1] Yet, my own research, along with Saratoga Institute's surveys of almost 20,000 workers from eighteen industries,[2] and the research of dozens of other studies, reveal that actually 80 to 90 percent of employees leave for reasons related NOT to money, but to the job, the manager, the culture, or the work environment (Figure 1-1). These internal reasons (also known as "push" factors, as opposed to "pull" factors, such as a better-paying outside opportunity) are issues within the power of the organization and the manager to control and change.

It is a simple case of "when you don't know what's causing the problem, you can't expect to fix it." This dismaying disconnect between what managers believe and the reality—the true root causes of employee disengagement and turnover—is costing businesses billions of dollars a year.

Saratoga Institute estimates the average cost of losing an employee to be one times annual salary.[3] This means that a company with 300 employees, an average employee salary of $35,000, and a voluntary turnover rate of 15 percent a year, is losing $1,575,000 per year in turnover costs alone. If, for the sake of illustration, 70 percent of this company's forty-five yearly

Figure 1-1.

Why people leave: what managers believe vs. the reality. *Source:* Unpublished Saratoga Institute research, 2003.

89%
of **managers** believe employees leave for more money.

11% of managers believe employees leave for other reasons.

12% of employees leave for more money.

88%
of **employees** leave for reasons other than money.

voluntary turnovers—thirty-one employees—is avoidable, then the company, by correcting the root causes, could be saving $1,102,500 per year. This should be enough to raise the eyebrows of most CEOs and propel them to take action.

Just looking at turnover costs doesn't tell the whole story, however. Long before many employees leave, they become disengaged. Disengaged employees are uncommitted, marginally productive, frequently absent, or in some cases, working actively against the interests of the company. The Gallup Organization reports that 75 percent of the American workforce is either disengaged or actively disengaged (Figure 1-2).[4]

The 15 percent of actively disengaged workers can be particularly destructive to morale and revenues, for these are the workers who disrupt, complain, have accidents, steal from the company, and occupy the time and attention of managers that would be better spent dealing with other workers. As we know, some turnover is good turnover, and rather than struggle to re-engage actively disengaged workers, it is usually wiser, kinder, and more courageous to let them go.

The cost to the U.S. economy of disengaged employees is estimated to be somewhere between $254 billion and $363 billion annually.[5] The cost of absenteeism alone, a signal symptom of disengagement, is estimated to be $40 billion per year.[6]

Most of this mind-boggling cost accumulates from the loss of sales revenue caused by customers' disappointing interactions with disengaged employees, many of whom are turnovers waiting to happen. Simply put, employee disengagement leads to customer disengagement, and employee defections eventually lead to customer defections.

Figure 1-2.

Engaged vs. disengaged workers in U.S. workforce. *Source:* **The Gallup Organization, 2002.**

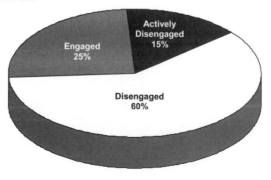

So, the best reason to be concerned about understanding the root causes of voluntary employee turnover and disengagement is an economic one. It's not just about being nice to employees just to be nice, although civility is a standard of behavior to be prized in itself. It's about taking care of employees so they will then feel good about taking care of customers.[7]

Hundreds of Gallup studies reveal that, on average, businesses units with employee engagement scores in the top half compared to those in the bottom half, have:

- 86 percent higher customer ratings
- 70 percent more success in lowering turnover
- 70 percent higher productivity
- 44 percent higher profitability
- 78 percent better safety records[8]

If we can commit to correctly identifying the root causes of employee disengagement, and if we can address these root causes with on-target solutions that increase the engagement of our workers, we will see tangible results in the form of reduced turnover costs and increased revenues.

Many managers will never get it. As Brad, another departed employee, told me during an exit interview, "It seems like most managers just don't care enough to go to any effort to retain good people." But many managers do get it, and do care. Now what we need are more organizations that make heroes of these managers, not just in terms of praising them, but also in terms of measuring and rewarding their contributions.

This book is for the managers, executives, business owners, and human resource professionals who care.

Turnover: Just a "Cost of Doing Business?"

To review, almost 90 percent of managers believe their employees are pulled out of the organization by better opportunities or more money, while almost 90 percent of employees say they were pushed down the slippery slope toward leaving by nonmonetary factors. Where lies the truth? As with many things in organizational life, it's all about differing perceptions. The question is, "*whose* truth?"

Many of today's managers still believe that turnover is an acceptable cost of doing business. Perhaps even you have said one or all of the following: "People come and people go" or "You can't expect to hold on to everyone forever" or "Good people get better offers and move on." There is a healthy realism in all these statements.

Let's also not forget that many of today's managers joined the managerial ranks in the 1980s and early 1990s, when there was a surplus of baby boomers in the workforce to take the place of employees who quit. Ever since the first boomers entered the workforce in 1968, the labor supply had always exceeded the demand. Then, around 1995, there came a tipping point. For the first time in recent memory, the number of jobs started to exceed the supply of workers. The end-of-the-century "war for talent" had begun.

For the next six years the war raged—companies made liberal use of signing bonuses and stock options to attract new employees. Some organizations vied to become "employers of choice" by offering everything from concierge services, to massages, to take-home meals, even letting their employees bring their pets to work. Employees had moved into the driver's seat.

Yet, a 1998 survey reported that although 75 percent of executives said that employee retention was one of their top three business priorities, only 15 percent had any plan in place to reduce turnover.[9] It was apparent, by their failure to act, that the majority of managers and executives were stubbornly hanging on to the mindset that had served them so well in their formative years: "Turnover is acceptable as a cost of doing business." Those who held on to this mindset soon found themselves competing for talent and losing to a minority of companies whose mindset—"Every turnover is a disappointing loss to be analyzed"—was very different, reflecting the same attitude about losing a valued employee as about losing a valued customer. Many of these companies were located in the Silicon Valley, where the war for talent was fiercest.

These companies formed the vanguard of employers across America who believed their people came first, built cultures of mutual commitment, lowered their tolerance for bad managers, and came up with clever and innovative best practices for keeping and engaging talent.[10] They were companies like Sun Microsystems, Cisco Systems, Southwest Airlines, SAS Institute, MBNA, Edward Jones, Rosenbluth Travel, Synovus Financial, Harley-Davidson, and many others. They were in the minority, as the best always are.

Then came the economic slowdown of 2001, when employees began "tree-hugging" their jobs and when replacements for those who quit were plentiful again, at least in most industries. CEOs began "high-fiving" one another in celebration of the fact that the war for talent was over. Employers had moved back into the driver's seat. One *Fortune* column featured the headline, "The war for talent is over . . . talent lost."[11] Once again it seemed entirely appropriate that managers and executives would re-adopt that comfortable old belief: "Turnover is acceptable as a cost of doing business."

It is understandable that managers' attitudes toward employees change as the employment market changes. It is also easy to see why managers would be less worried about employee turnover when there are plenty of unemployed or underemployed job seekers from which to choose. And when managers are not as worried about employees leaving, they are also not as likely to be concerned about *why* they are leaving.

When the Tide Turns, Mindsets Must Change

But what about when the economy improves, the rate of job-creation revs up, the 75 million Boomers start retiring, and the 45 million Generation Xers are too few to fill the available jobs? This is the scenario the U.S. Department of Labor (see Figure 1-3) now predicts at least through 2012.[12] If this prediction of dire worker shortages holds true—and most labor economists agree that it will—the war for talent will rage again. Employers of choice will once again fight hammer and tong for available talent, and the losers will not survive.

This means that no manager can afford to maintain outdated attitudes about turnover, especially when it is regrettable and preventable. Competitive managers will need to adopt a new mindset: that every voluntary avoidable employee departure is a disappointment to be analyzed, learned from, and corrected. Maintaining that mindset means managers can no longer just accept employees' superficial answers about why they quit, even though in some cases "better pay" or "better opportunity" may be the real reasons. Managers and senior executives need to know the truth about why they have lost valued talent, and they need to accept that maybe it was something they did or didn't do that pushed the employee out the door.

Of course there will always be managers who are too preoccupied, self-focused, or insensitive to notice the signs that employees are becoming disengaged while there is still time to do something about it. And when employees eventually do leave, managers may be too uncaring or in denial to confront the real reasons. Many cannot handle the unpleasant truth that the real reason employees are leaving may be linked to their own behavior. These managers are actually choosing not to see or hear the evil that plagues them.

Figure 1-3.

Projected growth of jobs vs. workforce. *Source:* U.S. Bureau of Labor Statistics, 2004.

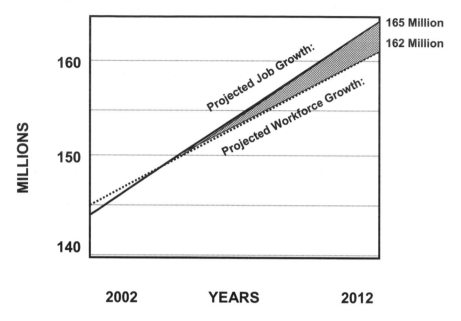

We cannot hope to keep all our valued talent. But good managers care enough to try to understand why good people leave, especially when it could have been prevented. Over the next several years, organizations must do everything they can to coach and train their managers in how to engage and keep re-engaging talented people.

What About HR's Role in Exit Interviewing?

Some managers may ask, "What about the human resources department—isn't it their responsibility to do the exit interviews, analyze the data, and report on the reasons employees leave? Traditionally, these certainly *have* been the responsibilities of HR departments.

However, available evidence suggests that in most organizations, HR departments and senior leaders are not providing the kind of meaningful data managers need about the root causes of employee turnover. A comprehensive Saratoga Institute study found that although 95 percent of organizations say they conduct exit interviews, only 32 percent report the data to managers, and only 30 percent follow up with some kind of action. Forty-two percent of HR departments surveyed admitted that their exit interview programs were not effective.[13]

To make sure that post-exit interviews or surveys are done and done effectively, HR professionals can play an important role by reporting findings to management, and by partnering with all managers to provide needed resources to assure that corrective actions are taken. For detailed guidelines on exit interviewing, see Appendix B.

What must *not* happen is for line managers to foist off on HR their own responsibility for keeping and engaging valued talent. HR is their partner in this process, but not the accountable party. The key is for the entire organization, beginning with the senior management team, to adopt a new mindset about managing all talent.

We have seen that the old mindset results in superficial understanding of employee turnover, leading to spiraling wage wars, and borrowing other companies' practices—usually tangible, but off-target quick fixes—which may not be the right aspirin required for the kind of headache the next war for talent will bring.

Notes

1. Marie Gendron, "Keys to Retaining Your Best Managers in a Tight Job Market," *Harvard Management Update,* June 1998, pp. 1–4.

2. Unpublished Saratoga Institute research of employee commitment, satisfaction, and turnover, conducted from 1996 to 2003, and involving 19,500 current and former employees in eighteen different organizations.

3. Barbara Davidson and Jac Fitz-enz, "Retention Management," study released by The Saratoga Institute, Santa Clara, California (New York: American Management Association, 1997).

4. Curt Coffman and Gabriel Gonzalez-Molina, *Follow This Path: How the World's Greatest Organizations Drive Growth by Unleashing Human Potential* (New York: Warner Business Books, 2002).

5. Ibid.

6. Ibid.

7. Hal F. Rosenbluth and Diane McFerrin Peters, *The Customer Comes Second: And Other Secrets of Exceptional Service* (New York: Quill, 1992).

8. Coffman and Gonzalez-Molina, *Follow This Path*.

9. Charles Fishman, "The War for Talent," *Fast Company*, August 1998.

10. Leigh Branham, *Keeping the People Who Keep You in Business: 24 Ways to Hang Onto Your Most Valuable Talent* (New York: AMACOM, 2001).

11. Geoffrey Colvin, "The War for Talent is Over . . . Talent Lost," *Fortune*, October 2002.

12. "Labor Market and Job Growth Outlook," U.S. Department of Labor, 2003.

13. Davidson and Fitz-enz, "Retention Management."

CHAPTER TWO

How They Disengage and Quit

Some quit and leave . . .
others quit and stay.

—ANONYMOUS

Before we identify the main reasons employees disengage, it is important to understand the dynamics of how they go through the disengagement process. Understanding the unfolding nature of employee disengagement helps us see how we can interrupt the process and salvage key talent at many points along the decision path.

The Disengagement Process

The first thing to realize is that employee turnover is not an event—it is really a process of disengagement that can take days, weeks, months, or even years until the actual decision to leave occurs (if it ever does). Here's what David, an accountant, told me three weeks after resigning:

"The very first day I started thinking of leaving. I was given an assignment and I realized very quickly that I was not going to receive any mentoring or support."

For Dave, it was all downhill from day one. Even though it was several months before he resigned, the first day was the turning point.

As the stair-step graphic in Figure 2-1 shows, there are actually several sequential and predictable steps that can unfold in the employee's journey from disengagement to departure. Of course, many managers are so busy or preoccupied that they wouldn't even notice if their employees walked around wearing sandwich boards saying, "Trying to Change Things!" or "Staying and Becoming Less Engaged Every Day!"—or whatever step in the disengagement process they happen to be on at the time. Not that it's only the manager's responsibility to take the initiative in this process—

Figure 2-1.

Thirteen steps in the engagement-to-departure process.

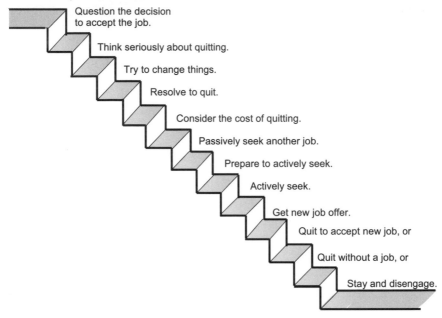

Start the new job with enthusiasm.

Question the decision to accept the job.

Think seriously about quitting.

Try to change things.

Resolve to quit.

Consider the cost of quitting.

Passively seek another job.

Prepare to actively seek.

Actively seek.

Get new job offer.

Quit to accept new job, or

Quit without a job, or

Stay and disengage.

employees also need to understand they have a singular responsibility to find ways of addressing their concerns and re-engaging themselves in the workplace. But many managers are just too slow to observe the telltale signs of employee disengagement until it's too late to do anything about it.

The obvious early warning signs of disengagement are absenteeism, tardiness, or behavior that indicates withdrawal or increased negativity. It is also useful to know that these early signs of disengagement typically start showing up after a shocking or jarring event takes place that causes the employee to question his or her commitment.

Here are some of the stimulus events that can trigger disengagement:

- Being passed over for promotion
- Realizing the job is not as promised
- Learning they may be transferred
- Hiring boss being replaced by new boss they don't like
- Being assigned to new territory
- Being asked to do something unethical

- Learning the company is doing something unethical
- Sudden wealth or sufficient savings to buy independence
- Earning enough money (grubstake)
- An incident of sexual harassment
- An incident of racial discrimination
- Learning the company is up for sale
- Learning the company has been sold
- Realizing they are underpaid compared to others doing the same job
- Realizing they are not in line for promotion for which they thought they were in line
- Realizing that their own behavior has become unacceptable
- An unexpected outside job offer
- Being pressured to make an unreasonable family or personal sacrifice
- Being asked to perform a menial duty (e.g., run a personal errand for the boss)
- Petty and unreasonable enforcement of authority
- Being denied a request for family leave
- Being denied a request for transfer
- A close colleague quitting or being fired
- A disagreement with the boss
- A conflict with a coworker
- An unexpectedly low performance rating
- A surprisingly low pay increase or no pay increase

Sometimes, departed employees use the term "last straw" in referring to these events. As a nurse named Karen told me:

> "I was happy there two years ago, but my manager left and my new manager was not a good mentor or coach. She was just coasting to retirement, but she was moody and unprofessional. And then one day she yelled at me. I went to her manager about it, but she just excused her behavior, saying 'that's just the way she is.' That was the last straw for me."

Here are excerpts from other post-exit interviews that illustrate the turning-point phenomenon:

- "The head of our department changed and I felt the new one didn't seek my input or recognize my contributions. Then, the work started becoming more administrative than technical. I felt like I was just shuffling papers and not designing anything. That's when I started looking elsewhere, and a coworker referred me to the company I now work for." (Dan, an engineer)
- "My managers made it very clear they didn't want my input. They could have made such good use of my foreign language ability, but I got the cold shoulder. They had an old boy network mindset. I went to a national company meeting because my manager couldn't attend—it was 95 percent male, and no one even came up and introduced themselves. That did it for me. After that, I started looking and I had a new job in six weeks." (Janine, business analyst)
- "I wasn't being challenged. And then I came across payroll information while doing some project costing and discovered that I was paid 15 percent less than everyone else in my group. That was the turning point." (John, financial analyst)
- "I had a degree from a prestigious university, and my manager would take pot shots at me in front of others. Then he started giving me menial work to do, like taking things to mail and FedEx. He would say, 'It's more cost-effective for you to do this than for me to do it.' I started looking for a job after only three months on the job" (Pamela, technical writer)

Dr. Thomas Lee, a business professor at the University of Washington, who has extensively researched what he calls "the unfolding model of turnover," reports several interesting findings about how and why people disengage and leave:

- The majority of voluntary turnovers—63 percent—are precipitated by some kind of shocking event.
- Very few employees start thinking of leaving because of shocking events related to pay.
- About 20 percent of departing employees leave without having another job in hand.
- Some leave when the job offer is "likely," not waiting until it is in hand.
- Temporary, part-time, and marginal workers are more likely to quit suddenly or impulsively after a shock rather than enter into a drawn-out period evaluating the situation.

- Many talented employees keep an eye out for other jobs while working, and decide to interview for outside opportunities just for practice, to create a "plan B," or to test their marketability.
- Many employees leave because of "personal shocks" unrelated to their workplace, such as marriage, pregnancy, inheritance, last child leaving home, decision to relocate, becoming a caregiver for a family member in health crisis, or paying off the mortgage.
- Exit surveying or interviewing that doesn't uncover the shock (turning point) and get the employee to discuss the deliberation process, if there was one, will not reveal the root cause.[1]

The Deliberation Process

Lee also points out that there are two distinct periods in an employee's process of thinking about leaving—the first period being the time between an employee's first thoughts of quitting and the subsequent decision to leave. As an example, one ex-employee said:

"After the merger I gave it a year to see what the company would be like, and I tried to keep my attitude positive, but things were no different, so I started looking."

Another man I interviewed told me that when he was promoted, no announcement went out, which he took as a personal slight. He first started thinking about leaving when he asked for more responsibility, but was turned down. He knew he had proved himself in his current position. The disappointment was made even more bitter because he had lived abroad for a year, apart from his wife and son, and he felt the company owed him a new opportunity. Instead of getting the job he wanted, he was transferred to another department. That's when he made the decision to leave.

The second period in the deliberation process is the time between the employee's decision to leave and the actual leaving. As you might expect, the chances of a manager re-recruiting and successful gaining renewed commitment from an employee are not as great during this second period as they might have been during the first. This is why it is important for managers to be alert to the signs that an employee is just starting to disengage when there is still time to do something about it.

Since most disengagements begin with some kind of shocking event like those listed above, managers need to keep their antennae up for signals that a valued employee may have recently received a disappointing shock Or better yet, because it is often hard to read the feelings of employees from the looks on their faces, managers should simply sit down with their direct reports on a regular basis and ask, "how are things with you?" Such simple, caring questions can help avoid turnovers like the one mentioned above, opening up discussions that can lead to a resolution of the precipitating issue.

Or, perhaps the employees could have done more on their own initiative to resolve the situations. Or, maybe they had done all they could. It may even have been impossible for the managers to accommodate the employees' wishes. We will never know. The point is, if the manager does not regularly initiate such discussions, and they never happen, it is the manager and the organization that risk suffering the loss of talent and the high costs of turnover.

When we consider the gradual, unfolding nature of employee disengagement and that, as research reveals, 75 percent of employees are disengaged, there can be but one conclusion: The need for managers to initiate action to engage and re-engage employees is urgent, and the daily opportunity to do so is ever-present.

Note

1. Adapted with permission from T.W. Lee, et al., "An Unfolding Model of Employee Turnover," *Academy of Management Journal* 39 (1996): 5–36.

CHAPTER THREE

Why They Leave:
What the Research Reveals

> Sometimes if we cut
> through the brain and
> get to the gut, we learn
> the truth.
>
> —JAC FITZ-ENZ

If you compiled an alphabetical list of all the reasons for leaving voluntarily from the exit surveys of dozens of organizations, it would look something like this:

Advancement opportunity
Benefits
Better-paying job
Bureaucracy
Career change
Commuting time or distance
Concerns about organization's future
Conflict with coworker
Discrimination based on race, gender, religion, etc.
Dishonest or unethical leaders or managers
Distrust of, or loss of confidence in, senior leaders
Excessive workload
Favoritism
Fear of job elimination
Geographic location of the job
Health concerns
Ideas not welcomed
Immediate supervisor

17

Inability to master the job
Inflexible work hours
Insufficient challenge
Insufficient or inappropriate training
Insufficient resources to do the job
Job elimination
Job itself
Job responsibilities
Job security
Limited earnings potential
Little or no bonus
Little or no empowerment
Little or no growth or developmental opportunity
Little or no performance feedback
Negative work environment
No authority to do the job
No career path
No consequences for nonperformers
No way to voice concerns
Not allowed to complete the job
Not allowed to do the job my own way
Not paid competitively
Not paid in proportion to contributions
Not recognized for contributions
Organization culture
Organization instability or turmoil
Organization politics
Outdated or inadequate equipment
Physical facility noisy, dirty, hot, or cramped
Poor communication
Poor teamwork
Retirement
Return to school
Self-employment
Sexual harassment
Spouse relocation
Stress
Timeliness of pay increases
Too many changes
Treated poorly

Uncaring leadership
Unfair pay increases
Unfair performance appraisal process
Unfair promotion practices
Unfair rules, policies, or procedures
Unwanted change in job duties
Unwanted relocation
Vacation policy
Work-life imbalance

These 67 reasons were, in fact, taken from exit survey responses completed by thousands of exiting employees. When you take away the unpreventable reasons (though some may have preventable origins)—advancement opportunity, better-paying job, career change, commuting time/distance, geographic location of job, job elimination, retirement, return to school, self-employment, and spouse relocation—you are still left with 57 preventable reasons for voluntary turnover.

While reading and categorizing the comments from among 3,149 employees who voluntarily left their employers, as surveyed by Saratoga,[1] I could not help being touched by the emotions expressed in them—disappointment, frustration, anger, disillusionment, resentment, betrayal, to name the most common. It occurred to me that very few of the "reasons" for turnover were based on reasoned thinking—they were mostly rooted in strong feelings.

As I analyzed and grouped the reasons for leaving, looking for common denominators, and peeling off layers from the onion in search of root causes, it became clear that employees begin to disengage and think about leaving when one or more of four fundamental human needs are not being met:

1. *The Need for* **Trust**: Expecting the company and management to deliver on its promises, to be honest and open in all communications with you, to invest in you, to treat you fairly, and to compensate you fairly and on time.

2. *The Need to Have* **Hope**: Believing that you will be able to grow, develop your skills on the job and through training, and have the opportunity for advancement or career progress leading to higher earnings.

3. *The Need to Feel a Sense of* **Worth**: Feeling confident that if you work hard, do your best, demonstrate commitment, and make

meaningful contributions, you will be recognized and rewarded accordingly. Feeling worthy also means that you will be shown respect and regarded as a valued asset, not as a cost, to the organization.

4. *The Need to Feel* **Competent**: Expecting that you will be matched to a job that makes good use of your talents and is challenging, receive the necessary training to perform the job capably, see the end results of your work, and obtain regular feedback on your performance.

Why Employees Say They Leave

When we look at the reasons employees give for leaving in Saratoga's confidential third-party exit surveys,[2] it becomes obvious that these basic psychic needs are not being met. As we see in the pie chart of reasons for leaving (Figure 3-1), the responses to the question "Why did you leave?" were classified into the following groups:

1. *Limited Career Growth or Promotional Opportunity* (16 percent), indicating a lack of hope.
2. *Lack of Respect from or Support by Supervisor* (13 percent), indicating a lack of trust or confidence.
3. *Compensation* (12 percent), indicating an issue of worth or value.
4. *Job Duties Boring or Unchallenging* (11 percent), indicating a lack of competence and fulfillment in the work itself.
5. *Supervisor's Lack of Leadership Skills* (9 percent), indicating a lack of trust and confidence.
6. *Work Hours* (6 percent), including comments ranging from undesirable work schedule, to inflexibility, to overtime (too much or too little), to undesirable shift—reasons indicating a lack of worth, inasmuch as the organization, in their minds, did not view their satisfaction as important enough to warrant a change.
7. *Unavoidable Reasons* (5 percent), generally considered unpreventable by the organization and including excessive commuting distance, retirement, birth of a child, child-care issues, relocation, other family issues, career change, too much travel, return to school, and death or illness in the family.

Figure 3-1.

Why they left. *Source:* Previously unpublished Saratoga Institute research.

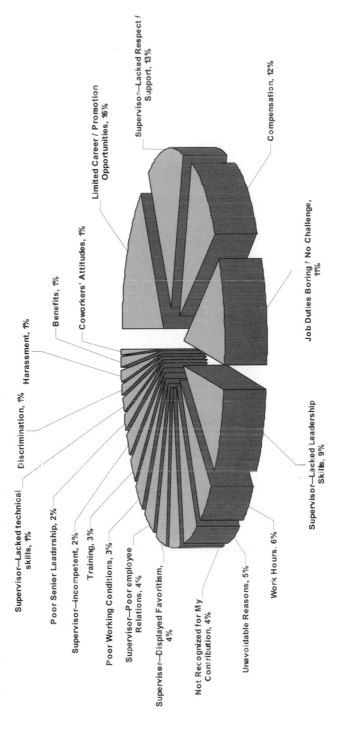

8. *Lack of Recognition* (4 percent), indicating a lack of worth.

9. *Favoritism by Supervisor* (4 percent), indicating a lack of trust.

10. *Supervisor's Poor Employee Relations* (4 percent), indicating a lack of trust.

11. *Poor Working Conditions* (3 percent), pertaining mostly to undesirable physical conditions, indicating a lack of worth.

12. *Training* (3 percent), pertaining mostly to insufficient offerings, poorly conducted training, or the denial of permission to attend training—all indicating the lack of perceived worth.

13. *Supervisor's Incompetence* (2 percent), indicating a lack of trust and confidence.

14. *Poor Senior Leadership* (2 percent), same reasons as those given for next level management, plus lack of clear vision or direction—indicating a lack of trust or confidence.

15. *Supervisor's Lack of Technical Skills* (1 percent), indicating a lack of trust and confidence.

16. *Discrimination* (1 percent), indicating a lack of trust and hope.

17. *Harassment* (1 percent), indicating a lack of trust.

18. *Benefits* (1 percent), indicating a lack of worth.

19. *Coworkers' Attitude* (1 percent), indicating a lack of trust.

To get below the surface of the exit survey responses, Saratoga conducted focus groups with respondents to probe further into their reasons for leaving, and analyzed the content of written survey comments. When employees are asked to give open-ended feedback, either in writing or open discussion, they are no longer just responding to prefabricated questions—they are speaking from their hearts about the needs that were not met.

Here are the ten most frequently mentioned issues identified in departed employees' responses to the question, "What did ABC Company (former employer) do poorly?"

1. *Poor Management:* The comments were mostly about uncaring, incompetent, and unprofessional managers, but also complaints about managers overworking them, not showing respect, not listening to their ideas, putting them in the wrong jobs, making no effort to retain them, emphasizing speed over quality, and being

abusive. There were also many comments about poor or nonexistent methods of selecting managers.

(Issues: Trust, Worth, Hope, and Competence)

2. *Lack of Career Growth and Advancement Opportunity*: Comments were mainly about having no perceivable career path, but also about the company's failure to post jobs or fill jobs from within, and unfair promotions or favoritism.

(Issues: Hope and Trust)

3. *Poor Communications*: Comments were mostly about top-down communication from managers and senior leaders (particularly the lack of openness with information) but also about miscommunication between departments, from the human resources department, from corporate offices to field offices, and following mergers.

(Issues: Trust and Worth)

4. *Pay*: Comments were mostly about not being paid fair-market value or not being paid in proportion to their contributions and hard work, but also complaints about pay inequities, slow pay raises, favoritism in giving raises and bonuses, and ineffective performance appraisals.

(Issues: Trust and Worth)

5. *Lack of Recognition*: This issue is connected to issues of pay and workload, but there were many comments about the organization's culture not being one that encourages recognition.

(Issue: Worth)

6. *Poor Senior Leadership*: The comments were mostly about lack of caring about, listening to, or investing in employees, but also about executives being isolated, remote, and unresponsive, providing no inspiring vision or direction, sending mixed messages, making too many changes in direction and organizational structure.

(Issues: Trust and Worth)

7. *Lack of Training*: Comments were mainly about not receiving enough training to do their current jobs properly, but also citing poor quality of training, being rushed through superficial training, lack of new hire training, poor management training, and lack of training for future advancement.

(Issues: Worth, Hope, and Competence)

8. *Excessive Workload*: The comments were mainly about being asked to do more with fewer staff, but also about sacrificing quality and customer service to make the numbers.

(Issues: Worth and Competence)

9. *Lack of Tools and Resources*: Comments cited a range of issues, including inadequate office supplies, malfunctioning computers, poor phone system support, outdated technology, and lack of human resources to relieve overwork.

(Issues: Worth, Hope, and Competence)

10. *Lack of Teamwork*: Comments were mainly about lack of coworker cooperation and commitment to get the job done, but also mentioning lack of coordination between departments or different locations.

(Issues: Trust and Competence)

What Caused Their Initial Dissatisfaction?

As noted in Chapter Two, employees often experience an initial shock or disappointment that may ultimately result in their leaving the organization. At one time, Saratoga Institute included the question, "What caused your initial dissatisfaction?" in its post-exit survey, but dropped the question after reviewing the first 950 responses. As it turned out, the nineteen reasons for leaving shown in the pie chart in Figure 3-1 were identical to the reasons for initial dissatisfaction and in the same order from top to bottom!

This lends added weight to the conclusion that most people ultimately leave for a reason that had as its genesis an event that may have occurred weeks or months earlier. Again, the key reminder and good news in this for managers is that there is a built-in period of "rescue time" during which they have the opportunity to identify the employee's dissatisfaction and try to correct it.

A Few Words About Pay

In spite of the fact that hundreds of employees surveyed had worked for companies that did not pay competitively compared to other companies in their industries, compensation issues still amounted to no more than 12 percent of all reasons for leaving.

This finding is consistent with the conclusion of Saratoga's comprehensive 1997 report, in which lead researchers Barbara Davison and Jac Fitz-enz, in their chapter on why employees leave, stated:

Pay . . . is often a smokescreen, not a primary reason that employees leave one organization and move to another. Saratoga Institute's ongoing research into retention shows that less than 20 percent leave for better pay.

Competitive pay is fundamental to retention; however, the ramifications of continually "buying" employees are not always in the best interest of the organization. The remaining employees are always affected, pay plans become ineffective, and the financial impact can be far-reaching . . . However, maintaining a competitive pay plan on the front end and facing up to job and working conditions has a greater positive effect.[3]

One of the first laws of retaining employees is to pay at or above what the market is paying for similar jobs. Competitive pay is the ticket to admission for organizations wishing to qualify as employers of choice, yet survey results make it clear that many companies have not yet purchased that ticket.

Regarding the individual employee's decision to stay or leave based on pay, Saratoga's director of research, W. Michael Kelly, observed, "The rule of thumb is that in a healthy job market an unhappy employee will bolt the company for a 5 percent pay increase, but it will take at least an increase of 20 percent to compel a satisfied employee to jump ship."[4] Of course, pay is more important to some than it is to others. We know that many employees who struggle to pay their bills can understandably be enticed to leave for increases of less than 5 percent.

Do You Know Your "Poach Rate?"

If you still think retention is mainly about money, find out how much it is costing your competition to get people to leave you. That's called your "poach rate." If your poach rate is less than 20 percent, it ain't the money, honey! People who love their work, love their boss, and love their company don't leave unless the offer is coming from the Godfather.

—John Putzier[5]

Several studies have also shown that, in general, salespeople are more money-motivated than most other workers. And, at the other end of the spectrum, we all know individuals whose loyalty to their employer, or to their manager, is so strong that they have turned down increases of 30 percent or more because they could not imagine being treated better, or finding a more satisfying job, elsewhere. Indeed, we can find plenty of these people happily employed at America's top employers of choice.

In reviewing survey comments about pay from both leavers and stayers, it is striking how few comments have to do with the actual amount of salary, bonus, or other incentive. Rather, the key issue seems to be fairness, or the lack thereof. Employees seem to be frustrated about pay because they have observed what they consider several kinds of inequities:

- Superior performance reviews have little effect on pay increases.
- Experience is discounted when new hires are paid as much as veterans.
- Higher education levels do not translate into higher pay levels.
- Increasing stress and aggravation aren't worth the money.
- More and more hours make the pay worth less and less.

As Michael Kelly commented:

"What is most disturbing about these beliefs is that they fly in the face of an employee's desire to know and understand the formal and informal rules for attaining higher pay levels—performance, experience, education, willingness to sacrifice and undergo hardships. If these factors are not linked to increases in pay, they ask, then what is? Pay policies and practices that do not encourage and support employee commitment present obstacles that even the most capable supervisor will find formidable, if not impossible, to deal with."[6]

Respecting the Differences

It's worth noting that these themes come from the comments of employees at all position levels in a wide range of industries—financial, pharmaceutical, medical devices, technology, manufacturing, distribution, insurance, health care, telecommunications, transportation, computer services, electronics, consumer products, consumer services, business services, consulting, and other services. The companies were widely distributed geographically as well, with every region of the continental United States represented.

In reading the exit survey comments, it quickly became apparent that two or three key issues were glaringly in need of fixing at each company surveyed. This is not unexpected, but it reminds us that, while most employees want the top ten things that bring satisfaction, every organization's culture is different, and each suffers from a smaller number of issues that cry out to be addressed.

We also need to keep in mind that, while all employees want trust, hope, worth, and competence, they may differ as to which ones are most important at any given time. This may depend on their age or tenure with the organization, for example, as with younger employees, for whom the hope and expectation of career growth in the company may be paramount. Older workers may be more concerned about health-care benefits. Computer designers will want the latest technologies. Some employees will want to be recognized in a public ceremony, while others will not. When it comes down to engaging and retaining one employee at a time, effective managers will respect these individual differences.

Who Has the Power to Meet These Needs?

It should be acknowledged that a manager or organization cannot always prevent a valued employee from leaving, or even delay the decision to leave. As we see in Figure 3-2, depending on the degree of employee control over the decision and the degree of employer influence over that decision, we have four possibilities[7]:

If we look back at the pie chart showing the reasons survey respondents left (Figure 3-1), and subtract the unavoidable reasons where the employer had little or no control over the employee's decision to leave—retirement, commuting distance, return to school, start own business, family illness/circumstances—we are left with 95 percent of the reasons fitting into quadrant A in Figure 3-2, *voluntary and preventable by the employer*. Of that 95 percent, more than 70 percent of the reasons are related to factors that are controllable by the direct supervisor. This conforms to what most of us already know—that the employee's direct supervisor has the major share of control or influence to prevent or correct these issues. As the saying goes, "people join companies, but they leave managers."

Well, sometimes they leave companies, too, and the senior leaders who run those companies. It is the senior leaders who set the direction, who shape the culture, who approve the pay ranges and the training budget, whose demands bring stress and overwork, and whose strategies can bring

Figure 3-2.

Degree of employer/employee control over decision to leave.

Employer Degree of Control
Over Employee Decision to Leave

	High	Low
High	**A** Voluntary departures where employer actions may prevent/delay turnover.	**C** Voluntary departures where employer actions are unlikely to prevent/delay turnover
Low	**B** Employer initiated (involuntary) departures.	**D** Employee initiated departures mostly unavoidable by employer or employee.

Employee Degree of Control Over Decision to Leave

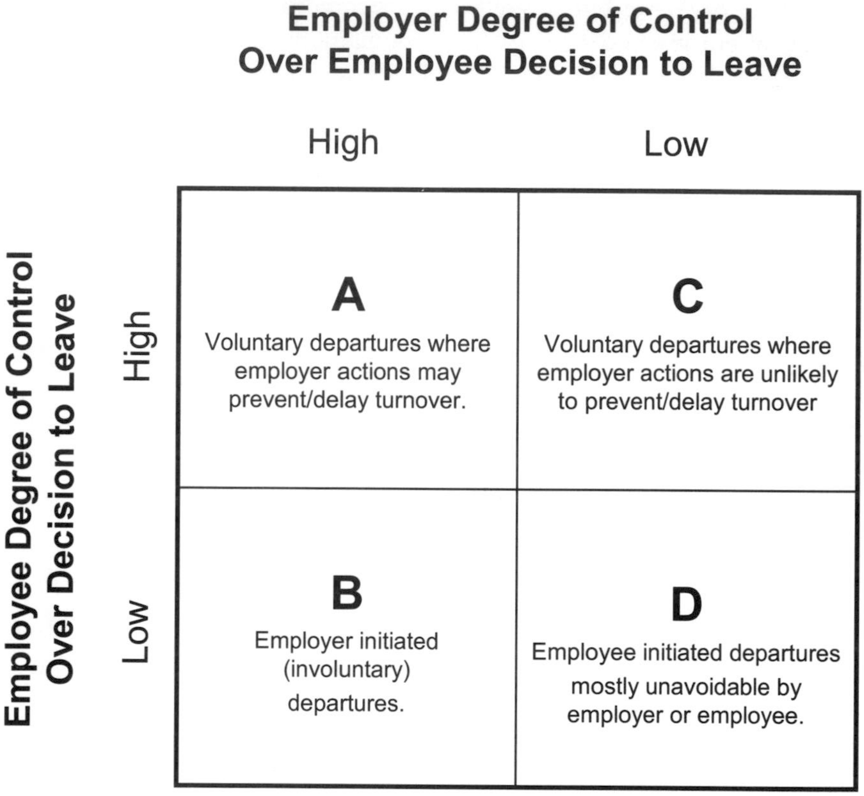

either growth (and career growth opportunities) or stagnation. For proof of the pervasive power of the senior executive, we need look no further than to companies like Southwest Airlines and the SAS Institute, where committed and caring CEOs—Herb Kelleher and Jim Goodnight—have built the two of the most remarkable "employer-of-choice" cultures in America today.

In upcoming chapters, it will become clear how managers, senior leaders, human resource executives, and yes, the employees themselves, can partner to create reciprocal commitment.

The Next Seven Chapters:
Hidden Reasons and Practical Actions

It is not a naïve platitude to point out that complaints are just negatively stated solutions. People complain of poor management when what they want is good management. They complain of favoritism when what they prefer is an even playing field. And so, in describing the seven main reasons employees leave, we come ever closer to pinpointing what it will take to make them want to stay and be more fully engaged. Delivering those engagement and retention best practices is the real purpose of this book.

Considering all the possible reasons that employees give for leaving, as presented in this chapter, you may wonder how I winnowed them down to a select seven. The truth is that this has not been that difficult, because the Saratoga findings generally confirm my own research and the findings of dozens of other studies on the causes of employee turnover.

Based on my desire to present root cause reasons that are simultaneously best-known and most-hidden, that are supported by the research findings, that are precisely identifiable and separable from one another, that managers or senior leaders can prevent or address, and that are few enough in number to be manageable, these are the ones I have chosen to dissect:

1. The job or workplace not living up to expectations
2. The mismatch between job and person
3. Too little coaching and feedback
4. Too few growth and advancement opportunities
5. Feeling devalued and unrecognized
6. Stress from overwork and work-life imbalance
7. Loss of trust and confidence in senior leaders

Each of the next seven chapters begins with selected survey comments that illustrate each hidden reason and also convey the depth of emotion surrounding it. Next, we will look at the visible signs that one or more of your employees may be disengaging for that reason. We will also take a look at predictable obstacles that stand in the way of preventing or correcting these root causes.

Most importantly, we will review 54 innovative ideas and practical, proven engagement practices that you and your organization can use to address each one. We will also focus on what employees can and must do to assume their own share of the responsibility for keeping themselves committed and engaged. As we know, sometimes the real reason employees leave—but one they rarely admit—is, "I left before they fired me."

It is also important to keep in mind that whether a company uses most, or only a handful of these engagement practices, the ones it does use need to be aligned with its strategic business objectives. In the final chapter, we will consider the process for building a comprehensive talent management strategy based on identifying the kinds of talent needed to execute the business strategy. A company may not be able, or even want, to implement all 54 of the engagement practices presented, but will want to select and apply the ones that will have the biggest impact on business success.

Notes

1. Unpublished Saratoga Institute research of employee commitment, satisfaction, and turnover conducted from 1996 to 2003, involving current and former employees in eighteen different organizations.
2. Ibid.
3. "Retention Management," a study released by The Saratoga Institute, Santa Clara, California, authored by Barbara Davidson and Jac Fitz-enz, and published by the American Management Association, 1997.
4. W. Michael Kelly, interview, March 17, 2004.
5. John Putzier, *Get Weird! 101 Innovative Ways to Make Your Company a Great Place to Work* (New York: AMACOM, 2001).
6. W. Michael Kelly, "Saratoga's Findings," unpublished report, September 2003.
7. Paul R. Ahr and Thomas B. Ahr, *Overturn Turnover: Why Some Employees Leave, Why Some Employees Stay, and Ways to Keep the Ones You Want to Stay*" (St. Louis: Causeway Publishing Company, 2000), p. 6.

CHAPTER FOUR

Reason #1:
The Job or Workplace Was
Not as Expected

Between the idea
and the reality
Between the motion
and the act
Falls the Shadow.

—T.S. ELIOT

Years ago when I was an employee career counselor at Disneyland's onsite career center, a young woman walked into my office one day, sat down almost in tears, and blurted out, "This is *not* the happiest place on earth."

I couldn't help being amused, but her disappointment was deep and sincere, almost as if she had truly expected that her work experience in the Magic Kingdom would be as carefree as that of a five-year old visiting the park for the first time. But alas, she had become disillusioned. She was having a conflict with her boss, who she believed had shown favoritism in promoting a coworker instead of her.

Disappointment about promotions was not uncommon at Disneyland, especially among summer workers, ride operators, and other entry-level and part-time employees. The fact was, the organization had an "Eiffel Tower" organizational structure—wide at the bottom but much taller and narrower at the top than a pyramid—and there were relatively fewer rungs on the promotional ladder to which younger workers could realistically aspire.

What this employee, and many others at Disneyland, needed to understand and accept was that there would come a time when it was best for them to let go of their illusions of long-term employment at "the happiest

31

place on earth" and move on. That was a key reason that Disney had created the career center in the first place—to help these employees assess their talents, develop new goals, even prepare new resumes, and make a successful transition to other employers. It was a smart strategy because it recognized that these young, disillusioned workers had become disengaged, and that disengaged workers cannot deliver the kind of world-class customer experience for which Disney had become famous.

Every day, new hires enter organizations with a wide range of illusions and unrealistic expectations. Some stay and adapt, some disengage and stay, and many disengage and leave. From Saratoga's surveys, here are a few word-for-word comments of some who had chosen to stay, but were less than fully engaged:

- "HR personnel lied to me about a wage increase and the bonus program just to get me there, then they never followed through with the wage increase! The rotating hours were never discussed."
- "Improper representation of job description and hours of work."
- "They do not deliver promises made as far as advancement, of potential growth with in the corporate ladder. This forces one to make some very hard internal choices on the reasons for staying."
- "Thing are not explained well by HR when you are hired."
- "When I hired on, it was with the clear understanding that I would be working three days a week for what I was being paid. Then, after I started the job, my manager said no, that we agreed to five days a week. He acted like we had never had the conversation. That made me really angry. I agreed to stay on full time because I needed the job, but I'm still looking for another part-time job."
- "Our manager makes a lot of promises that are not kept."
- "Supervisors do not keep their promises in terms of promoting employees."
- "I was not at all satisfied with the training I received when I started working for ABC Company. I was sitting at my desk for three or four hours a day for the first three weeks, and as a result I began looking for another job. I felt that management didn't care."
- "XYZ Company does not provide a training program course for any new employee. You are thrown into a new position and are expected to do all things that are required of your position immediately."

- "ABC Company is very good at lying to prospective employees during interviews. They deliberately misrepresent the position in order to get more qualified candidates than necessary for the position."
- "Length of time from interview to hiring was totally unacceptable. When you are told in the interview you will be hired pending check of references and drug test, six weeks is too long to wait."
- "They do not give to employees. For example, on my first day of work I was not able to take a lunch. Another example—I am not able to spend any money on my employees to show appreciation for a job well done."

At the root of all these comments is an expectation that was not met. In some cases, the employee's expectations may have been unrealistic, and in some cases they, no doubt, were not. In the big picture, it doesn't matter. The point is, unrealistic and unmet expectations cost a business untold millions of dollars. The cost of losing one professional is generally accepted to be one times annual salary. If the average salary is $50,000, then losing twenty employees over the course of a year because of unmet expectations adds up to a tidy total of $1 million.

You may never see an exit survey with a checklist of reasons for leaving that includes the choice "unmet expectations," but it may well be the number one reason most employees leave. It is the main reason 4 percent of employees walk off the job on the first day.[1] It is most certainly the main reason that more than 50 percent of American workers quit in the first six months.[2] And it is probably a key factor in the failure of 40 percent of new executives to last more than eighteen months in their new positions.[3]

A Disastrous First Day

"I'd said at the interview that I planned to take a holiday the following month, and my manager said that would be fine and to give him the dates when I'd booked it. On my first day, when I told him the week I planned to be away, he went bright red, slammed his fist on the desk, and barked that I clearly had no commitment to the company, and what message was it sending out to my team if I went away so soon? I survived another day and another showdown before I took one long permanent holiday."[4]

Hidden Mutual Expectations: The Psychological Contract

In his classic article, "The Psychological Contract: Managing the Joining-Up Process," John Paul Kotter defined the psychological contract as "an implicit contract between an individual and the organization which specifies what each expects to give and receive from each other in the relationship."[5] As shown in Figure 4-1, matches and mismatches can occur based on the four sets of expectations in this hidden contract.

For example, when a new hire expects to receive a promotion after one year on the job, and the employer is not prepared to give a promotion that quickly, there is a mismatch. When the employer can and does promote the new employee after a year, there is a match. Kotter's research confirmed what most of us would expect—that the greater the matching of mutual expectations, the greater the probability of job satisfaction, productivity, and reduced turnover.

Figure 4-1.

The psychological contract: two parties, four sets of expectations.

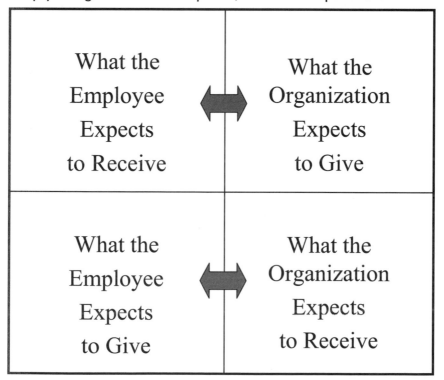

What the Employee Expects to Receive	What the Organization Expects to Give
What the Employee Expects to Give	What the Organization Expects to Receive

To illustrate further, here are some common mismatches that occur between what Gen Xers may expect to get from an employer and what Boomer managers may expect to give:

Gen Xers may expect to get:	*Boomer managers may expect to give:*
Plenty of vacation time	Three weeks vacation only after five years
Promotions based purely on merit	Promotions based largely on experience
Hands-off supervision	Close supervision
Self-paced computer training	Classroom training only
Frequent constructive feedback	Feedback only when they screw up

Not all mismatches occur because of generational differences, but most of us have certainly observed such situations and can vouch for the fact that, if not openly discussed, any single mismatch can lead to conflict, lost productivity, and turnover.

Allstate's Written "Psychological Contract"

Some employers, such as Allstate Insurance Company, have actually created formal statements outlining what employee and employer can expect from each other.

Because the company believes employee loyalty improves when both company and employees clearly know what is expected, Allstate provides this "partnership statement" to every employee:

You should expect Allstate to:

- Offer work that is meaningful and challenging.
- Promote an environment that encourages open and constructive dialogue.
- Recognize you for your accomplishments.
- Provide competitive pay and rewards based on your performance.
- Advise you on your performance through regular feedback.
- Create learning opportunities through education and job assignments.

- Support you in defining career goals.
- Provide you with information and resources to perform successfully.
- Promote an environment that is inclusive and free from bias.
- Foster dignity and respect in all interactions.
- Establish an environment that promotes a balance of work and professional life.

Allstate expects you to:

- Perform at levels that significantly increase the company's ability to outperform the competition.
- Take on assignments critical to meeting business objectives.
- Willingly listen and act upon feedback.
- Demonstrate a high level of commitment to achieving company goals.
- Exhibit no bias in interactions with colleagues and customers.
- Behave consistently with Allstate's ethical standards.
- Take personal responsibility for each transaction with customers and for fostering their trust.
- Continually improve processes to address customers' needs.[6]

When an employee realizes that the employer cannot meet a key expectation in the contract, there is often a feeling of having been betrayed, as if a real contract has been broken in bad faith. This can become the "shock" or turning point that begins the downward cycle toward disengagement and departure.

The more open the discussion that takes place about mutual expectations, the more probability of a satisfactory match. This doesn't happen as frequently as it should, partly because interviewees often feel powerless in the interview process and are reluctant to ask questions, and partly because interviewers are too rushed, or are simply afraid that if they tell the whole truth about the job or workplace, the recruit will not accept the offer.

The more clearly an employee understands his or her own expectations, the higher the probability of a match. Many new employees fresh out of college, however, are only dimly aware of their wants and needs.

The problem is compounded when the organization is also not clear about what it expects, which is often the case.

Companies frequently make the mistake of thinking in terms of offering "the most" or receiving "the best," when they would be better advised to think in terms of "fit." For example, many companies seek to hire only the "top graduates" with the highest grade point averages, when some of these individuals, because of their cerebral bent or analytical nature, may not fit the company's expectation that they become outgoing, street-smart sales people.

If an employee and an employer discover after the hire that they have a serious mismatch of expectations, it may be in their best interests to shake hands and part ways. Of course, this is not always easy to do.

The psychological contract changes over time as the expectations of the employee and the organization change. With each change in expectations, open communication serves to keep both parties in alignment, or may lead to a mutual agreement to renegotiate or break the contract.

How to Recognize the Warning Signs of Unmet Expectations

It is obviously far better to read the signs of *potential* unmet expectations prior to hiring than afterwards, so be alert to the following during the interview process:

- The interviewee asks few questions, or no questions.
- The interviewee asks lots of questions about one particular issue, and you have doubts about your ability or willingness to meet the implied expectation.
- The interviewee's previous employer had a culture and working conditions that are very different from your own organization.
- When you ask the question, "Why did you leave your former employer?" the interviewee mentions a reason that raises doubts about your own employer's ability to meet the implied expectation.
- You feel rushed to get through the interview.
- After the interview, you cannot recall discussing your expectations or those of the interviewee.

After hiring, look for these danger signs that the employee may have begun to disengage after realizing an important expectation will not be met:

- There is a sudden change in the employee's demeanor, indicating either suppressed anger or withdrawal.
- The employee avoids greeting you or making eye contact.
- The employee stops participating in discussions at meetings.
- The employee's performance drops off.
- The employee is increasingly absent.

Of course, you may not need to watch for any of these warning signs if the employee is assertive enough to come to you and directly voices dissatisfaction. However, as we know, many employees, especially younger and less experienced ones, are often reluctant to take that step.

Obstacles to Meeting Mutual Expectations

There are several obstacles to forging the unwritten psychological contract with a new employee, not the least of which is the fact that it is not typically put into writing, thus greatly increasing the potential for misunderstanding. Here are few others:

- The candidate lacks self-knowledge about wants, values, and expectations.
- The hiring manager is inexperienced or untrained at interviewing.
- The hiring manager is in a hurry to hire and rushes to get through the interview.
- The hiring manager and search team have created such a long list of ideal candidate characteristics that no single candidate could realistically possess them all.
- The hiring manager or other managers in the organization are increasingly unwilling to adapt to the changing expectations of younger generations of workers or to accommodate the expectations of diverse populations.
- The hiring manager believes that new hires should adapt to whatever is asked of them and be happy just to have a job.
- The organization's HR policies and management practices are outdated compared to competitors for talent in the industry and the community.
- The organization's recruitment advertising and related literature make implied promises that the organization cannot deliver.

- The candid interviewer faces the problem of getting the blame for failing to meet hiring quotas. "You told them WHAT?!!!" from an executive certainly puts a damper on honesty.
- The hiring manager is aware of negative working conditions the new hire will encounter, such as a pending downsizing or merger, or conflict within the immediate work team, and is afraid that mentioning it will cause the new hire to withdraw from the interview process or decline an offer.

Engagement Practices for Matching Mutual Expectations

The following practices for fostering realistic mutual expectations are frequently utilized by employer-of-choice organizations and have been found to significantly raise the probability of new hire success, satisfaction, and longer-term retention:

Engagement Practice #1:
Conduct Realistic Job Previews with Every Job Candidate

This practice is the most common way of addressing potentially unrealistic expectations. It involves initiating a frank and open discussion of job activities, performance expectations, immediate work team, working conditions, rules and policies, work culture, manager's style, and the organization's financial stability, or other topics where surprises need to be minimized. Because of the need to sell applicants on the position and the company, realistic job previews (RJPs) should obviously accentuate the positives, but not gloss over potential negatives that, when later experienced after hiring, could cause the new hire to abruptly quit or disengage.

This is a controversial practice among many managers who fear the risk of scaring off and losing talented candidates. The experience of companies who have implemented this practice has shown that some candidates will indeed withdraw when an organization's "warts" are openly discussed. On the other hand, candidates who turn out to be good fits for the organization and culture, tend not to be turned off by RJPs. Rather, in many cases, they are often actually more motivated to meet the challenge head on.

For example, GeoAccess, a Kansas City company, makes sure that all job applicants are made aware of the way people communicate in the company's fast-paced culture. It's a style of interacting that is direct, frank, spontaneous, and sometimes blunt. In meetings, coworkers give one another feedback that is honest, but may hurt. The company's human resource director, Greg Addison, wants to make sure that job applicants are made aware of this aspect of the company's culture. "Many companies don't understand their own culture," he says, "so they select misfits."

If you do lose candidates by divulging the truth about the job or workplace, then you probably would have lost them anyway within the first few months on the job. By discussing the truth up front, and allowing candidates to opt out, you have actually saved the cost of having to replace and retrain.

Some managers even go so far as to mention former employees who quit or were terminated because they could not adapt to a particular aspect of a challenging job, some working condition, or the company's culture.

Two important caution about conducting realistic job previews: First, before opening the company's kimono and showing its warts, interviewers should be trained to first ask the candidates about their expectations. Often, in listening to their answers, it is only too obvious that they would not fit the job or the culture, and you can save yourself the necessity of revealing the bad and the ugly to them. Second, be careful how you describe the negative aspects. Some hiring managers have been known to go overboard in describing the negatives, or describe them inaccurately because they have not personally experienced them. After all, what appears to be a negative to a hiring manager may actually be seen as a challenge to an applicant.

There is an art to conducting a realistic job preview without having it turn into a horrifying job preview. For example, it is honest, but not necessarily alarming, to say:

"You should be aware that there are negotiations going on that could result in the company being acquired. Should that happen, it could mean significant new career opportunities for many employees. It could also mean that a few people could lose their positions. Your position is one that we do not expect to be adversely affected. For those who might be impacted, we would provide career transition services to help them land on their feet in a new position."

On the other hand, interviewees would most likely be frightened off if you said, "You should be aware that our company might be acquired, in which case your job could be eliminated. There are no guarantees." Whatever is said in realistic job previews should definitely be approved at higher levels, so that managers are all delivering basically the same message in the best possible way.

To strengthen the RJP process, it is strongly recommended that organizations faithfully conduct exit interviews or exit surveys that allow departed employees to make comments. By analyzing exit comments, you can quickly determine what issues have been glossed over, over-promised, undelivered, and misunderstood. These are the issues that need to be more openly discussed during the pre-employment period.

Engagement Practice #2: Hire from Pool of Temp-to-Hire, Adjunct Staff, Interns, and Part-Time Workers

As the saying goes, before dyeing the whole cloth, it is best to first test a small piece of the cloth. When workers come aboard on a contingency basis, they have a chance to experience the ups and downs of the job first hand before they and the organization have made the commitment to a full-time relationship. Many of those who wouldn't fit the culture or would find it not to their liking can then decide to self-select out. Those who decide to stay and perhaps take on a full-time role will have gone through the most realistic job preview of all.

Engagement Practice # 3: Hire from Current Employee Referrals

The research shows that the first-year turnover rate for employees hired through employee referrals is significantly lower than for those hired through more formal recruiting methods, such as want ads.[7] Why? The main reason is that current employees tend to realistically describe the job and workplace to those they are referring. They have a vested interest in maintaining the friendship, and they are generally motivated to minimize surprises and "inoculate" the referred individual against possible disappointments.

Many companies have begun the practice of offering attractive monetary incentives or other types of rewards for successful referrals.

Engagement Practice # 4: Create a Realistic Job Description with a Short List of Critical Competencies

When search teams create too long a list of job requirements and competencies that the "ideal candidate" must have, they are unwittingly narrowing their pool of candidates, since fewer candidates could possibly pass the screening. They are also laying the groundwork for another problem later on—that the new hire will not be able to meet the performance expectations.

To prevent either of these problems, take care to create a realistic list of only the five or six most critical competencies needed for success, preferably stated as natural, motivated talents, not as technical or knowledge requirements. For example, a successful customer service representative needs not just the knowledge of the company's products, but also the natural ability to not take customers' anger personally. The more your organization has done to determine which competencies distinguish top performers from average performers in various job categories, the easier it will be to list them.

Engagement Practice # 5: Allow Team Members to Interview Candidates

When those who would work with the new hire as teammates are allowed to take part in the interviewing process without the manager being present in the room, they are free to answer the candidate's questions forthrightly. Likewise, the candidate is likely to feel less inhibited about asking questions of peers that might be uncomfortable to ask if the boss were present.

This practice has two added advantages: The "two-heads-are-better-than-one" factor typically leads to better candidate selection, and it also creates greater participation and "buy-in" from team members while sending them the message that their opinions count.

All interviewers need to be told up front that they are expected to provide solid reasons for voting "yea" or "nay" on a candidate. Some companies assign each interviewer a specific focus area for their questioning, such as fitting in, technical skills, business acumen, and so on.

Engagement Practice # 6: Hire from Pool of Current Employees

This one is easy to understand. When you hire or promote from within, you are taking less of a risk of turnover because the inside candidate is already wise to the ways of the organization. It's also a great way to increase morale by encouraging all workers about their career prospects within the company. However, be advised that, to be on the safe side, you still need to give current employees the same realistic job preview you would give to outside candidates.

Engagement Practice # 7: Create a Way for Candidates to "Sample" on-the-Job Experience

The traditional way of doing this is by asking the candidate a hypothetical question, such as "What would you do if an unhappy customer threatened to go to your manager and complain about your service?" An even better method is to ask a behavioral question, such as, "This job will frequently challenge you to deal effectively with unhappy customers. Can you tell me about a time when you dealt with a particularly unhappy customer and how you dealt with the situation?"

Better yet, many companies have begun using CD-ROMs that simultaneously test the applicant's aptitude for the position while also providing a glimpse of on-the-job realities. Wells-Fargo Bank, for example, requires bank teller candidates to watch a CD-ROM of an angry customer approaching to complain about an incorrect account balance, then freeze-frames the video and asks the candidate to select from among three possible responses to indicate how they would respond.

After Federal Express realized that 10 percent of first-time managers were leaving the company, it began conducting an eight-hour class called, "Is Management for Me?" that aspiring managers must attend before they can officially become candidates for management positions. During the class, current FedEx managers speak to the class, realistically describing the daily challenges of being a manager—the longer hours, increased workload, and the headaches relating to people management and discipline, plus the fact that they are never "off-the-clock." FedEx considers this program a success, partly because of the 20 percent dropout rate. They believe the program helps weed out management candidates who would not adapt well, and who might be motivated to get into management for the wrong reasons, such as their belief that it is the only way to advance.

Engagement Practice # 8: Survey or Interview New Hires to Find Out How to Minimize New Hire Surprises in the Future

In recent years many employers have started the practice of having recent hires complete evaluations of their experiences during the company's recruiting and new-hire orientation processes. Based on feedback received from written questionnaires, personal interviews, or both, the organization learns what the new hires were surprised to learn during their first thirty to ninety days on the job, what they expected and had not received, and things that were not discussed in interviews that should have been.

Why wait until after new hires have left to find out what they were disillusioned about—better to find it out while there is still an opportunity to do something about it.

How Prospective Employees Can Do Their Part

The main thing that a job candidate can do to gain a more realistic understanding of the job or workplace is ask questions. Some applicants will ask questions and others will not. A hiring manager must not wait for job candidates to ask questions, but should make it clear that all questions are welcome and that no question will be considered a stupid one. Hiring managers and everyone on the interviewing team should always invite more questions—in every job interview with every candidate—even after giving realistic job previews.

All recruitment materials should also invite candidates to ask questions, particularly the literature that is used in on-campus recruiting efforts and any that is distributed to entry-level recruits.

Here are other ways for employees to minimize the potential for disillusionment when starting a new job:

- Make a list of questions to ask before every interview.
- Ask friends and acquaintances what they know about the prospective employer.
- Research the prospective employer on the Internet.
- Ask to be interviewed by employees other than the hiring manager.
- Ask to be given a tour of the facility.
- Consider starting the job as a consultant or temp staffer, if possible, to gain a better feel for the workplace before making a full-time commitment.
- Directly ask everyone with whom you interview, "Is there anything about this job, the culture, or the work environment that new hires are sometimes surprised to find out after they start?"

Remember, you will be interviewed in a manner that tells you how employees are being treated. It is up to you to take or turn down the job, but at least you'll know what you're getting into.

The Beginning or Ending of Trust

Forging the psychological contract with a new employee in the interviewing and orientation phases is fundamentally a matter of establishing trust. If it is discovered that the employee lied about having a college degree, the trust is broken. If the employee realizes that the manager lied about how much travel would be involved in the new job, the opportunity for trust is lost.

Without trust, there can be no viable working relationship. Without taking the time and making the effort to establish trust from the start, managers are risking the waste of their most precious asset.

Employer-of-Choice Engagement Practices Review and Checklist

Review the engagement practices presented in this chapter and check the ones you believe your organization needs to implement or improve:

To Match Expectations with Reality:
1. ☐ Conduct realistic job previews with every job candidate.
2. ☐ Make a significant percentage of hires from pool of temp, adjunct, and part-time workers.
3. ☐ Make a significant percentage of hires from current employee referrals.
4. ☐ Create a realistic job description with a short list of most critical competencies.
5. ☐ Allow candidate's future coworkers to participate in job interviews.
6. ☐ Make a significant percentage of hires from pool of current employees.
7. ☐ Build into the interviewing process a way for candidates to gain a "sample" of on-the-job experience.
8. ☐ Survey or interview new hires to find out how to minimize new hire surprises in the future.

Notes

1. *"First Day at Work" Report*, Reed Company, UK, January 2003.
2. B. L. Brown, "Career Mobility: A Choice or Necessity?" *ERIC Digest* No. 191, ERIC Clearinghouse on Adult, Career and Vocational Educa-

tion, Center on Education and Training for Employment, Ohio State University, Columbus, 1998.

3. Kelly Beamon, "Just Say No," *National Business Employment Weekly*, Employment Briefs, November 24, 1998.

4. Emma Lunn, "Foibles . . . the First Day," *The Guardian*, September 29, 2003.

5. John Paul Kotter, "The Psychological Contract: Managing the Joining-Up Process," *California Management Review*, Spring 1973.

6. Source: Allstate Insurance, published in *Kansas City Star*, February 3, 1998.

7. Brown, op. cit.

CHAPTER FIVE

Reason #2:
The Mismatch Between Job and Person

> By treating people with diverse skills as an undifferentiated resource . . . companies forfeit the chance to make substantial gains in productivity, profitability, and personnel development.
>
> —VIVEK AGRAWAL

Research conducted over the last twenty-five years has shown that 80 percent of workers feel they are *not* using their strengths on a daily basis.[1] We hear the voices of these workers in the survey comments of both those who left and those who stayed:

- "Job functions are boring and monotonous."
- "My job responsibilities are not challenging."
- "ABC Company does not take full advantage of the employee skills that exist internally."
- "Employees are considered a billing number and their skill sets and hopes are not important."
- "ABC Company hires over-qualified employees into positions with low titles or grades."
- "They do not structure the positions to include job variety and challenge, which leads to a boring, routine job very quickly."

- "Employees are often in positions they are not qualified for."
- "XYZ Company doesn't understand the concept of utilizing their employees' skills to the fullest extent."
- "Our company just created a new training program for the operations group. In each department, they now have a skills coach. I am that person in my department. The thing is that I wasn't asked if this was something that I would like to do."
- "Job responsibilities are broken down too much. Too many people are doing jobs that can be combined with another job."
- "The company hires anyone."
- "They have the wrong type of people in certain positions."
- "Moving a person into a job that they don't want, even to prevent them from losing a job, is not a good policy. And if they don't take that job, then they receive no outplacement assistance."
- "In cross-training they give you the opportunity to learn a new task, but move you again before you learn it."
- "Managers are not good about giving employees extra responsibilities. They want to be in control of too much and don't want to let the employees help out once in a while."
- "There is too much control at the top and not enough delegation."
- "There was not enough authority pushed down. There were very talented people in the local office who truly had no authority."
- "My supervisor said I didn't deserve a raise because I didn't do anything new."

These are the comments of workers whose fundamental need to exercise competence has not been met. They are a sad testimony to an inestimable waste of human talent and loss of productivity. How does this happen? A closer look at the comments reveals some of the answers:

- Managers don't care or notice if their people are bored or unchallenged.
- Managers don't delegate enough to make jobs more interesting or challenging.
- Employees do not know their own strengths and the kind of work that would fit them best.
- Many organizations have no way of effectively assessing the talent of their employees.

- Employees are reluctant to discuss their dissatisfaction with their managers.
- Many jobs are so overly defined and narrowly drawn that almost anyone placed in those jobs would be underemployed.
- Managers are in such a hurry to hire that they end up just hiring warm bodies.
- Some organizations are simply inept when it comes to evaluating talent and matching people to the right jobs.
- For many managers, helping their employees grow and use new talents is not a high priority.

What's Missing: A Passion for Matching

With all these examples of talent management malpractice, it's almost surprising that 20 percent of the working population *does* get to use their strengths every day. It is also a reminder of how rare and special it is to have a manager who cares about the matching of talent to the job and does it well.

The key missing ingredient in so many companies is management's lack of passion for getting the right people in the right jobs. It has been said that the best managers are the best match-makers. This is truer today than it has ever been because of the preeminence of talent in an economy now dominated by service industries, encompassing everything from health care to retail, from business services to education. Distinguished business executives and management scholars have never been more in agreement about the importance of maintaining a relentless focus on talent:

> Over time, choosing the right people is what creates the elusive sustainable competitive advantage.
> —Larry Bossidy, chairman and former CEO
> of Honeywell Corporation[2]

> The best thing we can do for our competitors is hire poorly. If I hire a bunch of bozos, it will hurt us because it takes time to get rid of them then *they* start hiring people of lower quality. . . . We are always looking to hire people who are better than we are.
> —Miscrosoft recruiting director[3]

Leaders of companies that go from good to great . . . start by getting the right people on the bus, the wrong people off the bus, and the right people in the right seats.

—Jim Collins, *Good to Great*[4]

In acknowledgment of the new realization that talent is king, many large companies have even created senior executive positions with titles such as "chief talent officer," or "vice president, talent acquisition."

If matching people to the right jobs is generally recognized to be the key to business success, why do so many businesses lack the passion and commitment to get managers at every level to take it seriously and excel at it? There are many obstacles to consider, but the greatest of them all is a basic lack of understanding about the nature of human talent.

Common Misconceptions and Truths About Talent

- *Misconception No. 1: Employees are interchangeable parts to be moved into whatever slots most need to be filled.* It is truly amazing that so many managers seem to hold such a belief in this day and age, but judging by the way so many managers move employees around like stick figures, they obviously still do. As a corollary to this belief, many managers also believe that anyone can do certain jobs, especially lower-level ones, so they end up just hiring warm bodies, many of whom are not well matched to the work and end up as turnover statistics.

  Truth: People are "hard-wired" to perform certain activities better than others and to prefer using a handful of these talents more than others.

  These preferred natural gifts and talents are sometimes referred to as "motivated abilities," meaning that people are naturally self-motivated to use them and will make every effort to use them in their jobs, even if their jobs do not appear to require them. If a job does not allow employees to use their motivated abilities, they will find a way to use them in their leisure time because it is intrinsically satisfying to exercise these select few talents.

- *Misconception No. 2: Skills and knowledge are more important than talents.* It is easy to understand why so many managers believe this. It all begins with the hiring process when someone sits down to make a list of job requirements and writes down the basic requirements for eligible candidates. At the top of that list are the minimum skills, knowledge, certifications, degrees, or training needed to perform the job. Because these requirements are so often the primary focus for screening candidates out and in, many managers frequently lose sight of the natural abilities that will ultimately determine excellence in the job.

Truth: While job-content skills and knowledge are important as basic job requirements, they are much less important for long-term success on the job compared to natural talent. Most taxi drivers, for example, can learn the streets and how to get from here to there, but the most successful taxi drivers have vital native abilities: friendliness, being a good listener, the ability to sense when customers want to talk, a good sense of direction, observation skills, tact and diplomacy, eye-hand-foot coordination, to name a few.

Hiring managers frequently fail to make the distinction between eligibility to do the job based on trainable skills and suitability to do the job based on personality factors and natural talent. The problem is that natural talents are so much more difficult to identify than trainable skills, causing many managers to make very little effort to do so; many more simply do not know how. The result is the hiring of trained applicants who lack the native talents to achieve true competence, and the screening out of or failure to consider many trainable external applicants or internal candidates who do possess the right talents for success.

- *Misconception # 3: With the right training and coaching and the proper attitude, people can learn to do well in almost any job.* This myth is related to that great American idea that "you can do anything if you just set your mind to it." Many managers confront their employees with this very challenge, urging competent employees to take on "stretch" assignments outside the range of their natural talents, and even promoting them into management positions when what they truly enjoy is doing the work, not delegating it.

Truth: Yes, people are extremely adaptable, and can be "bent, folded, and mutilated" to perform many roles adequately. But, unless they are in the roles that match their motivated abilities (natural talents), they will not excel or enjoy the work. Instead, they will become disengaged, possibly burning themselves out, or search for ways to change the role, or leave the job altogether.

What's really going on here, in many cases, is that managers are far more interested in their own needs to fill a slot than they are in the best use of employees' talents. They may say they are trying to develop their people by challenging them, and they may even convince themselves they are doing the right thing, and feel very self-satisfied and well intentioned, but the fact is, they are misusing and disrespecting their most precious asset.

Employees also buy into in this process by not being sufficiently aware of their own best talents, or confident enough in them, to turn down an inappropriate assignment, or proactively seek a better fit when the job has gone stale.

The bottom-line assumption in all three of these misconceptions about talent is that the needs of the organization supersede the needs of the individual, and that it is the individual who must adapt. Of course, individuals have always adapted, especially during economic hard times, and they always will adapt when job security and survival are at stake. And organizations are certainly limited in their ability to accommodate every employee's talents.

But when times get better and companies are competing for talent, people will have other choices outside the organization, and they will pursue them. At that point, organizations start waking up to the fact that perhaps a way can be found to meet the employee's needs *and* the needs of the organization, and both parties are better served for having made the effort. That can be a turning point in their becoming true employers of choice.

Recognizing the Signs of Job-Person Mismatch

An employee may be mismatched with the job if he or she:

- Did not seem excited when first assigned to the job.
- Complains that the job content is not what was expected.
- Is not achieving the results or standards you expected.
- Starts making uncharacteristic mistakes.
- Is stressed and overmatched by the demands of the job.
- Starts asking that some job tasks be reassigned to coworkers or outsourced.

- Appears bored or unchallenged.
- Keeps coming around asking for a new project.
- Keeps mentioning a talent they would like to use in the job.
- Starts spending discretionary time on an activity that is more satisfying to perform but may not be important to the job.
- Requests a reassignment or starts lobbying for a promotion.
- Starts applying for other jobs in the organization.
- Generally appears less engaged or energized on a daily basis.

Obstacles to Preventing and Correcting Job-Person Mismatch

Many of the obstacles to effective job-person matching are based on deficiencies of organizational leadership and the human resource department, while some are attributable to the manager and others to the individual employee:

- The organization does not have basic job descriptions.
- The organization is using outdated job descriptions as the basis for screening, interviewing, and hiring.
- The organization has so narrowly defined the activities of a job that employees who occupy that job feel they have no room to perform the job in a way that makes best use of their strengths.
- The organization has not forecasted critical talent needs based on clear strategic business objectives.
- The organization has not analyzed jobs based on key targeted results to determine the critical few talents that distinguish top performers from average performers in each role.
- The fast pace of the organization and/or the manager has created a tendency to rush through the interview process and make hires without careful evaluations.
- Senior leaders have failed to establish a rigorous talent evaluation process, both for new hires and for current employees, as part of the career/succession planning process.
- Senior leaders and managers have overpromoted the idea of "selecting the best" instead of "selecting the best fit," which often results in the hiring of college graduates with the best grades or from the

best schools who do not always fit the culture or excel in the roles for which they were chosen.

- There has been an excessive focus on eliminating employee weaknesses through coaching and training when it would be wiser in many cases to put those employees into new roles where they can better capitalize on their greatest strengths.

- Organizational values, structures, and policies have reinforced the idea that the only way to grow professionally is to be promoted.

- Hires made from a limited talent pool have greatly limited the chances of finding an acceptable match.

- There has been a failure to delegate.

Companies with strong reputations for selecting the right talent and keeping employees well matched with their jobs do seem to have certain best practices in common. These practices fall into four main areas: selecting, engaging through job task assignment, on-going re-engagement as needed, and job enrichment.

Best-Fit Selection Practices

Engagement Practice # 9: Make a Strong Commitment to the Continuous Upgrading of Talent

The best employers do not have a cavalier, seat-of-the-pants approach to recruiting and interviewing. Instead they have a serious and resolute mindset about talent that begins with a fundamental belief that the organization's future depends on getting and keeping the right people in the right jobs. This means they leave little to chance.

Most companies do not take such a determined and proactive approach to the acquisition of talent. In fact, in a McKinsey survey of corporate executives, only 8 percent agreed with the statement, "Our company is always looking for talented people, even if we are not trying to fill a specific position."[5] In a war for talent, this is the mentality that is needed among all managers and executives.

It usually begins with a CEO who is driven to create an intense focus on strengthening talent levels across the organization. The CEO makes it clear that this is the top priority of every manager and typically insists that every manager not delegate hiring. This means that the hiring process is owned by the hiring managers, not by human resources, which operates as a key resource and full partner to support the hiring managers.

The Hartford: Managers as Talent Scouts

Like most companies, The Hartford used to depend on classified advertising and headhunters to fill positions. Gradually, they realized they were spending too much valuable time and money screening candidates. Vice president of human resources, John Madigan, had been receiving referrals from managers for years, but the company had not been making the most of the referral information.

Madigan hired a researcher to identify and evaluate each previously referred candidate as well as those that had been identified through other sources. He then promised managers that all their referrals would be thoroughly checked out and stored in a referral database. When managers refer candidates, they are contacted and invited in for an interview, after which their data is added to the database. When an appropriate job becomes available, the right candidate can be much more quickly identified.

As a result of creating the candidate tracking system, managers feel better about putting their energies into scouting talent instead of screening. The Hartford also lowered its recruiting expenses and Madigan believes it has also increased retention. "These people have been courted and there is a familiarity," he said. "And since they didn't knock on the door to begin with, when they make the decision it is because the fit is right."[6]

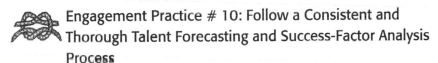

Engagement Practice # 10: Follow a Consistent and Thorough Talent Forecasting and Success-Factor Analysis Process

Before beginning the recruiting process, the best companies engage in a talent forecasting process based on key business objectives. The business objectives drive talent needs, with special attention focused on pivotal jobs that will create the most value for the organization. For auto dealerships, these are general managers, sales people, and finance managers. For grocery stores, these are store managers, department managers, and checkers. For mutual fund companies, these are fund managers. Often, they are lower- to mid-level workers who have the most direct customer contact. In some service-driven organizations, 80 percent of the value (revenues) derives from the results generated by 20 percent of the jobs (talent) in the organization.

The next phase of the preselection process involves understanding what makes top performers successful in all positions, but especially those that create the most value. Many companies validate a selection instrument by having their top performers—the ones they would clone if they could—take a battery of personality and ability assessments, then look for common traits and capabilities. The more top performers who take the assessments, the more valid the conclusions that can be made from them. Many organizations find this process helpful, but it is fallible in one sense—not all successful people use the same talents to succeed in the same job. Still, top performers tend to share a select few critical characteristics that are worth the effort to uncover.

Capital One:
A Semi-Automated Assessment and Screening Process

Many large companies, in an effort to screen thousands of applicants, have created semiautomated hiring processes that help screen candidates based on their suitability for various positions.

Capital One Financial Corporation, with a payroll of more than 15,000, screens candidates by having them take a battery of tests that have already been validated by 1,600 top-performing employees, from call center operators to executives. Employee test results are fed into a database with detailed profiles of the tested workers' job performance. Capital One's staff psychologists and statisticians then analyze the results to design new tests that predict on-the-job success.

This highly efficient process allows a call-center employee to be screened, tested, tried out, and subjected to one face-to-face interview, all in five hours' time—a process that used to take twenty hours.

But does it result in a better matching of people with jobs? The company believes so. Capital One's attrition rate has dropped from 45 percent to 10 percent, also due partly to better pay and benefits.[7]

The idea is to supplement an in-depth interviewing process by using the same battery of assessment instruments to screen job candidates in search of those whose profiles look most like the top performers.

Some companies add depth to the validation process by conducting focus group interviews with top performers. One large hotel chain gathered eight of its best housekeepers from around the world into a room to find out what they had in common. They described how they try to see the rooms through the eyes of the hotel guests (empathy), and put on a show for the guests by doing things like arranging children's toys and stuffed animals on the bed to make it look like they were interacting (desire to please and delight).[8]

Other companies may go one step further and conduct one-on-one "behavioral event" interviews with "water-walkers" in key jobs, in which they are asked to tell detailed stories about exactly how they achieved a previous successful outcome for a customer or client. Interviewers listen carefully, probe with clarifying questions, and take notes about the talents the worker was using in each achievement. Still others use consultants to observe successful workers while they go about their daily business, taking notes and questioning as appropriate to gain a deeper understanding of why the workers do what they do.

Whatever combination of methods is used, the desired outcome is a short list of critical success factors for each job, no matter how low it is in the organization's hierarchy. The mistake most companies make here is that they invite too many people to help construct a list of skills, talents, and traits they would like the ideal candidate to possess. By the time the employment requisition and job ad are written, there are so many job requirements that not even Superman could meet them all. As a result, many perfectly qualified candidates are screened out, and the job goes unfilled for weeks or months.

Finally, it is a cardinal rule that no outdated job descriptions will be used as the basis for constructing employment ads and interview questions. In an ideal world, every job description would be updated every time a new person is hired, reflecting the particular needs of the organizational unit at that moment in time.

What Qualities to Look for and Why

Hire and promote first on the basis of integrity; second, motivation; third, capacity; fourth, understanding; fifth, knowledge; and last and least, experience. Without integrity, motivation is dangerous; without motivation, capacity is impotent; without capacity, understanding is limited; without understanding, knowledge is meaningless; without knowledge, experience is blind. Experience is easy to provide and quickly put to use by people with all the other qualities.

—Dee Hock[9]

Engagement Practice # 11: Cast a Wide Recruiting Net to Expand the Universe of Best-Fit Candidates

The logic is simple—the larger the selection, the greater your chances of finding the right fit. There are three ways to expand your labor pool: first, by not imposing too many restrictions in terms of your job requirements; second, by changing the job itself; and third, by creatively considering new sources of talent that you have never before tapped. Here are guidelines for each of these:

1. *Loosening Job Restrictions*: As mentioned previously, many organizations create job descriptions with too many requirements, many of which are optional but not really essential. This means you may need to challenge many of the technical requirements that often appear on the long laundry lists that circulate prior to beginning the recruiting process. This is especially important when the labor market is tight or when the supply of talent for the position to be filled is limited.

2. *Changing the Job Itself*: Every time you fill a job you have the opportunity to take a second look at the way the job is done. "Because we've always done it that way" is not the answer you are looking for. The next time a position opens up, don't just rush to fill it. Instead, start with a clean slate by asking yourself, "What is the work that needs to get done?" and take a fresh look at the needs behind the job, not just the job description.

   It may be that doing the job in a new way will actually result in increasing the availability of applicants. United Parcel Service, for example, was experiencing excessively high turnover with its drivers. When they asked drivers why they were leaving, the overwhelming response was that they hated having to load and unload the delivery trucks. UPS decided to eliminate loading and unloading as a job requirement for drivers, and to create a whole new job category—loader. Their reasoning made perfect sense—the supply of drivers is less than the supply of potential loaders, so why unnecessarily restrict that supply? As it turned out, the rate of turnover among loaders was also high, but they were easier to replace than drivers, so the solution was a good one.

3. *Creatively Considering New Sources of Talent*. In my previous book, *Keeping the People Who Keep You in Business*, there is a list of 54 creative sources for expanding the talent pool. One of the most

overlooked is the pool of internal candidates. Many hiring managers can actually become victims of their own limited perceptions. Failing to consider administrative assistants for management positions because of having stereotyped them as second-class workers is a common one.

Another self-imposed way of restricting our own talent supply is to persist in keeping a job requirement that has become outdated, such as continuing to demand specific programming knowledge when today's software packages have made it easier for more internal workers to learn the software and be redeployed into those jobs. The same holds true for job restrictions related to heavy lifting and words-per-minute requirements for word processors, which may no longer be needed. Another example is loosening dress code restrictions in call centers that may have previously screened out workers who prefer a more informal way of dressing.

According to John Sullivan, former chief talent officer at Agilent Technologies and recruiting guru to many forward-thinking employers, "only 10 percent of the recruiters in business today are using innovative methods to help their companies attract and retain talent. The other 90 percent of companies are still using old tools." Here are some of the newer practices that Sullivan recommends more companies consider:

- Host open houses by invitation, by asking current employees to bring in friends they believe would be good employees.
- Build a Web site that puts prospects into e-mail contact with current satisfied employees. Put streaming video on the Web site showing the work environment.
- Make your Web site more interactive, offering applicants the opportunity to list their ideal job criteria, then showing jobs that most closely match, and linking them to current openings.
- Train all hiring managers to be more proactive as talent scouts, by coaching them on where to look for new recruits and how to sell them on the company and the job.
- Build a contact database of the best talent in your industry and reach out to build relationships with them through e-newsletters or by phone so they will think of coming to work with your company when they are ready to make a job change.
- Make every employee a recruiter by creating or revitalizing employee referral programs, as this method remains by far the most effective method of attracting talent that stays.[10]

Engagement Practice # 12:
Follow a Purposeful and Rigorous Interview Process

Most companies with excellent track records for keeping a high percentage of the people they hire use a highly focused and systematic interviewing process and have trained all hiring managers to follow the process religiously. Here are some of the most effective components that these companies use:

- *Train all hiring managers in "behavioral interviewing."* This means that the company must first make the commitment to thoroughly analyze each job in terms of critical success factors, and have hiring managers develop questions that require applicants to respond with stories of how they demonstrated those success factors in their past experiences. Most behavioral questions will be asked in the form of, "Tell me about a time when you . . ."—as in, "Tell me about a time when you had to deal with a difficult customer and how you did it." If an applicant does not have a story to tell, it is quite difficult to make one up on the spot. Well-qualified applicants can usually come up with illustrative stories to tell right away, while unsuitable candidates cannot.

   The principle that makes this method effective is that actual past behavior accurately predicts future behavior. Companies considering use of behavioral interviewing should realize that it requires discipline for a manager who is in a hurry to fill a position to slow down enough to create behavioral questions and remember to conduct a behavioral interview with every hire. Human resource staff can be valuable partners by assisting with the pre-employment job analysis and the preparation of behavioral questions.

- *Use multiple interviewers.* The chances of hiring the right person go up when several interested parties are invited to participate in interviewing candidates. The interviewing team typically consists of peers and others with whom the new hire will have frequent interaction. It is a good way to involve team members in an important decision process while also getting valuable input and differing perspectives from those with a vested interest in seeing the right person hired.

   Whether done by having serial one-on-one interviews or with the interviewee facing a panel, it is highly recommended that the interviewing team meet beforehand to plan what questions will be asked, how, and by whom. Afterward, the team will need to meet and discuss each candidate as well.

At Whole Foods the Whole Team Hires

At Whole Foods Markets, teams—and only teams—have the power to approve new hires for full-time jobs. Store leaders screen candidates, then recommend them for jobs on a specific team. After the team interviews the candidate, a two-thirds vote is required for a hire, then the candidate doesn't become a full-time employee until after a thirty-day trial period. Teams routinely reject new hires before the thirty days are up if they turn out not to have the right stuff. Not everyone fits the Whole Foods profile, which is people who are "serious about food, have a knack for pleasing customers, and can tolerate the candid give-and-take that's necessary for a [workplace] democracy."

Another reason Whole Foods team members are so tough on new hires—the company's gainsharing program ties directly to team performance. If team members vote for someone who doesn't perform, their bonuses will be less.[11]

- *Check several references without fail.* Many managers do not check references because of the time it takes, and because many references are reluctant to speak for fear of a lawsuit. Still, smart hiring managers know how to overcome these obstacles and they know that the information to be gotten is worth taking the extra time. There are several books that provide tips for better reference-checking, among them Pierre Mornell's *Hiring Smart!* and my earlier book, *Keeping the People Who Keep You in Business.*

Engagement Practice # 13: Track Measures of Hiring Success

Many companies track cost per hire, but fewer than 10 percent of companies track the most meaningful hiring measure of them all—quality of hire.[12] Here are recommended ways of tracking the measure that comes closest to quantifying the match between person and job:

- Each hiring manager sets quarterly and first-year performance objectives for the new hire expressed in terms of expected quantifiable results and, in partnership with human resources, tracks quality of hire based on the achievement of those results. Some organizations use the first-year performance appraisal to track quality-of-hire. How soon to measure quality of hire may vary from job to job based partly on expected ramp-up and learning curve.

- Results may be based on customer satisfaction surveys, achievement of on-schedule results, cost/quality targets, absenteeism rates, and achievement of targeted quantitative objectives.
- Track first-year retention rates of all new hires.
- Track employee engagement survey scores of first-year employees as a group.
- Each year hiring managers complete quality-of-hire ratings on all new hires.
- Gather 360-degree feedback ratings on all new hires at the end of their first year.

It is recommended that all hiring managers meet with human resources staff once a year to review quality of hires and to discuss any mistakes made, lessons learned, new strategies, and plans for improvement.

Best Practices for Engaging and Re-Engaging Through Job Task Assignment

There is potentially no more powerful motivator than the intrinsic satisfaction to be gained from using one's motivated talents. Managers can easily lose sight of this untapped source of motivational power by getting caught up in extrinsic factors like pay, bonuses, and benefits. Because so many workers have never had jobs that are inherently satisfying to perform, they, too, have come to accept external rewards as their due "compensation" for the trade-off they have made in job satisfaction.

Your job as a manager of people is to get the work done by allowing the maximum possible use of your employees' motivated abilities to achieve targeted results. This is not an easy task because it means taking the time to get to know each employee's unique combination of talents. It also means trying to dole out the available work so that it matches those talents, which is not always possible to do in a way that is perfectly acceptable to all, which can be frustrating.

The job of assigning the right tasks to the right talent becomes even more difficult when the manager's own style gets in the way, as when the manager:

- Believes there is only "one best way" to do the job and insists that the job be done that way.
- Doesn't trust people to make the right choices to reach the end result.
- Attempts to "idiot-proof" jobs by over-prescribing exactly how they will be done through detailed rules, regulations, and procedure manuals.
- Micro-manages employees because of constant fear that they might be doing the wrong thing or taking advantage.
- Exerts pressure on the employee to comply with demands instead of trying to gain voluntary commitment to performance goals (see Figure 5-1).
- Tries to correct employees' weaknesses at the expense of developing their strengths.
- Doesn't spend time trying to understand employees' best talents.

Admittedly, there are some jobs where safety, security, and financial accuracy dictate that they be done in a certain way, but in most jobs there is wide berth for the use of an individual's talent. With that exception, managers who engage in the above behavior are limiting their own ability to engage and retain their workers.

Organizations can step in to correct these kinds of management practices through implementing better processes for selecting managers in the first place, providing multirater feedback to all managers, training and coaching managers in better talent identification and people management

Figure 5-1.

Getting compliance vs. getting commitment.

Compliance	*Commitment*
Manager determines goal priorities.	Individual determines goal priorities.
Manager determines performance objectives.	Manager and individual together determine performance objectives.
Manager determines how the task will be performed.	Individual determines how to perform the task.
Manager defines job tasks.	Individual defines job tasks.

skills, rewarding and recognizing top talent managers, and holding all managers accountable for talent-related objectives.

Here are some practical tools and ideas that managers can use now to assign tasks so that workers can be more engaged through the use of their motivated abilities:

Engagement Practice # 14:
Conduct "Entrance Interviews" with All New Hires

Meet with the new hires during the first week on the job with the specific purpose of uncovering their greatest strengths and talents. Now that the employee already has the job, you can expect responses to be less calculated to impress you than when you asked similar questions in the job interview. Let employees know it is in your best mutual interests to get at the truth about their talents in order to put them to greatest use. Ask the following questions, even if you already asked similar questions in job interviews:

What do you consider your greatest strengths?

What do you consider your greatest weaknesses?

Which of your talents was most under-utilized in your last job?

Which of your talents would you most like to use in this job?

Which would you rather work with most—data, people, or things?

How would you like to be challenged in the coming year?

What other goals do you have for yourself in the coming year and beyond?

How often would you like to meet to discuss your progress?

In reading the job description, which activities appeal to you most and least?

Which of your talents would you most like to develop further?

Be clear that it may not be possible to make use of employees' talents in exactly they way they prefer, but at least they will know that is your intent. Let them know that you value their talents and look forward to helping them succeed. Invite them to come and let you know if they begin to feel that their best talents are being underused.

Engagement Practice # 15:
Work to Enrich the Jobs of All Employees

Years ago, job enrichment researchers Richard Hackman and Greg Oldham identified five factors that contribute to job enrichment:

1. *Skill Variety*: A desired mix of skills and activities is needed to carry out the work.

2. *Task Completion*: The job is undertaken as a whole, allowing the employee to complete an identifiable piece of work from beginning to end with a visible outcome.

3. *Task Significance*: The job has a recognizable impact on the overall mission or on other people inside or outside the organization.

4. *Autonomy*: The job offers substantial freedom, independence, and discretion in scheduling the work and in choosing the procedures to be used in carrying it out.

5. *Feedback*: The job provides feedback—by the observable progress and results of the job itself, or from customers, coworkers, and manager.[13]

Hackman and Oldham's research yielded strong evidence that employees display high levels of self-motivation, work satisfaction, performance, customer service, commitment, and retention when their jobs have all five of these elements.

Some jobs are more easily enriched than others, but it can be surprisingly easy to implement a change that has significant impact. A housecleaning firm, for example, started allowing workers to switch jobs as they moved from house to house (skill variety). This meant instead of having one individual vacuum all day long, they would swap jobs with the window-washer at the next house. After instituting this change, the company noticed increased productivity and retention among the workers.

Task completion, task significance, and autonomy can all be increased by one management decision, as when a manager decides to give sales or customer service people the authority and resources to resolve customer problems on the spot instead of passing them on to one person, then another. Customers seem to appreciate this as well.

Feedback can be increased simply by starting to have more frequent meetings with employees to give feedback on their performance, or by sharing customer satisfaction surveys, profitability figures, production re-

sults, and any number of other data now made available via company intra-
nets or through increasingly sophisticated information systems. One high-
tech manufacturing company even had each of its production teams stamp
its own phone number on every product shipped from the plant. The
phone calls received from customers who had problems with a product
served as a highly direct feedback mechanism that also served to motivate
workers to achieve higher levels of quality.

Here are a few other ways to enrich jobs:

- Combine several small tasks performed by separate people into one
  more fulfilling job.
- Place workers into teams or natural work units organized by the
  types of clients, industries, geographies they serve.
- Gradually give more autonomy to workers by delegating first one
  task, then another from a higher level job, or a manager's job, to
  workers at lower levels.
- Establish more direct contact between workers and customers.
- Create teams and task forces with the power to solve problems or
  create new products, services, or mini-enterprises.
- Allow people doing stand-alone tasks in various locations to connect
  with employees doing other phases of the work.

Very few jobs are fixed as they used to be. These days jobs constantly
change, and the opportunity to enrich them will be there if you choose to
take it. This also means that once a job has been enriched it will not stay
enriched without manager and employee working together to make it happen. Finally, it is considered a realistic rule of thumb that if 80 percent of a
job is enriched, it is probably a good job.[14]

 ## Engagement Practice # 16:
Delegate Tasks to Challenge Employees and Enrich Their Jobs

Today's younger generations of workers don't have the patience to "pay
their dues" as their parents had done. You may disparage their impatience,
but when they leave your company and move on to another one that may
be willing to give them the keys to the car as soon as they come in the
door, you are left high and dry without their talents. No matter how many
dues you paid as you climbed the ladder, no matter how gradually and

consistently you prepared yourself for a more meaningful role, and how deliberately you acquired valuable knowledge, that traditional model of gradually taking on incremental challenges is considered outdated by many Gen-Xers and Millennials. Most younger workers have a more short-term focus. They want meaningful work roles NOW.

This means you will need to employ the job enrichment guidelines above and, in many cases, start delegating tasks that you may have been uncomfortable delegating in the past.

Here are some reasons you may be reluctant to delegate:

- You're afraid they will screw things up.
- There's no time to train them to the point where you can trust them not to screw up.
- You believe they need to pay their dues first, as you did.
- You have some grunt work that needs doing.
- You like doing the work yourself too much to let it go.
- You're afraid that empowering your workers means giving up your power.

If you can identify with any of these concerns, you will need to work to overcome them. For practical guidelines on how to do that, refer to "23 Steps to Better Delegation and Empowerment" in *Keeping the People Who Keep You in Business*.[13]

The Employee's Role in the Matching Process

As in all the seven reasons employees leave, it's not just the manager that has all the responsibility. All employees need to be reminded that there is much they can do to achieve the best match of their own talents to the job:

- Ask questions during the interview to make sure the job is one that will make good use of your talents.
- Know your values well enough to resist being recruited into a work culture that would not be a good fit.
- If talent assessment workshops or inventories are not offered at the organization, seek assistance with identifying your talents through a private career coach, psychologist, community college, or university career center.

- If you feel the manager is not making good use of your talents, take the initiative to meet with the manager to discuss how you would like the job to be changed.
- Put yourself in the manager's shoes and be prepared to explain how enriching their own job will also benefit the work unit or organization as a whole.
- Seek whatever training you need to earn the trust of the manager to delegate more to them.
- Instead of getting too comfortable when you have mastered a job, keep yourself engaged by seeking new challenges.
- Ask for feedback when you feel you are not getting enough of it.

Employer-of-Choice Engagement Practices Review and Checklist

Review the engagement practices presented in this chapter and check the ones you believe your organization needs to implement or improve.

To Select the Right Talent for the Job:
9. ☐ Make a strong commitment to the continuous upgrading of talent.
10. ☐ Make sure that all hiring managers follow a consistent and thorough talent forecasting and success-factor analysis process.
11. ☐ Cast a wide recruiting net to expand the universe of best-fit candidates.
12. ☐ Follow a purposeful and rigorous interview process.
13. ☐ Track measures of hiring success.

To Assign the Right Task to the Right Person:
14. ☐ Conduct "entrance interviews" with all new hires.
15. ☐ Work to enrich the jobs of all employees.
16. ☐ Delegate tasks to challenge employees and enrich their jobs.

Notes

1. Marcus Buckingham and Donald O. Clifton, *Now, Discover Your Strengths* (New York: The Free Press, 2001).
2. Larry Bossidy and Ram Charan, *Execution: The Discipline of Getting Things Done* (New York: Random House, 2002).

3. Edward L. Gubman, *The Talent Solution: Aligning Strategy and People to Achieve Extraordinary Results* (New York: McGraw-Hill, 1998).

4. Jim Collins, author of *Good to Great: Why Some Companies Make the Leap and Others Don't* (New York: Harper Business, 2001), based on study of how eleven companies out of 1,435 went from good to great financial performance. Web-exclusive interview in *Fast Company*, October 2001.

5. Nana Rausch, "War for Talent II: Several Ways to Win," Peoplepalooza column, *Fast Company*, June 2000.

6. Bob Calandra, "Finders Keepers," *Human Resource Executive*, June 2, 2000.

7. "We Try to Minimize Face-to-Face Interviews," *Business Week*, November 22, 1999.

8. Marcus Buckingham and Curt Coffman, *First, Break All the Rules: What the World's Great Managers Do Differently* (New York: Simon & Schuster, 1999).

9. M. Mitchell Waldrop, "Dee Hock on Management," *Fast Company*, October/November 1996.

10. Jodi Spiegel Arthur, "Talent Scout," *Human Resource Executive*, June 2, 2000.

11. Charles Fishman, "Whole Foods Is All Teams," *Fast Company*, April 1996.

12. Quality Now, *Staffing.org Metrics Update e-newsletter*, January 8, 2003.

13. Richard Hackman and Greg R. Oldham, *Work Redesign* (Reading, Mass.: Addison-Wesley, 1980).

14. Edward E. Lawler III, *Treat People Right! How Organizations and Individuals Can Propel Each Other into a Virtual Spiral of Success* (San Francisco: Jossey-Bass, 2003).

15. Leigh Branham, "Guidelines for Better Delegation and Empowerment" (Retention Practice # 18: Give Autonomy and Reward Initiative), in Leigh Branham, *Keeping the People Who Keep You in Business: 24 Ways to Hang On to Your Most Valuable Talent* (New York: AMACOM, 2001).

Reason #3:
Too Little Coaching and
Feedback

The manager needs to look
at the employee not as a
problem to be solved, but
as a person to be
understood.

—Nigel Nicholson

Just in case you need more evidence that lack of performance coaching and feedback is a major cause of employee disengagement and turnover, here are some survey results to consider:

- The number one cause of performance problems in 60 percent of companies is poor or insufficient feedback from supervisors.[1]
- A survey of 1,149 people at seventy-nine different companies found that manager feedback and coaching skills were consistently rated as mediocre.[2]
- Forty-one percent of employees believe their managers have no effect whatsoever on their performance, and 14 percent said their manager actually made the job harder.[3]
- Only 39 percent of managers said that their company is very effective at providing candid feedback.[4]
- Only 35 percent of workers identified by their companies as highly talented feel the company tells them openly and candidly where they stand.[5]

It has been estimated that approximately 50 percent of the nonperformance problems in business occur because of the lack of feedback, and about 50 percent of what appear to be motivational problems in business are actually feedback problems.[6]

Saratoga's post-exit survey comments of voluntarily departed employees testify to the role that lack of feedback and coaching played in their decisions to leave:

- "Not enough feedback from supervisors."
- "There is not much feedback on job performance."
- "Managers need to coach employees."
- "There is no feedback from any of the supervisors on how jobs are being done."
- "In my three years of working at XYZ Company, I never had a job description or an evaluation."
- "ABC Company needs to pay a lot more attention to letting employees know how they perform."
- "As an employer, XYZ Company doesn't keep its employees updated enough on their errors, so that we know where we stand in our positions. We don't know what we've done wrong until an error is made because we aren't notified of process changes ahead of time."
- "Management needs to take a little more time to explain what they expect so I would be more inclined to work and perform."
- "The formal performance evaluations are geared more towards the number of mistakes rather than the number of positive contributions."
- "Managers are never around, never seem to keep up on reviews, and pay increases always seem to be delayed."
- "Managers don't handle issues with troubled employees well. They seem to not like confrontation with employees who don't produce or don't give good customer service."
- "This company tends to have managers who are more involved in the small time politics of the workplace rather than rewarding and disciplining based on performance. There have been times when supervisors have acted in a vindictive, self-serving manner."
- "Managers should start following up with disciplinary measures for those who blatantly disregard the rules."
- "The company will bend over backwards to keep employees that are performing below average."

- "ABC Company does not expeditiously hire, discipline, or terminate employees.
- "XYZ Company must pay more attention to letting employees know how they perform."
- "They tell you everything you do wrong and nothing you do right."
- "I'm not sure that this statement applies to all of ABC Company, but as far as the office I work in, they dwell too much on what an employee does wrong, far more than what an employee does right."
- "XYZ Company needs to address negative issues of employees because these negative issues affect the department as a whole."
- "ABC Company does not communicate expectations, provide timely feedback, or conduct timely performance evaluations. There is also a lack of trust between employees and management."
- "Performance reviews are given out on a whim, it seems."
- "I feel like nobody cares about the work I am doing."

These comments provide ample evidence that opportunities to build competence, trust, hope, and worth through coaching and feedback have been lost. They also reveal several underlying problems:

- Many managers are not paying attention to the people they supervise.
- Performance feedback is occurring irregularly or not happening at all.
- Basic expectations and changes in work procedures are not being communicated.
- Nonperformance is not being addressed.
- Too much emphasis is being placed on criticism and not enough on praise.
- Managers are allowing themselves to be influenced by politics, favoritism, and other factors besides objective performance.
- Employees themselves may be reluctant to seek feedback.

Why Coaching and Feedback Are Important to Engagement and Retention

Performance coaching and feedback is essential for employees because it helps them to answer four basic questions:

1. Where are we going as a company?
2. How are we getting there?
3. How do you expect me to contribute?
4. How am I doing?

The answers to these questions constitute much of what gives meaning to an employee's efforts. We all have a basic need to exercise competence and to know that our talents have been used to make a valuable contribution. At times, our own ability to see the impact of our contributions is clouded by the fact that we may be removed from the end result, or limited by our own narrow perspectives.

Companies need to give feedback and coaching to make sure that employees' efforts stay aligned with organizational and unit goals and the expectations of direct supervisors. This alignment is a necessary precondition for employee engagement.

One survey found that 80 percent of employees who had been coached by their managers felt a strong sense of commitment to their organization, versus 46 percent of employees who received no coaching.[7]

The goal of retaining employees through coaching and feedback is really a secondary one. The engagement of employees to enhance performance is the main goal. Much of the coaching and feedback managers do will always be directed at unsuccessful attempts to get nonperformers to meet expectations. Knowing when to continue coaching and when to discontinue and make the tough decision to terminate is a decision all managers will inevitably have to make. Just as you don't have a goal of making everyone you meet a lifelong friend, you will likewise not try to retain every employee you manage and attempt to coach.

Why Don't Managers Provide Coaching and Feedback?

There are many possible answers to this question. Generally, managers don't provide coaching and feedback because:

- They fear or dread confronting an employee with criticism without hurting, offending, creating defensiveness, alienating the employee, getting into an argument, or losing control of their own emotions.

- Too many of them are simply pressed into service on so many projects that they feel they have little time to actually observe an employee's progress over the long haul.
- They fear they will fail. True coaching and genuine, responsible feedback are higher-level people skills, but are not taught to managers as anything more complicated than "useful techniques."
- True progress is gradual, and managing step-by-step employee development requires far closer proximity—both physically and emotionally—to workers than most management jobs permit.
- Feedback in a world filled with virtual assignments, domestic and global travel, interminable meetings, and endless client contacts simply does not allow for the required immediacy of the effort—wait a day to give feedback on something and the effect is lost.
- They have never received skilled feedback or positive coaching themselves, or have worked too long in a culture that doesn't encourage it.

Reviewing this list makes one wonder how any feedback and coaching ever gets done, and it should raise our levels of appreciation and admiration for the managers who somehow do make time for it in their weekly schedules. Many managers actually believe they are providing sufficient feedback and coaching, but if you talk to their direct reports, you hear a different story.

Larry Bossidy, former CEO of Allied-Signal, believes that most CEOs are unaware of the lack of feedback their direct reports are receiving. "If you ask any CEO if their direct reports know what the CEO thinks of them," said Bossidy, "the CEO will slam the table and say, 'Absolutely! I'm with them all the time. I travel with them. We are always discussing their results.'" But he added, "If you then ask the direct reports the same question, nine out of ten will say, 'I don't have a clue, I haven't had a performance review or any feedback in the last five years.'"[8]

In the sports world, it would be unimaginable to think of a coach not giving feedback to a player for extended periods of time. Consider this ridiculous scenario: A basketball coach begins the season by telling his players, "OK, here's the deal. You're going to go out there and play thirty games, and at the end of the season I'll sit down with each of you and we'll go over how you did and how you can get better in the future." And yet, this is exactly what is happening in untold numbers of companies, where managers give feedback to employees once and only once each year—at the annual formal performance appraisal meeting.

Recognizing the Signs

Any of the following behaviors may indicate that your direct reports are not receiving the feedback and coaching they need to improve or maintain desired performance levels:

- You realize that the last time you gave feedback to one of your direct reports was months ago during their last performance appraisal.
- You have not spent at least one hour in the last three months giving performance feedback to each of your direct reports.
- You only give feedback when an employee requests it.
- You find yourself procrastinating on giving feedback to an employee until days or weeks after you first intended to give it.
- Your direct reports have tried to schedule meetings with you for feedback and coaching, and you have had to cancel or postpone them on several occasions.
- After you give feedback, things fail to improve or seem to get even worse.
- When giving feedback, you hold back for fear of hurting the employee's feelings.
- You feel uncomfortable with the whole idea of coaching and giving feedback because you have never been trained in how to do it well.

More Than an Event: It's About the Relationship

Giving good feedback and coaching is about more than having a series of meetings—it's about manager and employee building an open and trusting relationship. Most managers have built comfortable and satisfactory relationships with some employees, but have also experienced the opposite as well—relationships with other employees that never got off on the right footing, or went from bad to worse. Perhaps it is because we simply like some employees better than others, or we favor those who are most similar to us, but it is a common phenomenon to place a halo on the heads of some employees, and see horns growing on others.

Unknowingly, a manager may actually be contributing to the failure of an employee. As described in a classic article, "The Set-Up-to-Fail Syndrome," there is usually a triggering event that causes the manager to lose faith in an employee—losing a client, undershooting a target, or missing a deadline.[9] The syndrome is set in motion when the supervisor starts to worry about an employee's performance so much that she starts putting him on a "short leash"—constantly checking up on him, requiring approval for all decisions, and generally micro-managing him. The employee interprets this reining-in behavior as a loss of trust and confidence and, in the worst-case scenario, starts living down to the supervisor's low expectations. He begins to withdraw emotionally, may be paralyzed into inaction, and consumes so much of the supervisor's time that he is eventually fired or quits.

This is exactly the kind of downward-spiral disengagement process referred to in Chapter Two. It can be interrupted and reversed by a manager who is aware that it is happening and who is motivated to change the relationship. The prescription: a mixture of coaching, training, job redesign, and a clearing of the air. All this takes courage, an ability to be self-reflective, and more frequent contact and emotional involvement with the employee. But too many managers are not motivated to perform such transformations.

While listening to employees describe how they came to leave their past employers, I have heard many variations of the set-up-to-fail story. One very creative and talented employee I'll call Pam described a turning point with a manager, who was pushing her to tell a prospective client they could deliver a service that Pam knew they were not prepared to deliver. Pam saw this promise to the client as bordering on unethical, while her boss perceived Pam's reluctance as a lack of confidence. After that, the manager began withholding assignments from Pam and giving them to her peers instead. Eventually, the emotional chasm in their relationship became too great, and Pam was let go. With time to reflect, she realized she was quite relieved to be gone.

Could this employee have been salvaged with a different approach to coaching and feedback? Perhaps the disagreement about ethics would have been too great to overcome. But I sincerely believe that at least a third of all terminations could be prevented with better coaching and feedback, or by reassigning employees to managers with more compatible coaching styles.

The vast majority of bosses favor some subordinates, treating them as part of an in-group, while consigning others to an out-group. The manager may either totally ignore those in the out-group or over-supervise them to such an extent that they stop giving their best, stop taking the initiative, and become automatons, sending the clear message back to their managers,

"Just tell me what you want and I'll do it." This is the very definition of disengagement.

The effects on those in the in-group may also be highly negative. If the manager loses faith in a performer he perceives as weak, he may start overloading those he considers stronger performers, creating resentment on their part and eventually burning them out.

The dynamics of manager-employee relationships are complex, but in the best-case scenarios, with a good faith effort and the right approach to coaching, employees can be re-engaged.

Engagement Practices for Coaching and Giving Feedback

 ### Engagement Practice #17:
Provide Intensive Feedback and Coaching to New Hires

As the saying goes, you only have one chance to make a first impression. Starting the relationship with the right mix of coaching and feedback will pay big dividends later. As J. Sterling Livingston put it in his now-famous article, "Pygmalion in Management," "Something important is happening in the first year . . . meeting high company expectations in the critical first year leads to the internalization of positive job attitudes and high standards . . . If managers are unskilled, they leave scars on the careers of young people, cut deeply into their self-esteem, and distort their image of themselves as human beings."[10]

Good managers know that they need to proactively manage the new hires' joining-up process. Here are some specific steps that can jump-start a positive coaching relationship:

- Plan how you want the new hires to spend the first day on the job and arrange to spend quality time with them at the beginning and end of the first week.
- Meet with the new hire on day one to reaffirm how their job fits into the organization's mission and objectives.
- Conduct an "Entrance Interview," as presented in Chapter Five, focused on discovering in-depth the new hire's best talents and professional goals.
- During the first week, discuss your performance expectations in detail for the first ninety days, and ask the new hire to draft a perform-

ance agreement that summarizes the stated objectives as targeted results that are specific, measurable, achievable, and realistic.

- Pair up the new employee with a respected peer or senior coworker to be a mentor or buddy during the first six months or longer.

- Make it clear that giving feedback is your responsibility and getting feedback is the new hire's responsibility. In other words, new hires need to understand that when they feel they are not getting enough feedback, they needs to seek it out—from you, from a coworker, from a customer—instead of passively waiting for someone to give it.

- Look for opportunities to directly observe and debrief new employees as frequently as possible during the first few weeks. As events cause changes in first-quarter objectives, revise them as appropriate to make them more realistic or achievable.

- Meet with new employees at the end of the first three months to discuss progress on written objectives, and create new objectives for the next quarter. During this meeting, be sure to ask about any expectations that have not been met so they can be brought to the surface and openly discussed instead of being allowed to fester.

These same guidelines apply to employees you may inherit when you take over a new group of employees. It is worth keeping in mind that the scarcest commodity in most companies is the manager's attention. When days and weeks pass without new hires, especially younger ones, seeing or hearing from their managers, they tend to assume the worst. As Livingston so eloquently put it, "Managers often communicate most when they believe they are communicating least. . . . The silent treatment communicates negative feelings even more effectively, at times, than a tongue-lashing does. . . . Indifference says to subordinates, 'I don't think much of you'"[11]

Engagement Practice # 18: Create a Culture of Continuous Feedback and Coaching

Some companies have cultures where feedback flows freely and others have cultures where feedback is kept in reserve, saved for "a more appropriate time" that never comes, or kept until performance review time and dumped on the employee all in one sitting. General Electric under Jack Welch was a constant-feedback culture. As described in *Jack: Straight from the Gut,* "In GE every day, there's an informal, unspoken personnel re-view—in the lunchroom, the hallway, and in every business meeting."[12]

One study found that 64 percent of people prefer informal, on-the-job conversations with their supervisor over formal interviews.[13] Certainly a frequent-feedback culture is a reflection of a results-driven CEO who wants to make sure that employees have the feedback they need just in time to use it and make a difference for customers. The best way to make sure that feedback is given and received in a meaningful and productive way, however, is to train all managers in how to give it, and all employees in how to receive it. Here are some ideas on which to build a positive feedback culture through training:

- Begin with the assumption that every employee is responsible for getting feedback and not dependent or passively waiting for the manager to give it.

- It is the responsibility of every manager to give timely and frequent feedback to all employees, but the supervisor is not the sole initiator of feedback.

- Make sure that all managers are trained to understand the essential conditions for effective feedback—that the feedback giver is credible, trustworthy, and has good intentions; that the timing and circumstances are appropriate, the feedback is given in a personal and interactive manner, and that the message is clear and helpful.[14]

- Include a training module for employees on how to receive feedback that also encourages them to overcome any resistance they may have to seeking it.

- Emphasize the importance of managers making sure the feedback they are about to give is accurate before they give it.

- Communicate clearly and unequivocally that feedback is not to be reserved for periodic, formal occasions, but is expected to be given and sought on an ongoing, continual basis, driven not by the calendar, but by the situation.

- Look for logical times to give feedback to an entire team of people, such as at the end of a major project.

- Stress the importance of overcoming the natural defensiveness that people have about receiving feedback by giving positive feedback along with the negative. Encourage employees to build on their strengths as the preferred strategy for improving performance.

- It is not enough to point out shortcomings. Employees need help figuring out what actions they need to take in order to do better.
- Because feedback improperly given can have a negative impact on performance, training should include time for managers to practice giving it and employees to practice receiving it.
- Along with the training, offer a variety of feedback tools, such as internal and external customer questionnaires, 360-degree feedback instruments, and less formal feedback questionnaires.
- Make all managers and employees aware of available feedback tools and training.

Getting the Best Results from 360-Degree Feedback

Many companies have initiated the use of 360-degree, or multirater feedback that allows employees to receive formal feedback not just from the boss, but from one's peers, direct reports, and customers. The idea is to give employees a fuller picture of how they are perceived than they can hope to receive only from their direct supervisor. Most companies with experience using 360-degree feedback are reporting that best results are generally obtained when:

- The feedback is used only for self-development, not for rating performance or making decisions about pay or promotion.
- Employees are given the option of receiving 360-degree feedback, rather than having it mandated.
- Employees are allowed to select the raters in consultation with the direct supervisor.
- There are enough raters to assure anonymity to all raters.
- Those to be rated are trained in how to receive feedback.
- After receiving the feedback report, employees are encouraged to seek additional clarifying feedback through follow-up discussions with raters.

Engagement Practice # 19:
Train Managers in Performance Coaching

While there is no one right way to do performance coaching, most employees know a good performance coach when they have one. One study of great sports coaches found that what many of them describe as their secrets of success—"recruit the right players and inspire them to win"—is not what they do at all. Instead, they carefully observe their players in practice, stop practice and to give detailed feedback and teach the proper way, ask questions to make sure the player understood, watch the player perform the play or movement as instructed, and finally reward with simple praise.[15]

Joe Torre, manager of the New York Yankees, received wide public acclaim in an article that appeared in *Fortune* Magazine after he had guided his team to yet another baseball world championship. In the article, psychologist Daniel Goleman, author of the book *Emotional Intelligence,* said of Torre, "This guy is a textbook case of an emotionally intelligent leader.'" The article's author describes Torre's principal management tool as "not meetings or motivational talks, but regular one-on-one encounters with his players, which he uses to monitor and regulate their psyches." One of his players describes how Torre "watches and listens before he says a thing." Another says, "you never see him berating a player . . . or dropping his head in disgust."[16]

Torre and many other managers have the natural gift for coaching, but performance coaching can be learned. One of the best teachers of performance coaching is Ferdinand Fournies, whose book, *Coaching for Improved Work Performance,* outlines a systematic process based on principles of behavioral psychology. It is a process that provides a workable alternative to what he refers to as "YST Yelling, Screaming, and Threatening."[17]

> Instead of pushing solutions on people with the force of your argument, pull solutions out of them.[18]
>
> —Ferdinand Fournies

Fournies begins by confronting managers who believe falsely that employees' bad attitudes are unchangeable, and that employees choose, against their best interests, to underperform. Instead, he proposes that managers must do everything possible to prevent employee failure by pursuing a system of interventions. He presents sixteen reasons employees don't do what they are supposed to do:

1. They don't know what they are supposed to do.
2. They don't know how to do it.

3. They don't know why they should do it.

4. They think they are doing it (lack of feedback).

5. There are obstacles beyond their control.

6. They think it will not work.

7. They think their way is better.

8. They think something is more important (priorities).

9. There is no positive consequence to them for doing it.

10. There is a negative consequence to them for doing it.

11. There is a positive consequence to them for not doing it.

12. There is no negative consequence to them for not doing it.

13. Personal limits (incapacity).

14. Personal problems.

15. Fear (they anticipate future negative consequences).

16. No one could do it.[19]

When these sales managers fire someone they are saying, "I don't have one or two weeks to help you improve your performance, but I have thirty work days to devote to replacing you."[20]

—Ferdinand Fournies

A Five-Step Coaching Process

Fournies provides a coaching analysis chart that prescribes what a manager can do to intervene successfully, starting with identifying the unsatisfactory performance, not the *result* of the unsatisfactory performance. Finally, he presents a five-step coaching technique:

- Step 1: Get the employee's agreement that a problem exists.
- Step 2: Mutually discuss alternative solutions.
- Step 3: Mutually agree on action to be taken to solve the problem.
- Step 4: Follow up to measure results.
- Step 5: Reinforce any achievement when it occurs.

This process is not about placing blame or even assigning motives to employees for their behavior. Rather it is focused on producing positive behavior going forward. Companies wishing to upgrade the level of performance coaching to more fully engage employees would be well advised to design training for managers in a systematic process such as this one. As Fournies himself points out, "Training compresses time, making people smarter without getting older, and avoids the unnecessary bumps and bruises."[21]

Four Common Performance Management Routines of Great Managers

1. The routine is simple. (Simple formats allow manager to focus on what to say and how to say it.)
2. The routine forces frequent interaction. (Meaningful feedback happens when it follows on the heels of an event.)
3. The routine is future-focused. (Postmortems can lead to recriminations. Positive energy comes from discussing the future.)
4. The routine lets employees keep track of their own performance and learnings. (Creates more employee ownership of the self-discovery process.)[22]

 Engagement Practice # 20: Make the Performance Management Process Less Controlling and More of a Partnership

Over the past twenty years, most companies have been moving to a formal performance review process that reflects the growing trend to create more of a partnership between manager and employee, as the following comparison shows:

Traditional Approach	*Partnering Approach*
Manager-driven	Employee-driven
Parent-child model	Adult-to-adult model
An HR exercise	Manager's tool
Personality issues	Result-focused
Vague objectives	Specific objectives
Yearly event	On-going discussions
Rank for pay	Pay linked to goals

While more than half of all companies have no performance management system at all,[23] many of those that do still practice the traditional approach. This may help to explain why almost 90 percent of managers who do use performance appraisals do not believe they help to improve worker performance! If a company is trying to become an employer of choice based on creating a culture of reciprocal commitment, it is highly unlikely it will achieve that status using an outdated performance appraisal process that is based on anything other than an adult-to-adult relationship. Real commitment comes from partnering agreements in which employees suggest their own objectives and merge them with those of the manager, not from the imposition of goals and objectives from above.

Most experts on performance management systems report that companies achieve greatest overall satisfaction and effectiveness with systems that:

- Use no performance ratings or summary judgments, as these have been consistently found to increase defensiveness and reduce receptivity to constructive performance planning.

- Unlink performance discussions from salary discussions. Many companies have eliminated the yearly performance discussion focused on a "final" evaluation in favor of more frequent informal meetings. This avoids the inevitable "gunny-sacking" of supervisor criticisms over several months time until they are all dumped onto the employee in a yearly meeting.

- Further de-formalize the process by no longer requiring the employee's signature or placing the plan in a "personnel file." Some companies create more employee ownership of the process by allowing employees to keep the performance plan in their own files and give them the option of providing a copy to the supervisor.

- Call for meetings between manager and employee at least once per quarter and encourage frequent brief performance feedback-and-coaching discussions.

- Emphasize mutual performance analysis over performance appraisal.

- Give the employee the initiative in creating performance goals. Employee is the active agent, not the passive object of a supervisor's appraisal.

- Allow the employee to begin performance review discussions by evaluating personal progress toward self-created objectives.

- Train managers in a discussion process that is simple and memorable, such as "Get-Give-Merge-Go" (start by *getting* employee's perspective on performance, then *give* your perspective, then *merge* mutual perspectives into an agreement, then *go* forward with new objectives).
- Train managers in helping employees set appropriate objectives that are specific, measurable, achievable, realistic, and time-bound (S-M-A-R-T).
- Put the manager in the role of counselor and co-problem solver, not judge. Managers do not coerce or manipulate employees to accept organizational goals. The manager is responsible for assuring that the employee's objectives align with the objectives of the unit and organization.
- Hold senior executives accountable for following the same performance review and planning process as every other employee must do.
- Have built-in measures of the system to assure that it remains effective, with measures based on periodic quality and timing audits and on surveys of employee opinions about the process.
- Ditch elaborate and complicated ranking systems for determining salary increases. Many companies have managers use simple categories such as A-players, B-players, and C-players, or "walking on water," "swimming," and "drowning," as initial groups, then provide raises based on subjective judgments of overall value to the organization.

Engagement Practice # 21: Terminate Nonperformers When Best Efforts to Coach or Reassign Don't Pay Off

It may seem contradictory to recommend a practice devoted to the termination of poor performance after having recommended another practice encouraging the commitment to correcting poor performance. However, I do believe these two practices must coexist in employers of choice. Despite your best efforts to coach non-performers or change the nature of their job assignments, there will be times when it is simply best to let the employee go. The problem is that, all too often, other valued employees know when that time has come long before the manager does, and the manager's failure to act can adversely impact their commitment.

As one business columnist described the situation, "We're in the middle of a vast wave of nonfiring. . . . The damage to millions of lives, and the economy, is beyond calculating. . . . Keeping poor performers means that development opportunities for promising employees get blocked, so those subordinates don't get developed, productivity and morale fall, good performers leave the company, the company attracts fewer A players, and the whole miserable cycle keeps turning."[24]

This is a theme that appears in all the employee survey results I have seen—good performers consistently complain that underperforming employees are tolerated, even promoted and rewarded with raises, while they themselves are overworked or ignored. When McKinsey asked thousands of employees how they would feel if their employees got rid of underperformers, 59 percent strongly agreed with the option "delighted"—yet only 7 percent believed their companies were doing it.[25]

Jack Welch expressed his feelings on the matter quite clearly in a letter to GE's shareholders, customers, and employees before leaving his post as CEO, saying "Not removing the bottom 10 percent . . . is not only a management failure, but false kindness as well."[26] This stance opens a highly controversial door—whether to eliminate the bottom 10 percent each year. Some believe this helps to continually upgrade the organization's talent level, while many others believe the "rank and yank" approach eventually leads to the termination of competent employees who just happen to fall into the bottom 10 percent of highly performing teams, and can also result in litigation. Conversely, a mediocre employee in a struggling unit may come out looking great. To mitigate this concern, some companies reduce the percentage of employees to be weeded out in successive years, as in 10 percent the first year, 5 percent the second and third years.

Many proponents of forced ranking systems believe they force managers to be honest with their employees about how they are doing. Others argue that forced rankings can become a crutch for poor management, making the case that good managers should have the ability to make difficult decisions without having a system force it on them.

No matter where one stands on this issue, there is considerably less doubt about the need to step up and make tough decisions to cut nonperforming employees when all else has failed. Most managers would probably agree with Welch's point about "false kindness." As Debra Dunn, senior executive at Hewlett-Packard, put it, "There is no greater disrespect you can do to a person than to let them hang out in a job where they are not respected by their peers, not viewed as successful, and probably losing their self-esteem. To do that under the guise of respect for people is, to me, ridiculous."[27]

Engagement Practice # 22: Hold Managers Accountable for Coaching and Giving Feedback

If 60 percent of a manager's time is spent fixing people problems, you might think more companies would make special efforts to hold managers accountable for coaching and giving feedback to employees.

Some companies, such as The Security Benefit Group of Companies in Topeka, Kansas, have introduced "upward evaluation" systems that allow employees to give feedback on their managers' people management and coaching skills. When surveys are completed, results are reported both to the manager and the manager's manager for use in performance and development discussions. Security Benefit has noticed that evaluation results have become more positive since the practice was begun in 1995.

Many other companies have begun incorporating coaching and feedback competencies into the lists of key competencies they require of all leaders. For example, instead of listing "people management" as a single competency for managers, it is more meaningful to select, train and evaluate managers against competencies that are more specifically defined. This means that people management skills might be further broken down into more specific competencies, such as human resource planning, employee selection, performance coaching/feedback, training/development, and employee recognition/motivation—with clear definitions provided for each of these.

Management books such as Daniel Goleman's *Emotional Intelligence at Work* and *Primal Leadership* have also made many organizations more aware of the importance of emotional intelligence factors in selecting and promoting managers. Goleman describes the *Coaching* style of leadership as one of the most highly positive of six predominant leadership styles—the others being *Visionary* (most strongly positive), *Affiliative* (positive), *Democratic* (positive), *Pacesetting* (often negative), and *Commanding* (usually negative because it is so often misused). Yet, he concludes, "Despite the commonly held belief that every leader needs to be a good coach, leaders tend to exhibit this style least often."[28]

Regardless of how carefully we spell out competencies and study leadership styles, the only way to ensure that any new practices are working is to hold managers accountable and create new rewards and consequences. When corporate officers were asked if line managers should be accountable for the strength of the talent pool they are building, 93 percent said they should be, yet only 3 percent said that they actually held line managers accountable for this outcome.[29]

One company that is holding managers accountable for people outcomes is Applebee's International, which has installed balanced scorecard
measures for its restaurant managers based on results in three areas—
financial, people, and customer. In 2001, the company started holding its
area managers accountable for people results in four key areas with significant impact to the bottom-line—hourly staffing levels, percentage of employees retained among the top 80 percent of all staff, hourly new-hire
retention rates, and progress on succession management. Performance on
these four measures account for 30 percent of the formula used to determine pay raises. Applebee's also sponsored an annual contest among area
managers called "Turn Yourself Over to the Tropics," which awarded top
performers on low management turnover measures with vacations in Can-
cun and cruises to the Bahamas.

How have these new practices worked? The annual turnover rate
among hourly employees had dropped from 146 percent in 2000 to 92
percent in 2003, and turnover of restaurant general managers had fallen
from 20 percent to 8 percent over the same period. The drops in turnover
have to be attributed to more than a recessionary economy, as Applebee's
turnover rates have dropped further and faster than most of their competitors in the casual dining restaurant category. Based on avoided hard replacement costs for restaurant managers alone, the company conservatively
estimated a one-year savings of $1.6 million. Having achieved a cascading
positive impact by measuring area managers, the company hopes to realize
even greater dividends as it rolls out the same four people measures to
managers of individual restaurants.

Another effective way to create accountability among managers for
people results is to promote and select candidates for managerial and executive positions based on higher standards of management behavior. One of
the best-known examples of this came to the attention of the public in
early 2001, when Jack Welch, in his annual letter to stockholder, customers,
and employees, announced GE's new policy and practice regarding the
way managers treat employees.[30] The memo described four types of managers that existed at GE and at all companies (see Figure 6-1): The *Type 1
manager* treats employees with respect and makes the numbers (keep), the
Type 2 manager treats people with respect and doesn't make the numbers
(keep and coach), and the *Type 3 manager* doesn't treat people with respect
and doesn't make the numbers (terminate). The problematic type of manager had always been the *Type 4 manager*, the kind of manager who always
made the numbers but did *not* treat people with respect. In the letter, Welch
admitted that in the past GE had been guilty of keeping far too many of

Figure 6-1.

Four types of managers

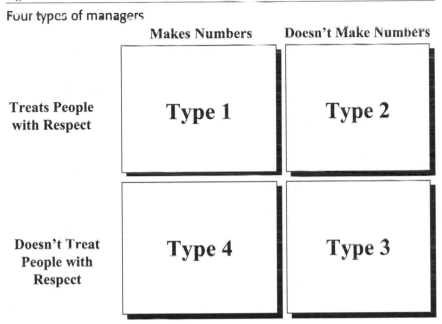

	Makes Numbers	Doesn't Make Numbers
Treats People with Respect	Type 1	Type 2
Doesn't Treat People with Respect	Type 4	Type 3

the Type 4 managers. In the future, he promised, these types of managers would no longer be tolerated at GE—they would be dismissed.

As new jobs are created faster than the supply of workers can keep pace, more and more companies will create "bad manager identification" initiatives. Finding themselves once again in a full-blown "war for talent" like they experienced in the late 1990s, many aspiring employers of-choice will realize, as GE has, that they can no longer afford the luxury of keeping any manager who drives talent out the door.

What the Employee Can Do to Get More Feedback and Coaching

The fact that we have covered so much territory encompassing all the things managers and organizations can do to improve performance through coaching and feedback by no means suggests that employees should depend on managers to take the initiative. Here are ways that employees should be expected to seek out and get the coaching and feedback they need when they need it:

- Whenever you believe you are not receiving the feedback and coaching you need, ask for it.
- If you find you are reluctant to seek feedback, start by asking those with whom you feel most comfortable.
- Develop the habit of asking for feedback from peers, customers, direct reports, task force coworkers, administrative assistants, and anyone with whom you might interact, not just the boss.
- If you receive feedback that is too general, or difficult to understand, ask for specific examples.
- If you have never been invited to write your own performance objectives or begin a performance evaluation by giving your own self-assessment, ask to do so.
- If you are not comfortable with your performance objectives or appraisal results, speak up. Try to reach a satisfactory mutual understanding with your supervisor.
- If you feel that changes in circumstances have necessitated that changes be made in your performance objectives, request a meeting with your supervisor to rewrite the objectives.
- If your company makes 360-degree feedback assessments available, consider asking if you can participate in the process.
- Ask whether your company provides off-the-shelf personality and work-style inventories, employee development planning guides, or competency assessments you can take.
- If you feel you are spending more time trying to improve weaknesses than building on your strengths, change your developmental objectives, your supervisor, or your job.
- If your company retains external coaches to assist current employees, ask if they would be willing to provide such coaching at your level.
- If your organization does not retain outside coaches at your position level, consider retaining an outside coach of your own.
- If you work for a supervisor who is not interested in coaching or giving the feedback you need, consider seeking a new position within the company where you can work for a manager who is, or leave the company.

Employer-of-Choice Engagement Practices Review and Checklist

Review the engagement practices presented in this chapter and check the ones you believe your organization needs to implement or improve.

To Provide Coaching and Feedback:

17. ☐ Provide intensive feedback and coaching to new hires.
18. ☐ Create a culture of continuous feedback and coaching.
19. ☐ Train managers in performance coaching.
20. ☐ Make performance management process less controlling and more of a partnership.
21. ☐ Terminate non-performers when best efforts to coach or reassign don't pay off.
22. ☐ Hold managers accountable for coaching and giving feedback.

Notes

1. Ron Zemke, "The Corporate Coach," *Training* Magazine, December 1996.
2. Ibid.
3. Ibid.
4. McKinsey Work Force 2000, Senior Executive and Midlevel Surveys, 2000.
5. Morgan W. McCall, Jr., *High Flyers: Developing the Next Generation of Leaders*, (Boston: Harvard Business School Press, 1998).
6. Ferdinand Fournies, *Coaching for Improved Work Performance* (New York: McGraw-Hill, 2000).
7. "Career Developments," Newsletter of Career Development Services, Inc., September 18, 2003.
8. Ed Michaels, Helen Handfield-Jones, and Beth Axelrod, *The War for Talent* (Boston: Harvard Business School Press, 2001).
9. Juan-Francois Manzoni and Jean-Louis Barsoux, "The Set-Up to Fail Syndrome," *Harvard Business Review on Managing People* (Boston: Harvard Business School Press, 1999).
10. J. Sterling Livingston, "Pygmalion in Management," *Harvard Business Review on Managing People* (Boston: Harvard Business School Press, 1999).
11. Ibid.
12. Jack Welch and John A. Byrne, *Jack: Straight from the Gut* (New York: Warner Books, 2001).
13. Richard Beatty, "Competitive Human Resource Advantage Through the Strategic Management of Performance," *Human Resources Planning*, Volume 12, November 15, 1989.

14. Tom Coens and Mary Jenkins, *Abolishing Performance Appraisals: Why They Backfire and What to Do Instead* (San Francisco: Berrett-Koehler, 2000).

15. Zemke, op. cit.

16. Jerry Useem, "A Manager for All Seasons," *Fortune*, April 30, 2001.

17. Fournies, op. cit.

18. Ibid.

19. Ibid.

20. Ibid.

21. Ibid.

22. Marcus Buckingham and Curt Coffman, *First Break All the Rules: What the World's Greatest Managers Do Differently* (New York: Simon & Schuster, 1999).

23. Danielle McDonald, "The Impact of Performance Management in Organization Success," Hewitt Associates Study, 1997.

24. Geoffrey Colvin, "Make Sure You Chop the Dead Wood," *Fortune,* April 2000.

25. Ibid.

26. Jack Welch, letter to shareholders, customers, and employees, January 2001.

27. Colvin, op. cit.

28. Daniel Goleman, *Primal Leadership: Realizing the Power of Emotional Intelligence* (Boston: Harvard Business School Press, 2002).

29. McKinsey Work Force 2000 survey.

30. Welch, op. cit.

Reason #4:
Too Few Growth and
Advancement Opportunities

In the end, it is important
to remember that we
cannot become what we
need to be by remaining
what we are.

—MAX DEPREE

Comments expressing disappointment with career growth and advancement fall into six categories: limited growth/advancement opportunities, unfair or inefficient job-posting process, not hiring from within, favoritism or unfairness in promotion decisions, insufficient training, and other. Here's a sampling of what departed employees had to say in each of these areas:

1. *Limited Growth and Advancement Opportunities*
   - "There is not much opportunity to move up. You get entrenched in a position and you're stuck there."
   - "Promotions and advancements outside a department within the company are not an easy thing to accomplish. One would think you should be able to advance within a company with ease."
   - "ABC Company's departments don't work together. In some departments people are promoted each year while other departments never have the money to promote employees."
   - "The company locks people into their positions for nine months, which stalls advancement. Nine months per position is far too long in most entry-level jobs, especially if the individual has extensive experience."

2. *Unfair or Inefficient Internal Selection Process*

- "They post positions and then take forever to follow through or proceed, and they don't communicate the status of the posted positions. I applied for a position almost a month ago and have not heard anything back."

- "The director was appointed without the posting of the position. Several other candidates had much more integrity, management experience and education than the director who was selected. It sickened the team."

- "XYZ Company did not seem to stick with their own rules. Example: I know that some posted jobs are tailored to fit one employee in particular and even some jobs are not even posted, but renamed and handed off as a promotion."

3. *Not Hiring from Within*

- "ABC Company hires too much from outside the company instead of promoting from within."

- "XYZ Company does poorly regarding promoting from within. We have internal candidates who could step in and do the job quite nicely."

- "Promote internally. I have seen four supervisors hired within one year—all of them from other companies."

4. *Unfairness/Favoritism in Promotion Decisions*

- "In certain cases the manager won't recommend an employee for another position because they do not want to lose that employee. It's not fair for someone to hold you back."

- "ABC Company is tainted with politics and favoritism. Employees were given management positions or promotions not for their skill sets but for how well they were liked in the firm."

- "I am a working mother of two, and I find it nearly impossible to move up within my department. My hours are structured (nine hours a day) but when I am in the office I work my hardest and strive to achieve my goals. When a project or on-going activities call for extended hours, I rearrange child care and work as needed. However, on a daily basis I am disheartened that the subject of my hours comes into play. My priority is my family, but my life also includes work that I enjoy. I know there is a delicate balance for working mothers within the workplace but I'm discouraged there is not more understanding and flexibility. I have heard several times that I need to work longer in order to complete my goals in order to become promoted. If my nine-hour days are not being counted or recognized, I feel worthless, as if my work doesn't matter."

- "Discrimination! Too many negative comments regarding women's weight, looks, etc. As a result many talented people are undervalued."
- "Supervisors hire friends as 'team leads' instead of the more competent of the group."

5. *Insufficient Training*
   - "I am disappointed that I am not able to take advantage of certain training/learning opportunities because they do not apply to my current position. I want to be able to grow and learn about all that the company has to offer, but they limit you to only the training that relates to your current job."
   - "I believe the biggest issue we have is training. I have many employees who would be more satisfied and willing to stay on if adequate training was provided."
   - "XYZ Company provides poor sales training. If the growth initiatives are to be the number one priority and there is no sales training, how can management expect different results or increased sales."
   - "Training!!! If you are not located at the corporate office, training is not available."

6. *Other Issues*
   - "Acknowledge and respect the employee's career goals when assigning work."
   - "They don't have a clear direction for those who do not know what they want to do. Clearly defined career paths are not available."
   - "Management and supervisors seem to only care for themselves and don't care about the growth or advancement of their employees."
   - "ABC Company does not have a career development workshop."
   - "Employees need more career counseling."

What They Are Really Saying

Look beneath the surface of these comments and you will see a number of issues faced by most organizations:

- There will inevitably be limited opportunities for career growth in every organization.
- Barriers between departments and position levels constrain internal movement and growth.
- No one at the top of the organization is coordinating internal talent management activities to create awareness of growth opportunities in all departments and units.
- Fixed time-in-grade policies keep employees from advancing when they are ready.
- Job posting processes are slow and unresponsive.
- Less qualified employees are being hired because of manager favoritism.
- Demand for long work hours limits promotional opportunities for single parents despite their sacrifice and hard work.
- Gender-based and other kinds of prejudice create obstacles to career growth.
- Training is restricted only to certain positions, departments, or locations.
- Training is approved only if it is related to employee's current position, and disapproved if it relates to preparation for future opportunities.
- Training is inadequate.
- There is no training at all, even when it is needed to achieve important company goals.
- Managers assign work without considering employees' talents and preferences.
- There is no process to assist employees with unclear career goals.
- Career path information is unavailable.
- Managers are concerned only about their own careers, not the career growth of their employees.

There are enough issues related to internal career growth and development in most companies to keep several consultants busy for months. Yet, employers of choice seem to have fewer such issues. They know that career growth and advancement consistently ranks among the top three reasons employees stay or leave in most companies. They understand that top performers seek out and pursue jobs and careers with employers that put extra effort into helping employees learn, grow, and advance internally.

Yet, in a survey by The Conference Board, limited career opportunities was found to be the number one driver of overall employee dissatisfaction, cited by 59 percent of workers.[1] In another survey, where managers and employees were asked to rate the performance of today's managers on 67 necessary leadership competencies, "developing direct reports" ranked 67th—dead last.[2] In a Towers-Perrin study, 85 percent of employees cited career advancement as a key reward, yet only 49 percent said their companies were providing it. Similarly, 80 percent said that learning and development programs are critical, but only 50 percent said their offerings are sufficient or effective.[3] These kinds of survey results remind us that, with about half of all companies not even trying to develop their people, there is ample opportunity for those who *are* trying to become employers of choice.

Employers of Choice Start by Understanding the New Career Realities

So much has changed in the worldwide business climate and in the way businesses now operate, that the impact of these changes on the careers of individuals working in organizations needs to be acknowledged.

Waves of downsizings have changed the loyalty contract and heightened the levels of stress and job security. The continuing focus on short-term, bottom-line results, particularly among public companies, has created tremendous pressure on managers to reduce costs and push workers to produce more with less. Resulting productivity gains have come at the price of reducing job satisfaction, eliminating rungs on career ladders, and forestalling job creation.

The September 11 attacks on the World Trade Center and Pentagon caused many workers to reevaluate the centrality of work in their lives and seek more time with family, leisure pursuits, or more personally fulfilling career options.

Fewer younger workers now seek traditional full-time jobs or long-term employment with any one company. Generations X and Y prefer short-term goals of job challenge, vacation time, and new skills acquisition over traditional rewards such as job security and long-term benefits.

More and more employees are choosing to work from home. Proven and valued older workers are now poised to retire in unprecedented numbers, inaugurating a new era of talent shortages, and leaving millions of companies with "leadership gaps" they are not prepared to fill.

While there will continue to be a shortage of skilled people to perform available jobs, the public education system will not be able to prepare workers with the skills needed to do tomorrow's jobs.

The cumulative effect of all these changes has been the creation of a new contract[4] between employer and employee, which many managers (who came of age when the old contract was in place) have been slow to recognize:

Old Career Contract	New Career Contract
Long-term employment is expected.	There are shorter term expectations, affected by changing business needs (no guarantees).
Reward for performance is promotion.	Reward for performance is growth, recognition, and self-satisfaction.
Management controls career progress.	Employees are in charge of their own careers.
Lifetime career is offered.	Employee-employer bond is based on fulfillment of mutual needs.
Clearly defined career paths are offered.	Career paths are less defined, more changeable.
Resulting in:	*Resulting in:*
Fixed job descriptions.	Changing jobs, more projects and task forces.
Compensation and benefits that reward tenure.	Recognition systems based on value creation and results.
Long-term career planning by the organization.	Short-term career planning by employee.
Plateaued workers.	Flexible, task-invested workers.
Dependent workers.	Empowered, responsible workers.

The reality is that the new career contract still has not materialized in many organizations, especially ones that value control over employee autonomy and self-direction. In these old-school organizations, many employees passively wait for managers to take the first step and never learn to manage their own careers. By contrast, most employers of choice clearly communicate that employees must take the initiative with regard to their own career development, but they also provide the tools and training necessary for them to do so, as we shall see in the best practices that follow.

Recognizing the Signs of Blocked Growth and Career Frustration

One of your employees may be experiencing restlessness and frustration with career growth and advancement if he or she:

- Indiscriminately applies for a succession of internal positions, for some of which they are unqualified or unsuited.
- Was recently not selected for another position in the company.
- Has been recently passed over for a promotion.
- Seems to be coasting and appears to be bored or underchallenged.
- Keeps asking for new challenges.
- Keeps asking for additional training.
- Asks for career path information.
- Has been in the same position long enough to have long since mastered it.
- Has applied for tuition reimbursement but is unclear about career goals.
- Has recently completed a degree and seems to expect a promotion.

Responsibility for employee career growth and development is shared equally by the employee, the manager, and the organization. Here is the way one organization divided the responsibilities:

Employee's Responsibilities

- Make job performance and creating value your first priority.
- Make your career aspirations known to your manager.
- Assess your own talents and get frequent feedback on your performance and potential.
- Continually seek new learning and growth opportunities.
- Learn to uncover hidden needs in the organization to create a new job.
- Seek growth through lateral movements and job enrichment, not just promotion.
- Learn how the organization fills jobs internally and how to use the job-posting system.

- Actively seek information about jobs of interest to make sure they are jobs you would truly enjoy, and that you would have a realistic chance of obtaining.
- Understand that you, not the organization or your manager, have the primary responsibility for managing your career.

Organization's Responsibilities

- Create systems, policies, and practice that facilitate professional growth for all.
- Provide training and resources to managers to help them develop employees.
- Conduct long-range strategic and human resource planning and communicate future talent needs to managers and employees.
- Create and maintain a fair and efficient internal job posting process.
- Provide necessary training to enhance performance and enable career growth.

Manager's Responsibilities

- Identify and continually reevaluate future talent needs in terms of the work to be done.
- Assess the strengths, motivations, and developmental needs of each employee and match them to the work to be done.
- Maintain person-job fit through frequent coaching, feedback, reassignments, or other corrective action.
- Assist employees in implementing realistic developmental goals and action plans.

If expectations and responsibilities become unbalanced, as when employees expect the organization to create their career plans for them, or when a manager fails to discuss career plans with a direct report, or when senior leaders fail to approve necessary training, the system breaks down.

Best Practices for Creating Growth and Advancement Opportunities

Here are the kinds of practices that serve to maintain a balanced approach to providing employees with the growth and development opportunities they need to stay, and stay engaged.

Engagement Practice # 23: Provide Self-Assessment Tools and Career Self-Management Training for All Employees

Smart companies recognize that employees can have a widely ranging degrees of self-awareness and that many highly talented performers may not understand, cannot articulate, and often underuse their greatest strengths. By misunderstanding their own talents, employees may seek jobs for which they are unsuited. They may also borrow the goals and ambitions of successful coworkers and pursue roles incompatible with their temperaments. They may create untold damage by becoming managers of people when the talent to manage people is missing or of little true interest, except as a means to getting a promotion.

Here are some of the practices in wide use by preferred employers to increase the self-awareness and enhance the realistic goal-setting of employees:

- Provide interactive software for self-directed career self-assessment inventories through the company's intranet.
- Offer voluntary career self-assessment and career self-management workshops, with career self-management guide, to *all* employees.
- Implement a self-assessment process that places a strong emphasis on identifying an employee's motivated talents and abilities through the

---

"PeopleComeFirst" at Lands' End

Lands' End has developed an online self-service career development and learning management system for its 8,000 employees called PeopleComeFirst. An employee can create a career development plan that will be available online for reference and revision. Employees typically meet with managers at least twice a year to work on their development plans, which serve as guides for training and career growth.

The company went to the online process after it found the manual process difficult to track. Now all information about employees' development and training activity is kept in a central location where both the employee and manager can access it. Lands' End has separated the career development planning process from the annual performance review in order to place the maximum focus on the employee's development.[5]

analysis of satisfying life achievements. Achievement analysis is especially empowering and confidence-building.

- Create a "virtual career center" containing self-assessment inventories along with career planning software programs, career path mapping scenarios, position competency definitions, job postings, talent bank profiles, training catalogs, recommended books, professional associations, conferences, courses, articles, and other information recommended by coworkers.

- Provide tools for independent career management and planning—career guides, individual development plans, and assessment inventories.

- Challenge employees to take the initiative and schedule meetings with their managers to discuss their assessment results and create a new individual development plan.

Engagement Practice # 24:
Offer Career Coaching Tools and Training for All Managers

Recognizing that the employee's direct supervisor is the primary agent for achieving employee commitment and satisfaction, more companies are providing tools and training to managers so they will be better equipped to fulfill their career coaching responsibilities.

Many companies now provide company-sponsored training with other managers on how to conduct career conversations, respond to frequently asked employee career questions, complete individual development plans, and follow through with sponsoring activity or accountability initiatives.-

---

How to Create a Job and Revitalize a Career

Bob Taylor had been with Charles Schwab & Company for twelve years, but was considering leaving the company. He had begun to lose interest in his work, but before resigning, decided to talk things over with his boss. With his boss' go-ahead, Taylor proposed the creation of a job that would combine his technology and business skills—organizational troubleshooter. "The key to my staying was to innovate my own job," said Taylor, whose formal title became vice president of the mobile trading project at Schwab's Electronic Brokerage Group. "To energize someone," advised Taylor, "let them work on what they absolutely love."[6]

Some companies provide individual development planning forms and feedback tools, such as voluntary manager skill evaluations that employees complete to give managers feedback on their employee coaching and development skills.

To help managers better understand the process that they will be recommending to employees, progressive companies also invite all managers to complete the employee self-assessment and career self-management process for themselves. After all, they are employees, too, and they will be more likely to encourage their employees to complete a process if they have benefited from it themselves.

Engagement Practice # 25: Provide Readily Accessible Information on Career Paths and Competency Requirements

Some companies understand better than others the need for employees to know how to prepare for future jobs. After using self-assessment tools to look within themselves at their own talents, preferences, values, and motivations, employees need to look outward at career growth options within the organization. This becomes much easier to do if the organization has invested in the creation of career paths and competency maps for all positions.

Employees need to have access to job descriptions, listings of competencies, and educational requirements they will need to qualify for other positions, whether these are shown on a company's intranet via a "virtual career center" or in hard copy form. Frequently, this information is made available on the company's Web site for outside applicants to view as well. Some companies even interview successful employees and publish "career path profiles," in which they tell the stories of their own advancement, key decisions they made, turning points, and give advice to newer employees about how to progress within the organization. Such stories make clear to anyone who reads them that successful employees in any company often do not progress upward in a direct, linear path, but make lateral moves, leave the organization and come back in higher-level jobs, and accelerate their careers through involvement on task forces, rotational assignments, and short-term projects.

Engagement Practice # 26: Create Alternatives to Traditional Career Ladders

If we truly value all talent for the value it brings to the organization, then we should not penalize top technical performers by forcing them to pursue management positions as their only route to higher pay. Many companies continue to provide only one path to higher pay—the line management career ladder.

Four Distinct Career Patterns

Michael Driver, professor in the business school at the University of Southern California, has conducted research showing that individuals are more or less hard-wired to have different concepts of career success, and that there are four distinct patterns:

1. *Linear:* These are people who are naturally motivated to move up the traditional corporate career ladder. They value power and achievement, but have been increasingly disillusioned and frustrated in recent years by the disappearance of rungs on career ladders in most organizations.
2. *Expert:* Rather than climb a career ladder, the expert wants to become known as an authority or the best in a selected field or craft. Experts tend to seek training and on-the-job experiences that deepens their expertise.
3. *Spiral:* These are people who aspire to broaden their careers by moving every five to ten years to a position that builds on previous positions, but may involve broader responsibilities. Spirals value growth and creativity and may seek rotational and cross-functional assignments.
4. *Roamer:* They define success by changing jobs often—perhaps every two to three years—and may move on to jobs unrelated to previous experience. Roamers are generally motivated more by variety and independence, not by security, and can play key roles in start-up situations in companies that are expanding.

Organizations may not be able to accommodate all four of these career patterns at all times. Still, understanding the different career styles that exist among the general population can facilitate the job-person matching process and help managers to assist employees in identifying best-fit advancement opportunities. Managers will need to understand the differing motives of employees through individualized career coaching and work to create career opportunities that meet employee needs and business needs in new ways.[7]

Other companies, especially those whose success depends on product innovations of engineers or other technical specialists, have created higher-level technical positions with increasing responsibility and commensurate pay. By doing so, these organizations provide individuals with technical growth aspirations the opportunity to realize them without leaving the company. They also prevent another damaging outcome: moving highly competent technical professionals into positions where their incompetence at managing people can have the unfortunate result of driving good employees out the door.

Off the Career Ladder and onto the SWAT Team

When Mervyn's department stores of California discovered that talented employees in merchandising were leaving because they were tired of patiently serving time on the company's one-size-fits-all career path, the company came up with a creative solution. Several managers suggested placing these restless individuals on unassigned status where they would be called on to fill frequently occurring staffing gaps in the company's nine different divisions.

Those put on this "SWAT Team," as it was called, found just what they were looking for—a varied mix of responsibilities, new contacts, new opportunities for growth and learning, and greater control over their own schedules.

In the first year, the SWAT Team grew from nineteen members to thirty-four. Several SWAT Team members have been recruited into higher-level positions because of their increased exposure across the company. By not holding to rigid ideas about traditional career paths, Mervyn's has created an exciting, prestigious, flexible alternative that has allowed the company to hold on to talent they would otherwise have lost.[8]

 ### Engagement Practice # 27: Keep Employees Informed About the Company's Strategy, Direction, and Talent Need Forecasts

The best employees seek reassurance that they have hitched their star to a company that will continue to be successful and have a need for their capabilities. This means they need to be kept informed about the company's evolving marketing and growth strategies, and the career opportunities that are likely to come with them.

Companies such as Sun Microsystems, IBM, Intel, Advanced Micro Devices, 3Com, and Microsoft have carried on the practice of giving open business briefings where senior executives regularly brief employees on decisions and plans that may impact jobs or skills required in the future.

Engagement Practice # 28: Build and Maintain a Fair and Efficient Internal Job-Posting Process

As we heard in the comments at the beginning of this chapter, employees are frequently suspicious about how jobs get filled inside the organization, particularly when they are filled without being posted, when qualified applicants are not interviewed or never even receive an acknowledgment from human resources that their applications were received, or when they are never told that they were screened out. Because hiring managers often make hires based on factors such as similarity of background, likeability, comfort, and chemistry, there will always be internal applicants who complain that they were more qualified. What is not excusable is hiring managers or HR managers not posting all positions, and not giving all qualified internal candidates sincere, open-minded consideration.

Much of the employee frustration with job-posting systems arises from the fact that in many organizations they appear to be the only valid way to find out about existing or developing positions. As we know, the reality is that by the time the job opening is formally posted, many internal candidates will have already found out about it through informal means and made themselves known to the hiring manager.

Many employees will be passive enough, naïve enough, or so overly trusting in the supposed fairness and efficiency of internal systems that they cannot see that using the job-posting system is often the last step in seeking a career opportunity, not the first. Companies who provide formal career self-management workshops and computer modules typically will include a section on how jobs are found internally. In these sessions, the importance of informal networking, doing informational interviewing about job and skill requirements, and building relationships with hiring managers can be openly discussed as legitimate career management activities. Such candid discussion can open the eyes of some employees to their own need to be more proactive and lessen their cynicism about favoritism and office politics.

Engagement Practice # 29: Show a Clear Preference for Hiring from Within

Few things are more frustrating for well-qualified employees than the company deciding to hire an outside candidate, or bringing in a consultant, without even giving them a shot at interviewing for the job. In fact, such an experience is often a predictable turning point in the disengagement and eventual departure of highly talented employees, who may feel taken for granted.

Employers of choice tend to hire outside candidates only when no internal candidate is available, consistently conducting searches for internal candidates as their first option. Some companies even maintain "talent banks" containing resumes and talent profiles of employees that managers can screen and match against job requirements.

Most companies recognize that it is more cost-efficient to hire a proven internal candidate rather than pay recruiter fees, relocation costs, and all the other avoidable costs related to new-hire orientation and training. Current employees already know the culture, have established relationships, and understand the way things are done. But the biggest advantage is the morale-boosting message an internal hire sends to all employees: "Your contributions and talent have not gone unnoticed."

 ## Engagement Practice # 30: Eliminate HR Policies and Management Practices That Block Internal Movement

One of the greatest obstacles to the career growth and advancement of high performers is the unwillingness of their own managers to encourage or approve their movement to positions in other departments. Such "blocking" behavior drives top talent out of companies, and has caused some

---

Getting Around the Manager's Career Roadblock

Cerner Corporation of Kansas City created a "career navigation center" where employees could confidentially seek a better position if they felt they were being stifled by the current manager. The company also held seminars for managers to teach them about their retention responsibilities and monitored unit turnover numbers. When numbers got too high, managers were called in for "what's wrong?" meetings.[9]

CEOs to issue directives to all managers that "there will be no hoarding of talent." Another way of expressing this is "the manager doesn't own the talent . . . the organization owns the talent."

Nevertheless, because some managers will always put their own self-interest before the interests of the organization, this will continue be an issue. One way to address it is to specifically include wording in competency descriptions, performance appraisals, and 360-degree feedback ratings, such as "encourages and approves the movement of employees when they seek professional growth opportunities that also serve the needs of the organization." Another effective way to discourage such blocking behavior is to confront these managers with performance coaching and feedback, and, if that does not work, to remove them from positions with responsibility for managing people.

New Way to Re-Engage and Retain Plateaued Employees

There will always be employees who reach a plateau and start looking for new challenges. AT&T re-engages and retains "plateaued" employees with a program called Resource Link, which functions as an in-house temporary service. Through this program, employees with diverse management, technical, or professional skills sell their skills to different departments for short-term assignments.[10]

Another kind of blocking that pushes valued employees out the door has more to do with outdated and rigid "time-in-grade" policies that require employees to remain in a job for a set period of time before they are allowed to seek other positions. Such policies were often designed to discourage internal job-hopping, but fail to take into account that top performers are often ready to move on sooner than average performers.

Engagement Practice # 31: Create a Strong Mentoring Culture

Formal mentoring programs have become a popular way for companies to meet three objectives at the same time: Increase opportunities for women and minorities, develop future leaders, and enhance the retention of employees at all levels. Mentoring programs have been found to be effective in increasing employee retention in 77 percent of the companies that implemented them.[11]

Successful mentoring programs are generally driven from the top down, with strong endorsement and involvement by the CEO to encourage involvement by managers at all levels. Some companies go with formal programs calling for regular meetings and frequent monitoring, while others prefer informal approaches where employees and mentors are free to decide how often to meet.

Mentoring managers tend to take their responsibilities as mentors more seriously when mentoring is one of the competencies for which they are evaluated on performance reviews. Training sessions for mentors and mentees to orient them to the process and clarify ground rules can be conducted to support the process. Peer mentoring and coaching is offered when a coworker has experience or knowledge to share.

Some large companies maintain databases of managers who have volunteered to serve as mentors. Employees may review profiles of mentors on file and submit their choices in order of preference. To relieve the time demands of having too many mentees, some companies facilitate small-group mentoring where four to eight mentees meet with one mentor. Often, such groups meet on a rotating basis with mentors who are expert in one area, such as e-commerce or cost accounting, and build their knowledge in a variety of areas.

Recognizing that many new leaders don't last two years in their new roles, many companies have also created "on-boarding" programs for newly hired executives to immerse them in the organization's culture.

Engagement Practice # 32: Keep the Career Development and Performance Appraisal Processes Separate

Traditionally, performance review forms have a section for summarizing appropriate career objectives for employees and writing developmental objectives designed to close the gaps in current and required competencies. It makes sense to discuss career advancement possibilities at performance appraisal time, but such discussions are often counterproductive in the context of a discussion that has salary implications and may arouse defensiveness against perceived manager criticism.

In recognition of these potential limitations, many companies have directed managers to have discussions with employees about career opportunities at the six-month interval between yearly performance reviews, or at least once a year separate from the discussion of performance. Managers and employees typically report more positive outcomes when there is a dedicated focus on the employee's career development.

Engagement Practice # 33: Build an Effective Talent Review and Succession Management Process

About one-fifth of all management positions across all functions, regions, and industries are expected to become vacant between now and 2010. As a result, the need for succession planning has gotten the attention of more companies in recent years.[12] Only 34 percent of U.S. companies report that they are effective at identifying future leaders,[13] and four in ten senior leaders fail in their new jobs within their first eighteen months on the job.[14]

Many companies are using new terminology, such as "talent review process" or "acceleration pool development," to describe what was traditionally called succession planning. These new terms reflect the increasing difficulty of preparing leaders and talented professionals for organizational opportunities that may not yet exist in a rapidly changing market environment. It is also widely acknowledged that many succession candidates are never promoted into the positions for which they were slotted.

Here are some succession management strategies that are proving to be effective:

- Create alignment between projected company needs and individual aspirations and abilities by conducting in-depth assessments of targeted employees against required competencies to assess promotability and developmental needs.

- Have the process codesigned by human resources and line management.

- Have higher levels of management review the assessments, eventually reaching a senior talent review task force headed by the CEO. The most successful succession management initiatives are usually driven not by the senior HR executive, but by the CEO, and owned by a senior task force or committee that includes the top HR executive.

- Have managers of targeted employees inform succession candidates that they have been identified to participate in a high-potential acceleration pool, being careful to make sure they understand that no promotions are promised and that changes in organizational plans may result in their removal from the pool.

- Have managers work with high-potential succession candidates to follow through on customized developmental plans, often including training, internal mentoring, 360-degree feedback, external coach-

ing, rotational assignments, global, and special exposure opportunities.

- Make sure that candidate progress reviews of developmental plans occur yearly and that potential is reevaluated for various future roles and positions. It is important to give honest and constructive feedback to candidates who have been determined not to be candidates for higher advancement, so they may use it to make more realistic alternative career plans.

Do these practices pay off? According to Hewitt Associates, top-performing firms as measured by total shareholder return are more likely to use a consistently formal approach to identifying, developing, and tracking the performance of potential leaders.[15] Yet, only 64 percent of companies have a management succession committee or process.[16]

What About the B Players?

In their effort to provide fast-track development to employees they see as A players, companies often overlook the development of B players—valued, stable contributors who comprise the backbone of the organization, but who often allow their own careers to take a back-seat to the company's well being.

One company that has made a concerted effort to develop its B players is the luxury hotel chain, Princely Hotels, which created a career development committee to give opportunities to all managers, not just the stars. The committee has developed a career track that offers "lateral promotions" to managers among its sixty properties and makes sure they are getting the coaching they need.[17]

Engagement Practice #34:
Maintain a Strong Commitment to Employee Training

Many managers question the wisdom of spending money on training, especially during down business cycles. They worry that the money they spend on training will be wasted when the employees they train leave to go to work for other companies. Their worst fear is that they will become a training ground for their competitors.

Here are some findings that might help to assuage such fears:

- Companies that spend $218 per employee in training and development have more than 16 percent annual voluntary turnover . . . while companies that spend $273 per employee have less than 7 percent annual voluntary turnover."[18]
- In a *BusinessWeek* survey of employees who say their companies offer poor training, 41 percent plan to leave within a year versus only 12 percent of those with excellent training options.[19]
- Eight of ten employees in a Gallup survey cited the availability of employer-sponsored training as an important criterion in considering a new job opportunity.[20]

It comes down to this—you have to train your employees so they can leave, or else they'll leave. Put another way, what if you don't train them and they stay?

Employers honored by their listing in *Fortune* Magazine's annual "100 Best Places to Work" issue provide an average of forty days of training per employee per year. As far as impact to the bottom line, firms in the top quarter of training expenditure per employee (averaging $1,595 per year) had profit margins 24 percent higher than those in the bottom quarter (averaging $128 per year).[21] More and more employers have concluded that training is an investment in employee productivity and retention and they are making it available in a variety of ways.

Self-paced online training programs are now in wide use. Employees utilize a Web portal to access course information and content as well as college courses offered online. Learning resources may be organized ac-

---

Cash Accounts for Employee Training

A great way to give employees more autonomy and choice in their own development is by providing individual learning accounts that provide employees with a set amount of training dollars they may spend per year from among a menu of company-sponsored training, including a course or two for pure self-enrichment.

The Horn Group, a public relations firm based in San Francisco, offers employees cash that they are free to spend on any type of training they feel would help them do their jobs better. Employees use the training dollars—called "a personal development fund"—to take courses in time management, writing, and many other subjects.[23]

cording to competencies needed by the employee. One survey indicated that up to two-thirds of companies planned to increase their investments in Web self-service between 2002 and 2005.[22]

Media such as CD-ROM, computer discs, videotapes, audiotapes, or textbooks have become popular means of delivering course content. Another effective practice is creating intranet-driven, knowledge-sharing networks where employees can ask and answer each other's questions via e-mail, bulletin boards, or in real time.

Many companies offer "soft-skills" training—in communication, giving feedback, and negotiation—to technical staff. Such training is typically offered in classes where new skills can be tried out in face-to-face situations.

Most companies now reimburse tuition for college courses completed onsite or through e-learning. Reimbursement policies usually require that course work relate in some way to an employee's current position or a foreseeable one.

Larger organizations often have internal corporate academies or universities, such as the one at Seagate Technology, which, in addition to formal training sessions, offers site tours, job shadowing, and team-building sessions at several locations. Truman Medical Center in Kansas City features a cyber café, which offers employees computer access and training. As an incentive, for every course an employee completes, Truman also gives "learning points' that can add up to paid time-off.

Smaller companies make the most of resources by having employees who attend industry conferences take detailed notes and make presentations to employees who could not attend. Others may start informal "brown-

---

When It's OK to Train 'Em and Lose 'Em

UPS realizes that many of its young part-timers won't want to spend the rest of their lives loading and unloading packages. But that doesn't keep the company from helping them pay their college tuition and offering Saturday classes for computer skills development and career planning discussions. UPS recognizes that college students are loyal to their own skills development more than to their jobs or supervisors, and that such perks will help assure a continuing supply of applicants. As for longer-term benefits to the company, Jennifer Shroeger, a UPS district manager commented, "I'd like all those part-time workers to graduate from college and start their own businesses—and become UPS customers."[24]

bag" lunch programs where employees brief each other on books they have read or share specialized knowledge on trends, products, processes, or clients.

Other trends in training include: just-in-time training for new hires and for quick reassignment; conducting training needs analysis to make sure it is tied to a real business need and can close a performance gap before offering the training; more outsourcing of training to outside vendors; and, for global companies, making all training accessible worldwide twenty-four hours a day, seven days a week

What Employees Can Do to Create Their Own Growth and Advancement Opportunities

We have reviewed many areas where the organization can create career growth opportunities for employees, but ultimately it is up to the employees to take charge of their careers. Managers can hold employees to their part of the bargain by challenging them to do the following:

- Master the job you have now, first and foremost. Remember that fortune favors those who do a brilliant job today.
- If you are in the wrong job, change to the right one. Love what you do, which means figuring out who you are in terms of talents, interests, values, and motivations.
- Know how the money flows through the organization, what factors cause profit and loss, and what part of that you can control.
- When no promotional options seem open, seek lateral or cross-functional assignments, or create a job that meets unmet company needs and makes use of your talents.
- Seek continual learning by formal and informal means.
- Familiarize yourself with career paths of those in positions to which you aspire, gain their advice, get realistic previews of their jobs, and ask them to be a mentor to you.
- If a position you desire is not currently available, seek mini-assignments that will help prepare you and try out pieces of the desired job.
- Exhaust all options for enriching your current job by seeking new challenges and satisfying activities in your current job before pursuing applying for other jobs.

- Communicate your aspirations, talents, ideas, and plans to your manager so he or she can provide appropriate feedback, coaching, or sponsorship.
- Re-energize your career by acting like an entrepreneur, by starting a new service or line of business for the company.
- Before deciding to leave the company, communicate to your manager or to a trusted mentor the source of your career frustration and ask for ideas and assistance.

Employer-of-Choice Engagement Practices Review and Checklist

Review the engagement practices presented in this chapter and check the ones you believe your organization needs to implement or improve.

To Provide Career Advancement and Growth Opportunities:
24. ☐ Provide self-assessment tools and career self-management training for all employees.
25. ☐ Offer career coaching tools and training for all managers.
26. ☐ Provide readily accessible information on career paths and competency requirements.
27. ☐ Create alternatives to traditional career ladders.
28. ☐ Keep employees informed about the company's strategy, direction, and talent need forecasts.
29. ☐ Build and maintain a fair and efficient internal job-posting process.
30. ☐ Show a clear preference for hiring from within.
31. ☐ Create a strong mentoring culture.
32. ☐ Eliminate HR policies and management practices that block internal movement.
33. ☐ Keep career development and performance appraisal processes separate.
34. ☐ Build an effective talent review and succession management process.
35. ☐ Maintain a strong commitment to employee training.

Notes

1. Human Resources Department, "Talent Management Emerges as HR Department's New Leadership Challenge," *Management Report*, November 2002.

2. Robert N. Llewellyn, "The Power in Being a People Developer: Who Is the Best People Developer in Your Organization? Why Isn't It You?" quoting study by Lominger Limited, Inc., *HR* Magazine, July 2002.

3. Maureen Minehan, "People Strategies, Rewards Are Keys to High Performance," *hr-esource.com*, Recruitment and Retention report, February 5, 2001.

4. Adapted from David Noer, *Healing the Wounds: Overcoming the Trauma of Layoffs and Revitalizing Downsized Organizations* (San Francisco: Jossey-Bass, 1993).

5. Paula Santonocito, "Lands' End to Use PeopleComeFirst Solution for Learning Management," *HR Professional*, May 20, 2002.

6. Leslie Goff, "Dream It, and They'll Be It," in "The Top 10 Retention Tactics," *Computerworld*, November 22, 1999.

7. Robert N. Llewellyn, "The Four Career Concepts: Managers Can Learn How to Better Develop Their People by Learning How They're Motivated," *HR* Magazine, September 2002.

8. Bruce Tulgan, *Winning the Talent Wars* (New York: W.W. Norton, 2001).

9. Diane Stafford, "Best Leaders Retain Key Employees," *The Kansas City Star*, August 10, 2000.

10. "Follow AT&T's Lead with This Tactic to Retain 'Plateaued' Employees," *Employee Recruitment & Retention*, Lawrence Ragan Communications, 2000.

11. Jodi Davis, "Leadership: The Role of Mentoring," presentation, Kansas City, Missouri, October 14, 1999.

12. "Developing Leaders for 2010 Report," The Conference Board, 2003.

13. Ibid.

14. Manchester Consulting survey, 2002.

15. Susan J. Wells, "Who's Next? Creating a Formal Program for Developing New Leaders Can Pay Huge Dividends, But Many Firms Aren't Reaping Those Rewards," *HR* Magazine, November, 2003.

16. Ibid., citing study of *Fortune* 1000 companies by Korn/Ferry International.

17. Thomas J. DeLong and Vineeta Vijayraghavan, "Let's Hear It for B Players," *Harvard Business Review*, June 2003.

18. Carroll Lachnit, "Training Proves Its Worth," *Training* Magazine, September 2001.

19. American Society for Training & Development, "Trends Watch," 1999.

20. Ibid.

21. Susan J. Wells, "Stepping Carefully: Attention to Staffing Levels, Compensation, and Training Will Help Ride Out a Slowdown," *HR Magazine*, April 19, 2001.

22. Santonocito, "Lands' End to Use PeopleComeFirst Solution."

23. "Create a 'Personal Development Fund,'" *Employee Recruitment and Retention*, Lawrence Ragan Communications, 2000.

24. Keith H. Hammonds, "Handle with Care: How UPS Handles Packages Starts with How It Handles Its People," *Fast Company*, August 2002.

CHAPTER EIGHT

Reason #5: Feeling Devalued and Unrecognized

Make people who work
for you feel important.
If you honor and serve
them, they'll honor
and serve you.

—MARY KAY ASH

It's really quite simple—everybody wants to feel important. So how do so many organizations manage to make so many people feel so unimportant? Selected comments from Saratoga's surveys show there are several way that working people are made to feel unimportant. Here are some of those ways, in their own words:

Lack of Simple Appreciation

- "They do not give to employees. On my first day of work I was not able to take a lunch. Also, I am not able to spend any money on my employees to show appreciation for a job well done."
- "It's horrid to hear about an employee who had been with the company for 20+ years and did not even receive a card showing the company's appreciation."
- "I believe ABC Company could do a better job of recognizing employees more. People tend to work better if there is an appreciation shown for what they are doing."

Too Much Focus on the Numbers, Not Enough on People

- "Everyone is treated as a number and not a person, you are a machine."

- "Company leaders should recognize employees or understand that despite all the focus on productivity, profits and customers, they also should be flexible and appreciate the employees. It does not surprise me that there is a high turnover rate at XYZ Company."

Feeling They Deserve Recognition and Don't Get It, While Others Do

- "The evening shift should be paid more!"
- "When you are in a remote office you are forgotten about."
- "They do not show appreciation to the people who do the work, they give praise to the managers of the people that do the work. 'Thank you's' are free."
- "ABC Company hires new employees [who are] making more money than the people that have been here a long time. Then they want you to train the new employees that make more than you."

Feeling That No One Even Knows or Cares if They Exist

- "This office never seems to receive any recognition in any kind of corporate newsletters or bulletins. Many of us feel isolated and ignored."
- "When I came to ABC Company my manager never paid attention to the times I was available to work. Once a week, if not more, I would have to bring it to her attention the hours that I was available to work. Two months in a row she scheduled me wrong and made changes in the schedule without even asking me. I will never work at ABC again."
- "Joining XYZ Company was the worst mistake I have ever made. When I was hired no one even knew I was starting."

Recognition Was Too Late in Coming to Be Meaningful

- "ABC Company rewards you for excellence, but when they do, it's months down the road before you hear anything."

Feeling That No One Is Listening to Them

- "We should be able to give input in regards to the new building. I believe that the employees know best how much meeting and storage space is needed."

- "ABC Company takes a bulldozer approach to management. It is 'this is the direction we are going,' period, without asking for input from employees."
- "XYZ Company initiates change without consulting the people who these changes will directly affect."

Feeling They Are Worth Less Than Employees at Other Companies

- "They don't stay competitive with other companies' pay scales. We have lost 75 percent of our employees to other employers that pay considerably more."
- "The pay for our jobs is not enough to keep well-trained employees away from the competition. The small raises enable the competition to steal the employees away."
- "Upper and middle management obviously don't have a clue what fair market value is for talented and experienced employees. After my two-year review I was so disappointed that I momentarily got nausea."
- "Compensation is below market. A software developer with the same experience and skill in this city is paid $53,000. However, I am only being paid $32,000. I have received two offers that are paying close to average."

Believing They Are Not Paid for Performance

- "I have been given no incentives and no bonuses to show that I am appreciated."
- "ABC Company needs a system to allow supervisors and managers to give raises based on merit or pay for performance. Their 'blanket' 2 percent and 3 percent raises are a joke and do nothing to encourage employees to strive for better performance."
- "Bonuses are only given to whomever the manager likes."

Some Feel That the Wrong Kinds of Rewards Are Being Given

- "Bonuses should always be an option for rewarding employees instead of certificates or plaques."
- "Forget all the cute gimmicks and 'jean day' and all the other childish improvements, and make the pay adequate enough to live off of—I have a mortgage to pay."

- "They had a company picnic for the employees and instead of giving the employees the whole day off, we got to enjoy the horrible food for only a half an hour, and then go back to work."

Slow Pay and Changing Pay Plans

- "There are too many changes in the compensation plans."
- "My last payroll change took six weeks. 401K deposits were inconsistent."
- "Reimbursement of tuition after four months is too long to have to wait!!"
- "Highly dissatisfied with delay tactics of HR in resolving payroll/ overtime issues. Instead of management resolving an issue, their words and attitude were 'if you don't like it—get a job elsewhere.'"

Feeling They Are Treated Like Children Instead of Adults

- "I did not appreciate having to keep tabs on every second of my time. I felt that as mature adults, we should be responsible for our time."
- "At the call center they make a big deal about the employees dressing appropriately when customers don't see even them."

The Company Doesn't Care About Their Physical Surroundings

- "The noise level makes it very hard to do my job properly."
- "A person cannot work in a 120-degree warehouse in the summer."
- The lack of workspace has become outrageous, to the point of employees having to sit on the floor to do necessary paperwork because lack of counter space. Yet requests for expansion (of existing services space) are continually denied. This has seriously impacted everyone and is the main cause of low morale."
- "We have beautiful signs in the front of our banking office, but the insides of most of our buildings are dirty, outdated and run down."

Not Provided with the Right Tools

- "Computers are horrible. They are always crashing."
- "I think ABC Company's biggest problem is skimping on equipment and amenities for doing our work."

- "It's like pulling teeth to get new equipment and supplies."
- "XYZ Company does not supply the necessary equipment, i.e., computers, adequate work space, or file storage, or reference books needed daily to be efficient and quick in the performance of job duties. Give people the tools necessary to efficiently do their job! Days and weeks are wasted waiting for computer bugs to be repaired."

In all these ways, companies are not only missing opportunities to engage their workers, they are also giving them cause to become disengaged. Because these are the comments of employees who actually left their organizations, they serve as strong evidence that disengagement leads directly to costly turnovers.

William James once said that "the deepest craving in human nature is the craving to be appreciated." If that is so, why is there such reluctance on the part of managers to give it?

Why Managers Are Reluctant to Recognize

Managers are reluctant to recognize because:

- The very qualities that result in people rising into management positions in most organizations often do not include empathy for others.
- They have worked for managers who taught them, "if you don't hear from me, that means you're doing a good job," or "don't expect me to pat you on the back just for doing your job—I expect you to do your job."
- They are not paying enough attention to the performance of their employees to know when they have done something worth recognizing. (This begs the question, what *are* they paying attention to, if not the performance of their employees?)
- They don't know enough about an employee's job to know the difference between average and superior performance.
- They believe their people will think they are phony and insincere when they try to praise them.
- They are afraid they will recognize some employees, and forget to recognize others.

- They believe that rewarding and recognizing employees is the responsibility of the human resources department.

It is rather discouraging to review these reasons. They are all too understandable. It makes one wonder how, with such obstacles, some companies are actually able to build cultures of recognition. The task of building such a culture is a formidable one, especially in organizations with a history of authoritarian leadership or in highly technical, scientific, or engineering organizations where thinking is more valued than feeling.

But thinkers have feelings too, and if their employers do not make them *feel* valued, they will exercise their options to move on to employers who do. After all, the comments of lost employees reveal that in all too many cases, disengagement really is about management's failure to consider the impact of their actions, or lack of action, on employees' emotions, especially when it results in an employee feeling *worth less*. It should be said that many employees have over-inflated views of their own worth. But I believe many more suffer from just the opposite affliction and need to be more frequently acknowledged as valued contributors.

Recognizing the Signs That Employees Feel Devalued and Unrecognized

Because there are so many factors that may cause an employee to feel devalued or unrecognized, there are just as many different indicators. Here are some suggestions of what to look for as precursors of potential disengagement:

- Valued contributor is overdue for a pay increase.
- Valued contributor is paid less than others in similar jobs in organization.
- Valued contributor is paid less than others in competing organizations.
- No bonus or incentive opportunity is available.
- Bonus or incentive offered is less than 10 percent of base pay.
- Nonperformers are receiving the same pay increases or bonuses as valued contributors.
- New recruits are making significantly more than more experienced, valued employees in similar positions.

- Valued contributor has not received informal recognition in the form of sincere expression of appreciation for contributions in the last 90 days.
- Employee is a "B" player—a solid contributor who may feel over-looked or taken for granted.
- New hires seem to be ignored and disconnected.
- A valued employee has recently been passed over for promotion.
- Valued employee works for manager who does not express appreciation or recognition.
- Valued employee works for abusive manager.
- Valued employees do not have the right tools or resources to do the job right.
- Valued employees work in cramped, noisy, messy, dirty, hot, cold, noxious, or unsafe physical environment.
- Employee survey indicates recognition and pay practices are top concerns.

Pay: The Most Emotional Issue of All

There is no more emotionally-charged issue for employees than what they are paid for their contributions. What we make doesn't just pay the bills—it measures our worth in the most material way. We cannot help defining ourselves by the levels of our income, yet we go to great lengths to keep the information private.

In reviewing the comments of ex-employees about pay, the root of their dissatisfaction runs deeper than the sums they were paid. They are bothered by the inequity of knowing that they make less than others who are no more qualified, or even less qualified, than they are. They feel the injustice of getting the same pay raises as those who have contributed far less to the organization than they have. They interpret HR's unresponsiveness to requests for payroll changes as a sign that they are unimportant. They have no chance to receive a bonus, while others do. It all adds up to feeling "less than."

This is why pay and recognition are combined in this chapter—they are both tools for acknowledging the worth of those who work for us. We will look at best practices in both pay and recognition, as they must be considered as "twins joined at the hip" in sending the right messages to employees about what we value. But it is helpful to remind ourselves of some key distinctions between the two:

- Recognition cannot replace pay; it can only add to it.
- Recognition is usually retroactive, acknowledging a contribution after the fact, while variable pay can be a powerful incentive for motivating future goal achievement.
- Recognition can happen at any time, reinforcing desired behavior more effectively when it quickly follows the accomplishment of a team or an individual.
- Recognition can be customized or personalized to fit the person receiving it, making it more meaningful.
- Recognition in the form of material possessions carries the additional motivational power of reminding the individual of the company's appreciation.
- Any employee can recognize another employee, while only management can pay.
- Recognition can take the form of celebration, bringing some needed fun and excitement into the workplace.
- Innovative recognition practices may bring positive publicity to the company.
- Contests—a common recognition practice—can give every employee an equal chance for a payoff.

Both pay and recognition are powerful tools for reinforcing organizational values or changes in personal behavior and work culture. Together, they are more effective than either can be separately.

Pay Practices That Engage and Retain

Companies spend millions of dollars per year on compensation consultants to make sure they are designing or redesigning their pay plans to fit their business cultures and objectives. So, it would be misleading to suggest that there are best practices that work equally well for organizations of all sizes and situations. However, there are definite trends in the way companies are choosing to pay their workers that appear to be more motivating and appropriate for the times and for newer generations of workers.

Companies have gradually replaced old pay practices with newer pay practices that meet new worker expectations. In the 1960s, 1970s, and even into the 1980s, most companies rewarded tenure over performance and created an entitlement mentality in much of the workforce. Workers "owned" their jobs and most companies were stable and paternalistic. Companies absorbed pay and benefit costs regardless of their ability to pay.

With the late 1980s and 1990s came downsizings and the flattening of organizations and with these, the loss of worker trust and loyalty. Workers were no longer entitled to their jobs, but had to learn new skills to stay employable. People found more flexible ways of working—from home, part-time, and temporary. Pay and benefit costs were cut along with jobs. There was a severe loss of workforce commitment that lingers today.

When talent became scarce compared to job growth in the late 1990s, companies actually started believing the words they had always mouthed— people really *are* a source of competitive advantage. Talented people had other options than working for companies that did not value them highly. Companies woke up to the fact that they needed to invest in their work-forces and form win-win partnerships. This meant more open communi-cation, more coaching, training, stock options, signing bonuses, creative perks, and generous benefits.

During the economic downturn of 2001, many employers began cut-ting back on perks, benefits, and signing bonuses. Employees started "tree-hugging" their jobs, in spite of the fact that they were asked to do more with less. At this writing, most experts believe the war for talent will return as the economy continues to grow while boomers retire in large numbers. If this happens, companies will realize anew that people work for more than just pay and benefits—they work for what we now call "total re-wards," the most meaningful of which are not related to pay.

Here then are some of the best pay practices that many preeminent employers have begun to embrace to better engage and retain their talent:

Engagement Practice # 35: Offer Competitive Base Pay Linked to Value Creation

The ongoing need to provide increased value to customers, combined with the need to control base pay increases, have led many companies to link base pay more to value creation and less to rank or years of service. This new emphasis has resulted in some companies paying lower-ranked em-ployees more than their managers, based on the judgment that their contri-butions brought more to the bottom line. At The Container Store, for example, consistently ranked among *Fortune's* "100 Best Places to Work in

America," it is not unusual for a sales associate to make more than a store manager.

Another key is to communicate clearly to all employees how "value" is determined when making decisions regarding base pay. For example, in many companies, overall sustained value is based on three criteria:

1. Skills and competencies needed
2. Labor market supply and demand
3. Ongoing value to the organization[1]

Yet, employees in most companies could not explain, if asked, how value is determined, because it has never been adequately explained to them. Besides communicating clearly how base pay decisions are made, managers need to also be held accountable for making hard decisions about which employees are creating more value for the business and are keeping their skills aligned with company needs. There will always be a degree of subjectivity in such decisions, and many managers will try to please everyone by spreading pay increases evenly (as with peanut butter) to all, often with disastrous results.

How salary decisions are made will depend on the goals of each organization. Some companies actually give base pay increases for lateral moves within the organization, thus reinforcing the company's emphasis on employee development and preparation for future assignments.

Here are some other notable trends in base pay:

- *Paying for Skills and Competencies.* This has been a growing trend, resulting in more emphasis on paying the person rather than the job. However, many companies have found that paying for results with lump sums and variable pay is the higher priority.
- *Less Emphasis on Internal Equity Based on Point Factors and Job Evaluations.* The more competitive the labor market, the more companies have de-emphasized internal pay equity in favor of staying competitive with other companies in the same industry. This can create problems of salary compression, as when new employees are recruited at starting salaries greater than those of experienced employees. Smart employers need to be disciplined enough not to get into bidding wars, remembering that pay is only one piece of the total rewards approach.

Some companies cannot afford to pay above-market base salaries, but can still compete effectively for talent by giving employees more mentoring, no-cost recognition, additional vacation days, or whatever nonpay reward might be important to them. When employers reach the point where they feel they must pay a premium to capture new recruits, they will simply have to find creative ways to reward more experienced workers.

- *Less Reliance on Salary Benchmarking.* More workplaces are becoming less structured and more fluid in the way the work gets done. This means some jobs are blended with other jobs, and some people are given broader roles, combining tasks that were formerly done by several others. This means that when companies look to make market-based judgments about employees' value, they need to keep in mind that, when looking at salary surveys and benchmarking with other companies, they may not be "comparing apples to apples."

- *More Broad-Banding.* Many employers have drastically cut the number of salary grades and created broad salary bands that reflect the fact that organizations may be flatter and less hierarchical than in years past. The growing popularity of broad-banding reflects the fact that it contributes to the attraction and retention of talent in several ways: It focuses employees on growing within a broad pay range, facilitates lateral career moves, emphasizes the person over the job, reinforces the use of dual career paths, and supports changes in work design.[2]

Increasingly, employers of choice understand that base pay, as a reward for individual ongoing value, is only one piece of a total rewards approach. Employers of choice have gravitated toward the mix of variable pay to reward current value and nonpay rewards to complete the total rewards package.

Engagement Practice # 36: Reward Results with Variable Pay Aligned with Business Goals

Because of the increased focus on productivity during the recent economic downturn, more companies turned to new pay practices that require employees to put more of their pay at risk in exchange for greater rewards if they help the company meet its business objectives. While many employees will be uncomfortable with assuming the increased risk, many others, including top performers, respond favorably to the opportunity for more "ownership" if it means being paid in proportion to their contributions.

Employee Ownership Reduces Employee Turnover

USA 800 Inc., a contact call center and fulfillment center with 400 employees across the United States, had experienced turnover rates as high as 70 percent, resulting in loss of significant training investment and in disruption of customer service. The owners decided to make the transition to 100 percent employee ownership. Since then, the company's revenues have increased by almost 30 percent and the employee turnover rate dropped to 23 percent. Company owners see another positive by-product of giving employees a stake in the company: 80 percent of the company's managers have been promoted from within.[3]

Three Types of Variable Pay

There are three types of variable pay that many companies use in combination: Short-term variable pay, long-term cash variable pay, and long-term equity variable pay.

Short-term variable pay, such as goal-sharing, win-sharing, gain-sharing, profit-sharing, team variable pay, individual variable pay, and combination plans, usually focuses on the achievement of business results within a one-year time frame. As a way of gaining more autonomy in directly rewarding employees for outstanding achievements, many managers now lobby for "spot award" money in their budgets.

Long-term cash variable pay is designed to reward business results over a sustained period of time, generally two or more years. Sustained performance requires a long-term focus, not just the short-term view adopted by so many companies in response to expectations of the investment community. The longer-term perspective can also help keep key talent for longer periods.

Long-term equity variable pay means stock options. By providing stock options to all position levels in the organization, companies spread the feeling of shared ownership, reinforce teamwork, and promote longer-term retention.

The major attraction of variable pay is that it has the potential to fulfill employees' expectations of being paid for performance while allowing businesses to make additional payouts only if they achieve business goals.

Generation Y Expects More Customized Pay Options

With the retirement of Baby Boomers in large numbers, employers will compete for Generation X and Y workers who will demand even more job freedom and flexibility. Also known as Millennials, Gen Y workers will have shorter job tenures, request work-from-home arrangements, and seek quarterly bonuses, not yearly ones. To meet the changing expectations of younger workers, companies will increasingly customize rewards programs to the individual preferences of workers. In 2001, only 2 percent of companies offered employees the ability to customize the rewards program to suit their preferences. By 2003, more than 20 percent of companies were expected to offer such customization.

Leaders of the Towers-Perrin rewards management consulting practice believe that "a customized rewards package will give companies a competitive edge in hiring and retention, increase the motivation (and therefore the productivity) of employees, and encourage creativity and innovation by empowering employees."[4]

For variable pay programs to work, they first depend on clear communication of the rationale, measures, and goals to be used both during and after the roll-out. This puts increased responsibility on senior leaders to openly discuss how bonuses will be figured and on the manager to do the measuring. Second, goals need to be realistic and achievable while still providing a reasonable stretch for the employee. Finally, goals have to change as the business environment and priorities change.

 ### Engagement Practice # 37: Reward Employees at a High Enough Level to Motivate Higher Performance

Studies have repeatedly shown that there is a certain level at which employees become more willing to put forth the effort to achieve higher goals. Some experts argue that an award of 10 to 12 percent above base pay is required, which is significantly higher than the 7.5 percent that most companies pay.[5]

Other experts report that variable pay in most companies averages about 10 percent of base pay for managers and sales professionals, 8 percent for exempt workers, and 5 percent for nonexempt workers.[6]

There are other factors to consider in determining the size of the variable pay opportunity. Generally, variable pay awards should be higher when:

- The bottom-line impact of the results is significant.
- The result is difficult to achieve.
- The result takes longer to achieve.
- Base pay is more at risk.

Engagement Practice # 38: Use Cash Payouts for on-the-Spot Recognition

Many top employers reserve 1 to 2 percent of their base pay budget for cash payouts or lump-sum payments to recognize top performers in the current time frame. One of the main reasons for the popularity of cash payouts is the increased motivational power that comes from giving awards as quickly as possible following an achievement. Such awards also give organizations more flexibility, in that they can be used to supplement team awards and recognize contributors whose value is acknowledged but who already have a high base pay, or those who may be designated to receive minimal base pay increases.

Engagement Practice # 39: Involve Employees and Encourage Two-Way Communication When Designing New Pay Systems

Research consistently shows that employee satisfaction goes up when employees know how their pay is determined. One study found that 74 percent of employees who understood how their pay was determined reported being satisfied in their jobs. On the other hand, of those who did not understand how pay was determined, only 42 percent were satisfied. The same study found that only 28 percent of employees saw a link between their pay and their performance.[7]

For those in military service, pay is seldom an issue with anyone, since all know how pay is determined and what everyone else is making. Thus, it is not the distraction it is in corporations, where so much time and emotion is wasted speculating, gossiping, and being angry about pay.

The best time, but not the only time, to start the process of creating employee understanding is when designing a new pay system. Inviting the input of employees is the best way to create an understandable system that fits their needs and gets their buy-in. Forward-thinking companies begin the process by linking business objectives with the employee behavior they want the new pay system to reinforce. After developing a preliminary design, they may survey the workforce, conducting one-on-one interviews or focus groups to surface and clarify key issues and ideas. The initial roll-out meetings should allow plenty of time for two-way communication, with most-commonly-asked questions solicited and answered.

Even if a pay system has been installed without going through this process, it is never too late to begin a campaign to communicate how pay is determined and solicit employee feedback. One survey reported that half of employees felt that discussing pay was taboo in their organizations.[8] This is an obstacle to engaging and retaining talent that may be an uncomfortable one to tackle, but is worth making the extra effort to overcome. We need to constantly keep in mind that when it comes to pay, employees are just as interested in "how" as they are in "how much."

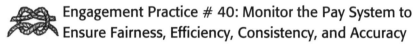 ## Engagement Practice # 40: Monitor the Pay System to Ensure Fairness, Efficiency, Consistency, and Accuracy

As we have seen in the comments of employees, there are always questions about pay systems, and there always will be. Employees should be surveyed on a regular basis about the pay system, including the effectiveness of managers in coaching them through the performance measurement and management process discussed in Chapter Six. Continued monitoring will also be needed to assure that pay practices stay aligned with business goals and that managers are making effective pay decisions.

The Total Rewards Approach to Scarce Talent

When talent is scarce, as was the case with IT professionals in the late 1990s, many companies respond by increasing levels of base pay and short-term bonuses. This popular, knee-jerk response often results in payment of generous sign-on bonuses, stay bonuses, and in making counteroffers to people after they announce they are leaving. Treating talent as a commodity may serve to attract talent, but often cannot keep it in the absence of other "total reward" attractions, such as having a great boss, attractive work-life benefits, challenging work, and opportunities for career advancement. Another downside to this approach is that it only serves to drive up pay costs and accelerate bidding wars with other companies.

Some companies put more of an emphasis on retaining scarce talent (as opposed to just buying it) by actually measuring their managers' success at keeping talent in the organization. "Percentage of employees retained" may be factored in to determine managers' pay. Other employers pay cash retention awards to key talent for each year they stay with the company. An employer may even pay stock options to employees who make referrals of scarce-talent candidates who are hired and stay for pre-set periods.

Employers who want to become true employers of choice typically pursue a more comprehensive strategy—they design a "total rewards" approach that balances pay as a key attraction equally along with a full range of non-pay factors. In other words, employers that pursue "total rewards" strategies focus on delivering a compelling value proposition to prospective and current employees based on practices like those presented in all the chapters of this book.

More Words to the Wise About Pay

Noncash rewards are the only real way to differentiate your employment offerings. Cash is a commodity, so it cannot differentiate one company's employment contract from another; it is the intangibles that distinguish. Besides, when it comes to money, someone will always pay more.

—Todd M. Manas and Michael Dennis Graham[9]

Nonpay Best Practices for Valuing and Recognizing People

The good news about showing people that we value them is that there are so many ways to do it that are absolutely free. At least they are free in the sense that you have to spend little or no money, but you do have to invest some time, energy, and imagination. So, the first key is to care enough to make those kinds of investments.

Next, it is important to understand what kind of recognition people want, that they don't all want the same kind of recognition, and that they don't all want the same kind of recognition as you do. Many studies on motivation and recognition have repeatedly found that managers thought employees valued good pay and job security, while employees themselves reported they most valued intangibles such as managers recognizing them, keeping them informed, and being interested in their professional growth. When workers and supervisors were asked to rank a list of motivators from one to ten in order of their importance to workers, workers rated "appreciation for a job well done" as their top motivator. Supervisors ranked it eighth. Employees ranked "feeling in on things" as number two in importance, while managers ranked it last at number ten.[10]

This means that managers simply need to ask their people how they would like to be recognized, which seems so obvious that it's puzzling that more managers don't do it. Of course, there are some forms of recognition that all employees value, which brings us to our first recognition best practice:

Engagement Practice # 41: Create a Culture of Informal Recognition Founded on Sincere Appreciation

Receiving simple and sincere thanks for their contributions is the primary form of recognition people want. In one recent study, 78 percent of employees said it was very important for them to be recognized by their manager when they do good work. Another 73 percent said they expected recognition to occur either "immediately" or "soon thereafter."[11] There are several ways of giving thanks, with face-to-face being the most preferred, but also including written, electronic, and public. Many employees like written expressions of thanks, as they can be copied and kept. Not all employees like public recognition, however, so it is always best to ask employees whether they mind being singled out in front of others.

Many managers find it hard to give this simplest of recognition because they have developed the habit of taking the contributions of their employees for granted, perhaps because their own contributions have gone unappreciated. It is difficult to get managers to develop the new habit of giving thanks for good work. It is probably easier to change to a culture of recognition by hiring managers whom we know to be good at giving thanks to their employees than it is to train managers to build new habits. Still, managers can be taught the art of giving thanks, and many companies do include modules on how to recognize and show appreciation in their basic supervisory training. It takes practice to build new habits, so most effective training requires managers to actually try out new ways of expressing appreciation during training sessions.

There are different ways to say thanks, such as:

- "I'm glad you're here."
- "Thank you for being who you are . . . your role here is vital and much appreciated."
- "You stayed late last night to finish that proposal, and I want you to know how much that meant to me and the whole team."

It also helps to have a list of different ways to express appreciation, like the following one:

- Send a gift certificate for dinner for two at a local restaurant with a note of thanks.
- Send out note cards for writing personal thanks with the words "You Done Good" or "Bravo" printed on them.
- Give employees a way to recognize their peers, such as having them pass around an old trophy to coworkers for doing something they view as outstanding
- Give employees an unexpected half day or day off.
- Take the employee to lunch.
- Give the employee a choice assignment.
- Pay for a massage or manicure.
- Send a gift basket to the home.

Whatever method you chose to use, keep in mind that recognition works best when it is contingent on desired behavior and performance. If you bring in donuts every Friday, it won't take long before employees see

---

A New Habit in Action

"I try to remember that people—good, intelligent, capable people—may actually need day-to-day praise and thanks for the job they do. I try to remember to get up out of my chair, turn off my computer, go sit or stand next to them and see what they're doing, ask about the challenges, find out if they need additional help, offer that help if possible, and most of all, tell them in all honesty that what they are doing is important: to me, to the company, and to our customers."[12]

—John Ball, service training manager,
American Honda Motor Company

it as entitlement. People actually value recognition more when they have done something to earn it. For more ideas on how to recognize employees, read Bob Nelson's best-selling book, *1001 Ways to Reward Employees*, a great resource for managers who wish to start building new habits of appreciation.

Focus on the People, Not Just the Numbers

There are more formal and elaborate ways of recognizing and saying thanks, which can require more sophisticated planning and financial investment. Yum Brands, the parent company of Pizza Hut, A & W Restaurants, KFC, Long John's Silver's, and Taco Bell, has marching bands march right up to employees in recognition of going the extra mile in the name of customer service. The recognition is just one part of the company's effort to "brand" itself as a great place to work, which also includes more extensive training in how to resolve customer issues and listen better. Since im-

---

Outdated Formal Recognition Programs

Here are three kinds of formal recognition that recognition expert, Bob Nelson, believes are out of step with the times and today's employees:

1. *Years of Service.* Although 93 percent of companies offer this one, it has become less meaningful in recent years as employee tenures average three years or less and organizations are less stable. Instead of rewarding endurance, companies should focus on rewarding performance

2. *Employee of the Month.* This award sometimes recognizes employees just because it is their turn to be recognized, even if they haven't done anything particularly outstanding recently. To quote Nelson, "We don't need employees-of-the-month as much as we need employees-of-the-moment."

3. *Attendance Awards.* The advent of telecommuting, flex-time, cell phones, pagers, and virtual work teams have made attendance awards obsolete in an increasing number of organizations. They reward employees for where they are rather than what they do.

plementing the recognition and training programs, the turnover in Taco Bell restaurants has gone down from 200 percent to 98 percent.[13]

Another example of a formal recognition program is the way Kinko's recognizes its best-performing stores. Each year all 1,200 Kinko's stores worldwide are ranked according to several criteria, including sales volume, performance against budget, annual sales increases, and customer satisfaction surveys. Employees of the winning store receive an all-expenses paid week at Disney World while top brass from Kinko's corporate office filled in for them.[14]

Nelson argues that many formal recognition programs have worn out their welcome because they look backward at what has been done instead of directing employees' attention forward to goals and the rewards they might find motivating to achieve those goals. In particular, he criticizes the incentive industry that continues to promote trinkets such as pen sets, coffee mugs, t-shirts, watches, clocks, paperweights, certificates of appreciation, and plaques, all of which today's employees value far less than being treated well on a daily basis.[15]

The bottom line is that informal no-cost recognition by an employee's direct manager, usually in the form of simple thanks in response to a job well done, does more to engage and sustain employee commitment than all other available options.

Engagement Practice # 42: Make New Hires Feel Welcome and Important

If we want employees to feel valued and important, the best time to start is during their first few days on the job. Increasingly, employers of choice are going to great lengths to welcome new hires in special ways:

- Sending gift baskets to their homes before they start
- Putting pastries or candy near their desks to encourage other employees to stop by, introduce themselves, and welcome them aboard
- Assigning "buddies," peer coaches, or mentors to coach new hires through the first few weeks on the job or help them get settled into a new community
- Training managers to manage the new hire's first few days so they know they are valued, that their contribution is vital to the company's success, and exactly what is expected of them

- Spreading out formal group orientation sessions so they occur over a period of weeks instead of bombarding new hires with more information than they can take in during their first few days on the job

Many organizations make a special effort to make sure new hires more fully understand the significance of the work they do. John Sullivan describes the process of helping new employees appreciate the true value of their contributions as "walking them downstream."[16] There are several ways to do this:

- Begin by first "walking them upstream" to see where the company's raw materials come from or how the customer makes first contact with the company. Then walk them downstream so they can see how the product or service has an impact on the customer.
- Let them talk directly with customers to find out how the product or service has an impact on them.
- Let them sit in on a sales call with a satisfied customer.
- Give the new hire testimonials and articles about the firm and its products or services.

Orientation Program Slows New Hire Attrition

The Mid-America Program Service Center of the Social Security Administration in Kansas City, Missouri had a new hire attrition rate of 9 percent in 2001 and expectations of losing 1,400 employees to retirement. The center conducted a survey of new hires and learned that new hires felt disconnected and did not understood how they fit into the big picture. Within three months a re-designed new hire orientation—NEON (New Hire Orientation and Networking)—was installed, focused on training managers how to interview and orient new hires. The program features interactive group presentations and one-on-one sessions with managers designed to familiarize new hires with the SSA's mission, its history, and career development opportunity. By the summer of 2003, new hire attrition had been reduced to 2.8 percent, and the center had saved over $400,000 in turnover costs.[17]

Engagement Practice # 43:
Ask for Employee Input, Then Listen, and Respond

A sure way to instantly know whether we are being taken seriously is to observe how well others listen to us. We all have a basic need to know that others care what we think. When people ask our opinion, we feel respected. Yet, only 36 percent of workers say that their companies actively seek their opinions.[18]

One problem here is that many managers are not very good listeners and they know it. Many managers became managers because they see themselves as leaders who already know the best way to proceed, and they don't want to be slowed down by having to check in with their employees to get their input. "The workplace is not a democracy," I have heard them say, and they are right about that.

The U.S. Navy is not known as a democracy either, and yet one of the best examples of a leader listening and acting on the input of the average worker comes from the destroyer *USS Benfold*, as told in the pages of the *Harvard Business Review*. When Captain D. Michael Abrashoff took command of this ship in 1997, its 310 crew members were mostly demoralized and the typical attrition rate in the Navy was 40 percent over the first four years. Captain Abrashoff set out to do something different to engage and retain his sailors.

What he did was to reject the Navy's traditional command-and-control approach to leadership. Captain Abrashoff had served under then-secretary of defense William J. Perry from 1994 to 1997 and had been impressed with the way Perry listened so intently to everyone he encountered. Abrashoff knew he wasn't a good listener, but vowed that he would "treat every encounter with every person on the ship as the most important thing in my world at the moment."[19] It wasn't easy to begin with, but Abrashoff began asking crew members what they would like to change on the *Benfold*. The sailors responded with creative, cost-saving, workable ideas that Captain Abrashoff implemented almost immediately in many cases. He set up "get-to-know-you" sessions and met in his cabin with every sailor on the ship, asking a series of questions designed to get to know them personally and soliciting their ideas for improving things aboard the ship. He started placing more trust and responsibility in their hands and they responded by doing their best so as not to let him down.

A result of Captain Abrashoff's steady efforts, the *USS Benfold* "set all time records for performance and retention, and the waiting list of officers and enlisted personnel who want to transfer to the *Benfold* is pages long. It's a long wait because very few aboard the *Benfold* want to leave."[20]

Employees are hungry to be heard, and you can't afford not to seek, listen to, and implement their ideas. Here are several ways that organizations of all kinds are giving their workers more of a voice and showing them the respect of listening well:

- Hold 50/50 meetings with employees, where management speaks for 50 percent of the time on their goals, strategies, and ideas, then gives the floor to employees to respond for the rest of the meeting time. These kinds of meetings can be conducted over breakfast, lunch, or during regular staff meetings.
- Conduct regular employee surveys and be prepared to act on key issues surfaced. This boosts morale by letting employees know you take their ideas seriously and respect their input. Conversely, nothing kills morale quicker than asking for input, then ignoring it. Surveys don't all have to be expensive undertakings. Some companies build morale by sending out e-mail surveys every month and acting promptly to correct seemingly small, but aggravating, problems.
- Conduct in-depth exit interviews that get to the root cause of why employees are disengaging and leaving, then take action to address the "push factors" that are driving good people out of the organization.
- Get out of the office and practice Tom Peters' MBWA principle—"Management by Walking Around." The key is you have to be sincere and prepared to act on their suggestions when you stop by and ask employees for their ideas on how to make things better.

A Manager Who's Paid to Listen

New York City's Tavern on the Green restaurant is known for maintaining a strong core of skilled workers in an industry known for high turnover. "We average 425 employees," says Tavern training director, Laura Vaughn. "About 150 have been here more than ten years, and some more than twenty." Although the restaurant's managing director's door is open to every staffer, he hired Vaughn partly to let employees know he cared about their concerns. "When I was hired, I said what we needed more than anything was a paid listener. . . . When we're busy, we are *so* busy. Even a manager who wants to listen has three other things going on and people feel brushed off."[21]

- Let employees give anonymous written feedback to their managers on how they can improve their people management skills, not as part of a formal performance review, but for developmental purposes.
- Publish the suggestions left in suggestion boxes and act on the good ones.

 ## Engagement Practice # 44: Keep Employees in the Loop

Few things say "you're not important" more loudly than withholding information that employees want and need to know. Keeping employees out of the loop creates disconnection, alienation, and disengagement. On the other hand, companies that feed their employees a steady diet of vital information about the company build ownership and commitment.

Most employers are familiar with the story of Springfield Remanufacturing Company's success with "open book management." After many frustrating years of working at a company where information was hoarded at the top, Jack Stack started Springfield Remanufacturing Company and founded it on a key practice— opening up the company's operations data and financial information and teaching his workers to understand it, thereby empowering them to make decisions based on it. Stack also gave each employee a financial stake in the game, which increased their sense of ownership in the business. The company's annual sales grew from $16 million to $83 million in just nine years, and Stack's book, *The Great Game of Business*, attracted such widespread interest that dozens of companies, such as Federal Express, Allstate Insurance, Exxon, The Body Shop, and Hostess Frito-Lay have adapted Stack's ideas to their own businesses.

One reason more companies have not adopted Stack's approach is their fear that giving information to employees would mean giving up their power. The thinking goes that "they wouldn't know what to do with it," or "they don't need to know," or "they will be overwhelmed with all this information," but too often underlying such statements is the assumption that employees are powerless children, too immature to be trusted with important information. The executive who hoards information may feel more privileged, important, and powerful, but the effect on the workplace is a negative one.

In the absence of information, employees fill the void with rumor born of anxiety. As rumors spread, productivity goes down and distrust goes up. Just the opposite occurs when the company decides to share information, often because the information it shares also happens to be important in achieving the company's goals. Cisco Systems openly reports all the bugs in its products on a public Web page as soon as any problem is reported. Rather than diminishing customer confidence in their products, this reporting builds trust and allows programmers to quickly correct the problem. Cisco's CEO, John Chambers, one of the most admired executives in American business, gives a Web-cast management update every few weeks during which he responds directly to employee questions. Chambers wants his employees to learn about company news firsthand, not in the media.[22]

Here are some ways to keep employees in the loop:

- Openly discuss the company's strategic plan and what it means to each department and employee.
- Share articles that you read about the company, industry trends, and competitors.
- Give briefings about upcoming events that may impact employees' career options.
- Share information as soon as you possibly can to nip rumors in the bud.
- Share information face-to-face when possible.
- There will be times when information is confidential, proprietary, or otherwise sensitive, and you will not be able to share it. Those times will be the exception, however, not the rule.

One final reminder, the more valuable and productive the employees, the more they want to be kept in the loop.

Engagement Practice # 45: Give Employees the Right Tools and Resources

Many employees are drawn to organizations by anticipation of great relationships with their manager and colleagues. Yet, in one survey, 44 percent felt they were not given the tools and resources needed to succeed in their first days on the job.[23]

Whether it's something as simple as a hotel manager making sure the kitchen workers have better knives, or a high tech company having the latest hardware, it's obvious that people need the right tools to do the job. When they don't get those tools they need, it's not just that they become less productive. They also feel less important.

We may look to save money on hardware, software, furniture, and equipment, but if we are thinking of them as costs only, we are being shortsighted. The right tools at the right time are investments—not only in productivity, but in sending a message to our employees that they are worth it.

Hal Rosenbluth, whose company, Rosenbluth Travel, depends on having the right technologies in place, believes in "continually reinvesting in technology, both in terms of people and the tools they need to stretch their talents beyond traditional limits. By the way, let *them* choose the tools they need."[24] The law firm, Alston & Bird, selected in 2004 as one of *Fortune's* 100 best places in America to work, was also selected as the "most wired" law firm in America in a survey by *American Lawyer.* The firm makes sure that all associates have all the wireless devices they need for staying in touch while away from the office.[25] Among Generations X and Y in particular, being able to perform their jobs while maintaining some semblance of lifestyle flexibility, is a value of prime importance. Over and above the practical aspect, having the right connectivity devices also makes employees feel vital to the organization.

If you are not sure what tools and resources to provide employees, simply ask. Send out a monthly e-mail survey asking the question, "What do you need that would make you more effective in your job?" If you're not sure whether it's worth the expenditure, ask employees to present the business case for the purchase, showing how the new tool would pay off in the long run.

Many of the things employees need to be more effective are easy and inexpensive to supply, and when you respond quickly, it builds even more commitment.

Engagement Practice # 46:
Keep the Physical Environment Fit to Work In

This one is so basic, you wouldn't think it would need mentioning, but time and again, departing employees complain of cramped, noisy, hot, cold, messy, dirty, noxious, or unsafe conditions. Ask yourself, "how would I like to work where my employees work?" Go to their workstations and spend some time talking with them about what in their physical surroundings could be improved. As with tools and resources, you may be surprised by how easy some solutions are—a fan, a heater, an occasional cleaning may be all that's needed.

The environment you provide for your workers tells them how much you value them. When Las Vegas casino mogul Steve Wynn designed a new hotel, he decided to spend the same amount of money per square foot to build the employee cafeteria as he spent on the hotel coffee shop. Wynn also decorated the back corridors that employees use in the same bright and cheery colors he used to decorate the guest corridors. Again, the message he sent was "you are important, you are worth it . . . because if you are happy, you will take care of the customer."

What Employees Can Do to Be More Valued and Better Recognized

There may be good reason why some employees don't feel valued or recognized—perhaps they have not made themselves as valuable to the business as they think they have. Research has consistently shown that the vast majority of employees feel underpaid and believe they are in the top 25 percent of all performers, which, of course, cannot be the case. This means that many employees have an inflated view of their value or that they feel unduly entitled to receive what they have not earned.

Here then are some guidelines for employees for getting more recognition and pay:

- Ask your manager to define what results are required for excellence in your job.
- Ask yourself if you are willing to work hard and pay the price to achieve those results.
- Ask what criteria are used to determine bonuses and raises.
- Ask yourself if you are willing to put more of your pay at risk, to be paid bonuses based on achieving targeted results rather than getting annual pay raises.
- If so, make them part of your performance plan and commit to achieving them.
- Compete against yourself to achieve key results, not against your peers.
- Ask what new skills would make you more valuable to the organization.
- Tell your manager how you prefer to be recognized for your contributions.
- Ask to sit in on a sales call with a satisfied customer to better understand the value of your job.
- Present a cost-benefit analysis to your manager making the case for the purchase of tools and equipment you believe you need.

- If you feel you are being kept out of the loop, ask for more information.
- Don't wait for your manager to ask for your input—give him or her the benefit of your views and ideas.

Employer-of-Choice Engagement Practices Review and Checklist

Review the engagement practices presented in this chapter and check the ones you believe your organization needs to implement or improve.

To Make Employees Feel Valued and Recognized:

36. ☐ Offer competitive base pay linked to value creation.
37. ☐ Reward results with variable pay aligned with business goals.
38. ☐ Reward employees at a high enough level to motivate higher performance.
39. ☐ Use cash payouts for on-the-spot recognition.
40. ☐ Involve employees and encourage two-way communication when designing new pay systems.
41. ☐ Monitor the pay system to ensure fairness, efficiency, consistency, and accuracy.
42. ☐ Create a culture of informal recognition founded on appreciation.
43. ☐ Make new hires feel welcome and important.
44. ☐ Ask for employee input, then listen, and respond.
45. ☐ Keep employees in the loop.
46. ☐ Give them the right tools and resources.
47. ☐ Keep the physical environment fit to work in.

Notes

1. Patricia K. Zingheim and Jay R. Schuster, *Pay People Right! Breakthrough Reward Strategies to Create Great Companies* (San Francisco: Jossey-Bass, 2000).
2. Ibid.
3. Ruth Baum Bigus, "Ownership Option Helps Curb Employee Turnover," *Kansas City Star*, September 18, 2001.
4. Hara Marks, "The Future of Total Rewards," HR e-source, May 14, 2001.
5. Steven Kerr, "Risky Business: The New Pay Game," *Fortune*, July 22, 1996.

6. Zingheim and Schuster, op. cit.

7. Compensation study, Mercer Consulting, 2002.

8. Jeremy Handel, "Can Communication Boost Employees' Pay Satisfaction?," *HR Focus*, July 2002.

9. Todd M. Manas and Michael Dennis Graham, *Creating a Total Rewards Strategy: A Toolkit for Designing Business-Based Plans* (New York: AMACOM, 2002).

10. Bob Nelson, "The Top 10 Ironies of Employee Motivation Programs," *Employee Benefit News*," June 19, 2001.

11. Ibid.

12. Bob Nelson, "Why Formal Recognition Programs Don't Work," *Update on Employee Recognition*, April 2004.

13. "Yum Stresses Trust, Recognition," *Work and Family Newsbrief*, December 2003.

14. Diane Stafford, "A Reward Truly Worth Copying," *Kansas City Star,* March 25, 2004.

15. Nelson, "Why Formal Recognition Programs Don't Work."

16. John Sullivan, "Walk Them Downstream: Showing Your Employees They Make a Difference," *Electronic Recruiting Exchange*, April 1, 2002.

17. Ruth Baum Bigus, "Orientation Program Stems New-Hire Attrition," *Kansas City Star*, July 22, 2003.

18. Catherine D. Fyock, "Retention Tactics That Work," citing Labor Day survey by Watson-Wyatt, White Paper, Society for Human Resource Management, March 1998.

19. D. Michael Abrashoff, "Retention through Redemption," *Harvard Business Review*, February 2001.

20. Ibid.

21. Deborah S. Roberts, "Two Companies Battle High Turnover—and Win!" *Employee Recruitment and Retention*, undated sample issue, 2000.

22. Frederick F. Reichheld, *Loyalty Rules: How Today's Leaders Build Lasting Relationships* (Boston: Harvard Business School Press, 2001).

23. Barbara Morris, "The Cost of a Bad Start," *Marketing* Magazine, October 27, 2003.

24. Hal F. Rosenbluth and Diane McFerrin Peters, *The Customer Comes Second: And Other Secrets of Exceptional Service* (New York: William Morrow, 1992).

25. Lynne C. Lancaster and David Stillman, *When Generations Collide* (New York: Harper Business, 2002).

CHAPTER NINE

Reason #6: Stress from Overwork and Work-Life Imbalance

> What my business
> experience has taught me
> is that the key to
> competitiveness is
> innovation, and the key to
> innovation is people.
> Taking care of people,
> therefore, is an essential
> way of taking care of
> business.

—Randall Tobias, chairman of Eli Lilly

> The thing to remember is
> that, for great workplaces,
> there *is* no shortage of
> talent. Companies that are
> short on talent probably
> deserve to be!

—Jeffrey Pfeffer

The fact of stress in corporate America is no surprise, but it is sobering to consider all the things there are to be stressed about—overwork, personality conflicts, forced overtime, disorganized supervisors, gossip, harassment, prejudice, poor teamwork, manager abuse and insensitivity, other employees who don't pull their weight, inflexible work hours, illness in the family, child care, elder care, long commutes, sacrificing family dinners to stay late, and the list goes on. The comments of Saratoga survey respondents are poignant reminders of the frustration and conflict that take their daily toll:

Doing More with Less

- "ABC Company does not recognize the employees that work hard on a daily basis and take on extra responsibilities to compensate for the lack of manpower."
- "XYZ Company does not employ enough staff. This results in high stress and high turnover of employees."
- They were not proactive in taking care of and keeping good employees. I have watched too many good employees leave ABC Company because they are not appreciated. The motto 'Do more with less' has been taken to the extreme.
- "XYZ Company will go long periods of time without filling empty positions. This puts massive amounts of stress on the employees and product development is stifled."

Abuse/Harassment/Insensitivity

- "Does not deal well at all with sexual harassment and freaky, nasty remarks made by other employees."
- "Management was the worst I have ever experienced in my fifteen-year nursing career. I had a death in my family, and the time was taken from my vacation time, that was incentive enough to start looking for another job."
  "We're not getting paid enough for the type of abuse we take from the customers."

Sacrificing Family/Personal Life

- "My number one complaint is that I do not get to spend enough time with my family. I have so much trouble being able to schedule time-off for certain events. All I would want is leave without pay. I will continue to give XYZ Company 110 percent, but I need more time."
- "ABC Company does not acknowledge the fact their there is life outside of work."

- "I feel that XYZ Company is a workplace for single people. It does not accommodate employees with families in regards to scheduling."
- "I think they need to work on scheduling more weekends off."

Inflexibility of Work Hours

- "Make working hours more flexible for those going to night school."
- "Need to have flex-scheduling—something like any eight hours between 6 A.M. and 10 P.M. you pick."
- "There were not enough chairs for the RNs to sit and do their charts. Despite working on your feet for up to fourteen hours without sitting, we did not get breaks and were told that we didn't get paid for them. I was required to be in the building at lunch but without pay unless I took an urgent phone call. If I needed to leave at lunch, I needed to find a medical doctor willing to take calls and inform the receptionist. If you spoke what was on your mind you were considered a troublemaker."
- "Family comes second to ABC Company—mandatory overtime on Saturdays!"

Impact on Customers

- "XYZ Company expects employees to increase production while failing to realize that increased production may lead to unsatisfied customers."
- "We are so short-staffed that we talk to one customer right after the other with no time in between. Customer service is decimated due to this fact."
- "Our manager short-staffed us to the point that it jeopardized patients. She only cares about saving money in her budget."

No Fun

- "We used to have Christmas parties and gifts. We never see anything like this anymore. Work should be a little fun, not so stressful."

Inadequate Benefits

- "One personal day per year?! Other employers give as many as three."

- "Employees should not have to wait five years to get more than two weeks vacation."
- "I was very frustrated by ABC Company's health benefits. I was diagnosed with breast cancer—and I feel I have had to fight to get the bills paid."
- "When people are sick they should not be penalized for it by receiving an occurrence. In fact, when there is a death in the family you should not be given an occurrence. We are given a certain amount of paid sick days and those should not be held against us in our raises. They are!!!!!!"
- "Maternity leave is poor. An employee has to be with the company for a year before receiving any maternity leave."

How Big a Problem Is Stress?

These kinds of comments indicate that stress is indeed a problem in the workforce, but how big a problem is it really? Here are some findings from several surveys:

- 55 percent of workers said they sometimes felt overwhelmed by how much work they had to do.[1]
- 40 percent of workers report that their jobs are "very or extremely stressful."[2]
- 26 percent of workers say they are "often or very often burned out or stressed by their work."[3]
- 29 percent report feeling "quite a bit or extremely stressed at work."[4]
- 25 percent of employees view their jobs as the number one stressor in their lives.[5]
- Health care expenditures are nearly 50 percent greater for workers who report high levels of stress.[6]
- 25 percent of employees do not take all of the vacation to which they are entitled because of the demands of their jobs.[7]
- Lost work time due to depression costs companies $31 billion to $41 billion per year in lost productivity.[8]
- 49 percent of employees who experience high levels of feeling overworked say they are likely to seek employment elsewhere within the

coming year, compared to only 30 percent who report low levels of feeling overworked.[9]

- 79 percent of employers think they take care of their employees, yet only 44 percent of employees agree.[10]
- 70 percent of employees don't think there is a healthy balance between their work and their personal lives.[11]
- 61 percent of workers would give up some pay for more family time.[12]

Causes of Increased Stress

Judging by these survey results, it seems clear that one quarter to one half of all workers are feeling some level of dysfunction due to stress, which is undoubtedly having a negative impact on their productivity and the probability they will stay with their employers.

Several factors are contributing to current levels of employee stress: companies squeezing as much productivity as they possibly can from all workers in a hyper-competitive global economy; the impact of downsizing the workforce while not proportionately downsizing the work to be done; continuing worries about job security as employees read about downsizings, mergers, and acquisitions; heightened levels of free-floating anxiety that have persisted since the 9/11 terrorist attacks; and the continuing increase in two-career couples, working single parents, and workers with elder care responsibilities.

Signs That Your Workers May Be Stressed-Out or Overworked

There are a wide range of symptoms, when it comes to watching for overstressed and overworked employees. Here are some that show up sooner or later:

- Consistently work late
- Work through lunch
- Work through sickness
- Seem more fatigued than usual
- Take work home

- Rush to meet deadlines
- Express frustration
- Don't take vacations
- Appear increasingly cynical, forgetful, or irritable
- Try too hard to please a new boss
- Have relocated from a distant location
- Have recently experienced a disappointment or failure at work
- Have experienced a significant family transition or trauma

While most researchers agree that some workers are more easily stressed than others, most agree that negative working conditions spread the stress among all workers. Many of these conditions have been touched on in previous chapters—mismatch of the individual to the job, lack of worker participation in decisions, feeling left out of the loop, frustrations about the lack of career advancement, and unpleasant physical environments, to name a few. Other factors include: infrequent rest breaks due to constant work demands, a constant hectic pace, stultifying routine, seemingly senseless tasks, and conflict and resentment among coworkers

The ultimate question is whether the issue of worker stress is on the radar screens of managers and executives. Certainly it is from a personal perspective—most managers and professionals report feeling overworked, and work significantly longer hours than other employees.[13] But do managers care enough to actually make plans to reduce worker stress as a means of increasing productivity, engagement, and retention? As we shall see, there are many managers who do, and whose success stories inspire others to act in new ways.

Healthy vs. Toxic Cultures

An organization's culture is a fact of life that must be faced, and many organizations need to face the fact that their cultures are toxic. Toxic cultures are simply unhealthy environments, often characterized by the following:

- Forcing workers into choosing between having a life and having a career

- Seeing workers as costs, rather than assets in which to invest
- Viewing workers merely as resources, not as people
- Treating employees as if they are lucky just to have a job
- Attempting to control employees rather than empower or form partnerships with them
- Hoarding information at top levels of management as means of maintaining power and control
- Leaders so self-involved or isolated that they are out of touch with employee attitudes and feelings
- Infighting and conflict between departments
- Behaving in ways that are inconsistent with their professed values, or rewarding and tolerating such behavior
- Blaming others for one's own mistakes or seeking credit for others' accomplishments and ideas
- Lying, covering up the truth, or otherwise behaving unethically
- Constantly changing direction, frequently driven by management fads, but not committed to a consistent long-range strategy
- Believing that employees cannot be trusted

Any list would be incomplete, as there are any numbers of ways a toxic organization might manifest its toxicity. As we know, an organization

---

What's Your Organizational Civility Score?

Envisionworks, a Geneva, Illinois, management consulting firm, has created what it calls an Organizational Civility Index that surveys employees on how they treat each other. Questions on the index ask whether employees are reprimanded when they "are rude and disrespectful to other employees," and whether coworkers "shout at each other," or "block each others' success" or "compliment each others' work."

Founder and president Kevin Schmidt says that most of the companies that score poorly are headed by executives who put harsh demands on employees and belittle rather than praise staff. Schmidt says he has never met a monster boss, but says he has told executives, "It must be awfully hard to be you because people hate you." When hit with this feedback, some break down.[14]

might have a generally healthy culture, but have managers who create toxic subcultures in their departments. Conversely, a manager might have built a healthy culture in a generally toxic organization, although this would be less likely and more difficult to achieve.

The growing cost of health care is causing many companies to actually start assessing their "organizational health." A senior executive with Medstat Group, a health-care information management company based in Ann Arbor, Michigan, told the *Wall Street Journal* that corporations are starting to realize their "psychological health" can be a major driver of costs. Their "health and productivity management study" of forty-three large corporations found that in 1999, during the height of the talent wars, "turnover-related costs rose to 37 percent of the health and productivity dollar."[15]

More Than Just the Right Thing to Do

Increasingly, companies are realizing that taking care of their employees as people is not just the right thing to do, it's also good for business. In the past decade, an overwhelming body of evidence has accumulated showing a strong connection between treating people right and business profitability.

James Heskett, Earl Sasser, and Leonard Schlesinger, in their book, *The Service-Profit Chain*, persuasively diagrammed the links in the chain that leads from a starting point of internal quality of work life, to employee productivity, loyalty, and satisfaction, to quality customer service, to customer satisfaction, to customer loyalty, ultimately resulting in greater revenues and profits (see Figure 9-1).[16]

In his book, *Treat People Right! How Organizations and Individuals Can Propel Each Other into a Virtuous Spiral of Success*, Edward Lawler presents evidence strongly supporting the logic of these links, but also makes an astute observation: "At the core of many people's concern about the wisdom of treating people right is the belief that there is an irreconcilable conflict between what is good for the business and what is good for employees."[17]

Some business leaders have been reluctant to embrace the idea that benevolent people-management practices can be a driver of profits. They know that treating people well is a good thing, but also believe that nice guys finish last, that the toughest and meanest survive, and that if employees

Figure 9-1.

Links in the service–profit chain.

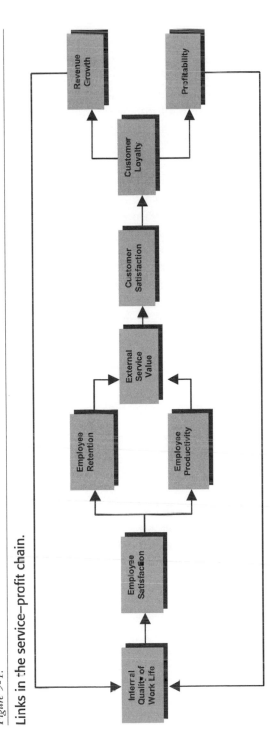

don't like it, they can leave. I once worked at a company where the vice president of manufacturing, when asked if he was stressed, responded, "I don't *get* stress, I *give* stress." For such individuals, caring for people as a business strategy seems weak and soft-headed.

There is a fast-growing information systems company that once made *Fortune's* top 100 employers list, but fell off it largely because of its demand that employees work 60 to 80 hours per week. There seems to be no shortage of young professionals who are attracted to working those hours in exchange for rapid advancement and good pay. A woman who worked there told me that, when she told this company she wanted to work part-time, the employment representative responded, "a part-time job in this company is 40 hours per week." In spite of this, young, talented professionals continue to be drawn to this company, attracted by the fast-track experience. They generally stay a few years and move on. The company has a good product and is profitable. But the question remains—are they building the kind of employment brand that will serve and sustain their business interests long-term?

The Best Places in America to Work

Here are profiles of a few companies that have taken a different path.

- *The Number One Place in America to Work: Smucker's!*

The J.M. Smucker Company, Orrville, Ohio, made it to number one on *Fortune's* list of the 100 best places in America to work by continuing to do what they have done for years—live by a simple code of conduct: "Listen with your full attention, look for the good in others, have a sense of humor—but not at the expense of others, and say thank you for a job well done."[18] Lots of companies have similar values statements, but few adhere to them the way Smucker's does.

One employee said she had been thanked more in her two years at Smucker's than she was at the three other mega-food companies where she had worked the previous nine years. Managers routinely hand out gift certificates and buy lunch for their teams. Employees can recite the company's strategy and corporate values. Workers say there is a commitment to each other founded on the Golden Rule. The result is a positive work environment where people feel respected, challenged, and valued.

Ernestine Wilson, who works in the packing line, told a reporter that when her husband had cancer, the company let her come to work when she could and park close to the shop so she could leave quickly if she had to. "They have been so good to me," said the 32-year veteran, "I can't say enough." Another employee said, "I don't worry about somebody asking me to lie. That's a good feeling. If it means working twelve hours a day, that's OK."[19]

The company has no stock options, no onsite day care center, no concierge services, or other such flashy perks, but it does offer flex-time and provides an average of seventy hours of training per employee per year. Employees consistently say it's the intangibles that make Smucker's special. The company also puts a lot of energy into hiring the kind of people who fit the culture and will work well with long-term employees.

Is there a bottom-line pay-off? The company's stock has had a total return of 100 percent over the past five years, and it has only a 3 percent voluntary turnover rate.

- *The Second-Best Place in America to Work: Alston & Bird*

This Atlanta law firm grants mothers three months of maternity leave, and the same to fathers if they are the primary caregivers. The firm also charges a reasonable $500 per month for its onsite child-care center, and it averages fifty hours of training per employee per year.

Average yearly job growth—8 percent, with turnover of only 7 percent.

- *The Third-Best Place in America to Work: The Container Store*

This retailer has been among the top employers for several years now. It offers weekly yoga sessions free to employees, with 25 percent of the company's workforce attending. The company's official mascot is Gumby—a fitting symbol for the company's value of bending over backwards to please their customers *and* their coworkers. The Container Store averages 162 hours of training per year per employee and is known for its exuberant staff morale. Other perks include: monthly chair massages, stretching classes, and an online exercise and nutrition diary that is personalized for every worker.[20]

What They Have in Common

What all these employers have in common is a philosophy of "give first, get second." In other words, these preeminent employers believe that if they take the first step in giving a desirable employment experience to its employees, those employees will respond by giving back. Thus begins a virtuous cycle of reciprocal commitment. Employers of choice understand that they are competing with other employers—both large and small—for talent, and realize the importance of "branding" themselves as preferred places to work. It's no longer about passively recruiting by selling during job interviews—it's about proactively marketing one's organization as a great place to work.

Contrast this approach with that of employers who start employees on probation, wait to see if the employee is worthy of respect, judge new hires guilty until proven otherwise, and wait for employees to prove their commitment to the organization before demonstrating the organization's commitment to them. This is certainly the traditional. approach, but in a war-for-talent economy, it can no longer keep your company competitive. The new employers of choice resolve to give before getting back, and usually go to extra lengths to select the right people. This makes it so much easier to trust the employees they hire to return their commitment in kind.

Interested in Becoming One of the Best Places to Work?

If your company is interested in applying to be selected as one of *Fortune's* 100 best places in America to work, you can start by sending an e-mail stating your case to: *100best@greatplacetowork.com*

It's Not Just the "Big Boys" You're Competing With

When Tom Creal started his own company—First Biomedical—he had already given seventeen years of his life to a large company before he was let go in the fifth of five rounds of layoffs. The big-company environment had transmogrified into one where employees were no longer loyal to the company. It was a culture Creal didn't like. So he decided that someday he would operate his own company in a totally different way.

He didn't want to become a father figure, but Creal did want to develop company loyalty among his workers. He decided he would provide:

- Full medical, dental, life and health insurance for the whole family
- 15 vacation/sick days, with carry-over of unused days
- IRAs with 3 percent match and first-day vesting
- A seven-hour workday

- Free cell phones for employees on call
- Free snacks and Costco cards paid for by the company
- A new onsite gym
- A new incentive-driven wellness program
- Open sharing of the company's financial situation
- 2 percent of employees' annual salaries paid any month the company has a record gross-profit
- A year-end bonus of 4 to 5 percent of annual salary
- No job descriptions, with the freedom to move on to different positions

Since opening its doors in 1998, this employer of fifteen people has lost only four, a record that Creal believes has significantly increased productivity and revenues. "We started at zero and we'll be a $3.5 million company this year."[21]

Whether benefits-driven, culture-driven, or great-manager-driven, employers of choice choose the right employment branding strategy for their business objectives. The branding goal they choose is to be known for having cultures that are both high-performance and high-caring (see Figure 9-2). High-caring cultures never forget that employees are people, with basic human needs and widely varying family situations. They know

Figure 9-2.

Your culture equals your employment brand.

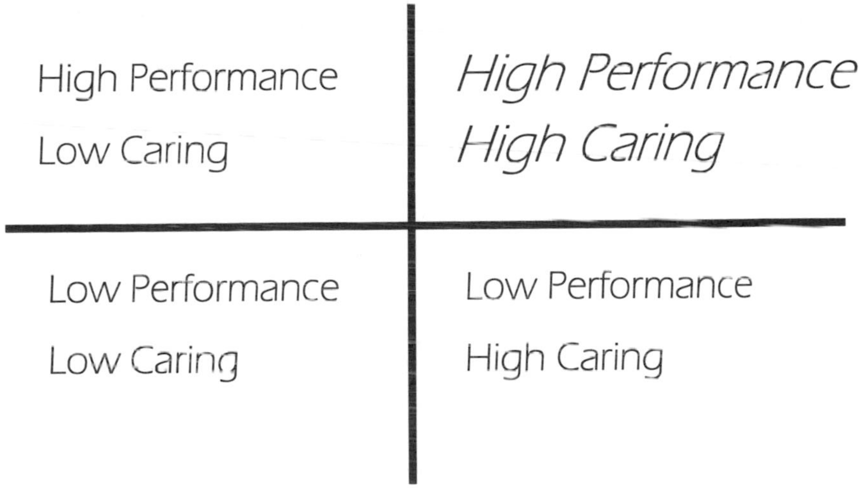

High Performance Low Caring	*High Performance* *High Caring*
Low Performance Low Caring	Low Performance High Caring

that their employees want to have time to live rich lives beyond the bounds of work.

Employers of choice also seem to have the following engagement practices in common:

Engagement Practice # 47:
Initiate a Culture of "Giving-Before-Getting"

Some companies initiate generous work-life and health benefits for their employees out of genuine, warm-hearted caring, and others do so more as a means to an end—capturing and keeping talent. My research and experience tell me that employers with the former motivation generally build more caring everyday cultures and arouse more commitment from their employees. That does not mean that taking a more calculating approach based on generous benefits cannot succeed. I believe it can, especially if the decision to provide those new benefits signals the beginning of a cultural transformation based on a more caring and respectful treatment of the workforce.

In researching the best practices of employers of choice in the late 1990s for my first book, I was struck by how often the companies identified as employers of choice were led by CEOs with a sincere passion for taking care of their employees as people: Jim Goodnight at SAS Institute, Quint Studer at Baptist Hospital in Pensacola, Herb Kelleher at Southwest Airlines, Hal Rosenbluth at Rosenbluth Travel, and Wilton Connor at Wilton-Connor Packaging Company—to name a few out of a growing number.

What I noticed in all these leaders was their "if-we-build-it-they-will-come" faith in making the first move. What they all seemed to know intuitively was that if they demonstrated an initial willingness to trust their employees by giving valued services, then the employees would willingly reciprocate. As astute business executives, they also certainly realized that well-treated employees take better care of customers, but that realization did not seem to be the driver of their generosity.

A Big Menu of Benefits and Services

The question most employers ask is, what benefits and services can we afford to give that will allow us to attract and keep the talent we need while also helping to reduce their stress at work and lead fuller and healthier lives

Owners Work Hard to Help Employees Battle Burnout

Working for a company like D3 Inc., a small, Kansas City-based strategic marketing communications firm, sometimes requires long hours, including nights and weekends to finish projects for big clients like Sprint and Hallmark. For owners David Svet and Mark Schraad, employee burnout is a very real concern. Both owners had previously worked for other marketing firms where creative staffers would get burned out and leave. They were determined not to create the same kind of environment in their business.

"A steady diet of this schedule dulls your senses and the ability to think outside the box," said Svet. To prevent such burnout, the owners established regular working hours of 8:30 A.M. to 5 P.M., and they try hard to enforce that schedule, clearing the office in the evenings if necessary. When client projects call for longer hours, employees are compensated with time off to refresh themselves. Svet and Schaad also take D3 workers on regular outings to parks and museums to stimulate their creativity and break the routine of the workweek. The owners also pay for training conferences around the country and give spot bonuses and twice-yearly salary reviews.

Since implementing these new ideas, D3 reports very low turnover and a noticeable improvement in morale. Employees appreciate having the extra hours for their lives away from work. The owners have actually turned away business because they knew it would impose an unhealthy workload on staff.[22]

outside of work? With the cost of benefits hovering at around 45 percent of total compensation, most companies look carefully at the cost/benefit equation and carefully consider the needs of their current and desired labor pool according to its demographic make-up.

Here is a breakdown of some of the most popular employee benefits as reported by the Society for Human Resource Management (SHRM) in its latest annual benefits survey, showing the percentage of surveyed companies offering each benefit in 2003 compared with 1999:[23]

Family-Friendly Benefits:	2003	1999
Dependent-care flexible spending account	71 percent	65 percent
Flextime	55 percent	54 percent

Family-Friendly Benefits:	2003	1999
Compressed workweek	31 percent	26 percent
Job-sharing	22 percent	22 percent
Elder care referral service	20 percent	14 percent
Child care referral service	18 percent	15 percent
Adoption assistance	16 percent	14 percent

Health Benefits:		
Prescription drug program coverage	98 percent	93 percent
Life insurance	98 percent	97 percent
Dental insurance	96 percent	93 percent
Preferred Provider Organization	87 percent	81 percent
Mental health insurance	76 percent	78 percent
Vision insurance	71 percent	64 percent
Flexible medical spending account	70 percent	65 percent
Employee assistance program	67 percent	64 percent
Wellness programs	57 percent	57 percent
Health Maintenance Organization	54 percent	65 percent
Health care premium flexible spending account	52 percent	50 percent
Long-term care insurance	47 percent	36 percent
Well-baby program	42 percent	47 percent
Health screening programs	40 percent	49 percent
Smoking cessation program	32 percent	32 percent
Fitness center subsidy or reimbursement	31 percent	23 percent
Accelerated death benefits (for terminal illnesses)	33 percent	23 percent
Retiree health care benefits	30 percent	42 percent
Prenatal program	27 percent	35 percent
Weight loss program	24 percent	23 percent
Onsite fitness center	22 percent	20 percent
Stress reduction program	21 percent	21 percent

Personal Service Benefits:		
Seminars, courses, conferences	93 percent	94 percent
Professional memberships	85 percent	85 percent
Casual dress one day per week	58 percent	56 percent

Family-Friendly Benefits:	*2003*	*1999*
Casual dress every day	44 percent	44 percent
Food services/subsidized cafeteria	26 percent	38 percent
Legal assistance services	25 percent	17 percent
Dry-cleaning services	13 percent	12 percent
Massage therapy services	11 percent	8 percent
Self-defense training	6 percent	7 percent
Concierge services	2 percent	4 percent
Leave Benefits:		
Paid holidays	98 percent	NA
Paid bereavement leave	91 percent	93 percent
Paid jury duty	90 percent	95 percent
Long-term disability	88 percent	89 percent
Paid vacation	87 percent	95 percent
Short-term disability	81 percent	78 percent
Paid sick leave	76 percent	87 percent
Paid time-off plan (sick, vacation, personal)	68 percent	35 percent
Paid personal days	40 percent	57 percent
Unpaid sabbatical program	19 percent	19 percent
Paid maternity leave not covered by short-term disability	14 percent	51 percent
Paid paternity leave	12 percent	12 percent
Paid sabbatical program	6 percent	6 percent
Financial Benefits:		
Full flexible benefits plan (formerly cafeteria plan)	23 percent	24 percent
Parking subsidy	12 percent	13 percent
Onsite check cashing	12 percent	14 percent
Transit subsidy	12 percent	10 percent
Carpooling subsidy	4 percent	5 percent
Business Travel:		
Employee keeps frequent flyer miles	74 percent	90 percent
Paid long distance calls to home while on travel	71 percent	77 percent
Compensatory time given for travel time	25 percent	23 percent

Family-Friendly Benefits:	*2003*	*1999*
Paid dry cleaning while on travel	24 percent	30 percent
Paid health club fees while on travel	5 percent	9 percent
Housing and Relocation Benefits		
Temporary relocation benefits	44 percent	45 percent
Spouse relocation assistance	21 percent	21 percent
Cost-of-living differential	21 percent	20 percent
Rental assistance	15 percent	9 percent
Mortgage assistance	12 percent	9 percent

Much of the decrease in the percentages was due to belt-tightening as a result of the slumping economy during the intervening years, and the fact that 1999 was the peak of the talent-war years. If the war for talent returns again, as many predict, the percentages are likely to go up in most benefit categories.

It is worth noting that many new benefits were reported in 2003 that were not even surveyed by SHRM in 1999, such as: infertility treatment coverage (41 percent), telecommuting on part-time basis (34 percent), un-paid release time for volunteering (24 percent), domestic partner benefits (23 percent), spot bonuses (22 percent), travel planning services (20 per-cent), scholarships for members of employees' families (19 percent), paid release time for volunteering (17 percent), telecommuting on a full-time basis (17 percent), grief recovery program (14 percent), time bank of vaca-tion leave that can be donated to other employees (13 percent), free or discounted Internet service (12 percent), nutritional therapy (11 percent), onsite medical care (11 percent), loan to employee for purchase of personal computer (8 percent), free computer for personal use (5 percent), already prepared take-home meals (2 percent), and "boomerang" bonus to rehired employees (2 percent).

For a copy of SHRM's latest yearly benefit survey, which also in-cludes comparison data based on company size, industry, and geo-graphic areas, visit their Web site: *www.shrm.org.*

Over the past several years, dozens of companies have conducted inter-nal cost-benefit studies, which tend to link work-life programs to improved employee satisfaction, productivity, and attendance. Washington-based Fannie Mae, with 4,000 employees, conducted a study of its elder care services to evaluate the cost-benefit of having hired a full-time clinical social worker. In the first two years on the job, the elder-care director saw 10 percent of employees, which equates to about $3.5 million per year in avoided lost productivity due to elder-care responsibilities.[24]

First Tennessee National Corporation of Memphis, which has been honored for its pioneering work-life programs, found that since introducing flexible hours, it reduced its response time to customer requests at its operations centers to four days from ten days. The cost savings were neutral, but customer satisfaction was increased, and employee retention rates were twice that of offices where managers were less supportive of flextime. The biggest finding was that customer retention rates were 7 percent higher in the offices with flex-time.[25]

New York-based financial services company, Deloitte & Touche, estimates that the flexible work arrangements it provides to its 30,000 U.S. employees helped the firm avoid $41.5 million in turnover-related costs in 2003 alone.[26]

Even during a long-term economic slump, most companies were willing to risk eliminating the very programs they have positioned as marquee items in their campaigns to brand themselves as good places to work. Many companies—such as Xerox, Charles Schwab, PriceWaterhouseCoopers, Lucent Technologies, and Sara Lee—kept their work-life programs intact during major layoffs.[27] Many other companies certainly have realized that maintaining benefits and services is even more important when they are asking their employees to work harder because of cutbacks.

Reducing stress and overwork is not all about providing formal benefits and services; it's also about creating an informal culture where executives and managers are thinking about what they can do for their employees, at least as much as they are about what those employees can do for the company's customers.

Engagement Practice # 48:
Tailor the "Culture of Giving" to the Needs of Key Talent

Selecting the kinds of benefits and work-life services to offer workers is not simply a matter of looking at benefit surveys and matching what other employers provide. The fact is that you may not be able to afford the kinds of benefits that other companies in your community provide, and yet you must still compete with them for the available talent. This means you must figure out a way to compete for talent that is more cost-effective, so instead of offering onsite child care, you might choose to focus on recruiting, selecting, and training managers so they will manage people with respect and caring.

The other key to selecting the right benefits and services is matching them to the needs of your applicant pool and your current employees. Consider the case of Financial Associates, a 25-year-old insurance broker-age firm that employs twenty-five people. The owner, Charles Stumpf, is a veteran in the insurance business, and understands how competitive it can be. That is why he resolved to treat employees in such a way that they would not want to leave. "I made the conscious decision," he said, "to treat the people around me as family, not employees." So he put several practices into place that he thought would accomplish that end, including keeping records of employees' birthdays and hiring anniversaries and send-ing them cards on those special occasions, providing treats in the company kitchen, and putting signs on staff office doors in recognition of their ac-complishments.

Stumpf also thought about the fact that several of the women who work at Financial Associates have school-age children and some of them would prefer to work part-time. So, he tailored a nontraditional work schedule to accommodate their needs. Working mothers are allowed to arrive a little later in the morning so they can be home when their children leave for school. Others come in earlier in the morning so they can get home and be with their children at the end of the school day. Stumpf also worked it out so employees wanting part-time work could share the same jobs. He points out that one employee who works three days a week is one of his most productive workers.

When Stumpf made up his mind to move to a new location, he asked his employees what was most important to them in an office location. Their answer was, access to a major interstate highway and windows that opened. He asked them what features they wanted in a break room, and throughout the office, and he put them in place. The new office had a kitchen, and access to a patio with picnic table, grill, and a telephone jack.

Stumpf also recalled that, early in his own career working for a trucking company, he always worried about whether he would have enough money to take along on a trip, so he gives employees a cash bonus before they go on vacations. He also gives them extra days off around the holidays.

As you might imagine, employee turnover is not an issue at Financial Associates. Stumpf knows he has saved time and money by maintaining a stable workforce. "When you have to hire and retrain people, you know they won't know their jobs for a year, and that's time lost," he said. "By treating your people so they want to stay, you don't have to go through that cycle."[28]

Know Your Workforce!

The key is understanding the needs of the workforce. One of the best known examples of this is SAS Institute, Inc. in Cary, North Carolina, where CEO Jim Goodnight has built one of the most successful software companies in the world by giving the right things to the right people. Goodnight knew that every other major software company gave stock options to its employees, yet he chose not to offer them. He knew that most other software companies offered extraordinary salaries, yet he decided to offer salaries that were merely competitive. Goodnight also knew that the work pace and style in most software companies was crazy and frenetic, so he deliberately set out to create a sane and relaxed campus environment.

What Goodnight understood was that there were hundreds of talented software professionals who were more interested in a sane working environment and some semblance of balance between life and work. So that is what he created. At SAS, there is no limit on sick days. SAS operates the largest onsite child-care center in the state; a 3,600-square-foot company gym; tennis and volleyball courts; soccer and softball fields; massages; classes in yoga, African dance, and tai chi; ping pong and billiards; a ten-lane swimming pool; casual dress; art on every wall; piano music playing in the cafeteria where meals are free; a full-time elder-care coordinator; free immunizations; and work hours dictated by the fact that the company gates don't open until 7 A.M., and close promptly at 6 P.M. Yet, the company's environment is anything but lax—the work culture is built on accountability and results.

By its own calculations, the company saves $67 million per year in avoided turnover costs due to the fact that it maintains a 3 percent turnover rate in an industry that averages 20 percent turnover. This means the company can afford to keep adding new benefits, which it does on a regular basis. The strategy is working. SAS Institute, Inc. has carved out a niche—an employment brand—by creating a work environment unlike any others in its industry. In so doing, the company has become a magnet for talent, especially Generation Xers who value a saner, more balanced life and tell stories of turning down higher salaries to come to work for SAS.[29]

Whether your company surveys the workforce yearly, as SAS does, or simply asks employees face-to-face, the key is to ask. Smart companies design their benefits, perks, employee services, rewards, cultures, and management practices to attract and keep the specific desires of the talent segments they need to meet their business objectives. In other words, they align their human capital strategies with their business strategies. In scanning *Fortune's* profiles of the 100 best companies in America to work for, one is struck by the way so many top employers appear to have matched the right offerings to the right talent:

- Construction company *TD Industries* of Dallas offers upward mobility and respect to construction workers by calling them "partners" and paying 100 percent tuition reimbursement.
- *W.L. Gore*, inventor of Gore-Tex fabric and Elixir guitar strings, is a company built on innovation, so it offers the kind of work environment in which independent, creative people thrive. Workers get to choose their projects, and the process for selecting leaders is highly unstructured—most leaders are not appointed, but rather emerge based on the fact that other workers seem to follow their lead.
- *Starbucks* knows that many of the younger workers it needs to attract will only work part-time, but would not get health coverage for part-time jobs with other retailers. So, they offer health coverage to all workers who put in 20 hours a week and give stock options to those who stay for a year.
- Wireless tech supplier, *Qualcomm*, has employees in more than 100 countries, so they offer a flexible holiday policy that allows them to use ten company-approved days to suit their needs.

In all these examples, the common thread is the matching of what is given with what is valued, and a faith that if it is given, employees will give back.[30]

Engagement Practice # 49: Build a Culture That Values Spontaneous Acts of Caring

So far in this chapter, we have focused on benefits and aspects of culture that are within the power of business owners and chief executives to decide. But great employers are also characterized by managers who are empowered to act with spontaneous acts of generosity and caring. Here are some examples of how individual managers have helped relieve employee stress and generate more loyalty in return:

- Letting the team go out for a long lunch at the manager's expense on the condition that they not talk about work
- Sending cards, free movie tickets, or restaurant gift certificates to the homes of employees who worked long hours to complete a project
- Bringing meals to the homes of workers who are grieving the death of a family member
- Providing a sympathetic ear when employees are going through divorces or child-custody problems
- Creating a Thursday ritual—free pizza in the office
- Giving an employee the rest of the day off after a particularly stressful morning
- Allowing employees to work from home when it isn't essential that they be at the workplace
- Pitching in to help with the workload on especially busy days
- Stopping communicating by e-mail, having real conversations with employees, and concentrating on listening with genuine interest
- If they have been insensitive in the past, offering a sincere apology

The point here is not to provide a prescriptive list of things to do, but to describe the kinds of things managers do when they are being spontaneously sensitive to the needs of workers. Employees can tell when managers are going through the motions, following a tip they read in a book, and when they are acting sincerely in the moment. Like so many other practices already covered in this book, the first requirement is paying attention to the people you manage.

Engagement Practice # 50: Build Social Connectedness and Harmony Among Employees

There is little doubt that part of the glue that binds people to workplaces comes from the relationships they form with other employees. I have heard employees say to coworkers, "You people are what's keeping me here," even as things are going from bad to worse in the other aspects of their work lives. Human beings have a basic need for belonging, as Maslow pointed out, and more employees look to the relationships they form at work as a source of the "family feeling" that might otherwise be missing.

We live in an increasingly transient society where workers stay in their jobs less than three years on average, and yet workers long for connection with coworkers. We spend one third of our workdays communicating by e-mail—time that in years past we spent in direct human contact. Many people now work from home or from remote locations and feel isolated from coworkers and alienated from their organizations. In toxic workplaces employees often experience anxiety, distrust, unspoken conflict, petty jealousy, departmental in-fighting, incivility, and outright nastiness—conditions that make teamwork almost impossible.

What can a manager do about all this? Perhaps it is easier to start with what a manager cannot do—change the culture or suppress all conflict. Conflict, if openly and constructively expressed, can actually have positive consequences, leading to higher levels of trust and quicker, more open resolution of disagreements. Managers cannot expect employees to always get along, nor should they view themselves as referees in every personal dispute. Although manager interventions may sometimes be required, employees need to be able to resolve their own conflicts whenever possible.

What managers can do is work to actively encourage harmony and social connectedness among workers. Here are some of the ways managers can help bind employees together in a positive way:

- Allow employees a reasonable amount of time to meet in the halls or at the water cooler to have personal conversations. Try not to always look at such gatherings as a drag on productivity, but rather, as time spent building connectedness with each other.

- Assign teams to work on projects together when possible, especially when there is an opportunity to bring together workers who have not worked together before.

- Create cross-functional teams, mixing staff from your department with employees from other areas or functions.

- Invite people from other departments to your staff meetings.

- Take the initiative to organize group outings such as picnics, softball games, offsite work sessions, group volunteer work, holiday parties, birthday parties, lunchtime card games, trips to sporting events, regular breakfasts or pot-luck lunches together, or informal meetings on Friday afternoons to review the week.

- Encourage several employees to join professional associations and attend meetings together.
- Ask employees to get up and go speak to one another more often, or take each other to lunch more frequently instead of depending on e-mails as their primary mode of communication.
- When an employee seems bogged down trying to solve a difficult problem, bring together several coworkers to brainstorm new ideas and possible solutions.
- Encourage the formation of employee interest groups, such as investment clubs, book clubs, informal parenting discussions, or travel discussions where employees can share photos from recent vacations.
- Get to know all your employees on a personal basis so you will know enough to link those with common interests or to refer one employee to another who can help with a practical everyday issue, such as finding a good real estate agent.
- At staff meetings, ask each member of the team to introduce themselves by mentioning one fact about themselves that most people would not know.
- As often as possible, bring onsite workers together with those who work from home or remote locations.

Research shows that employees who have better relationships with their coworkers are also more committed to the organization.[31] There may be times when those relationships are in need of repair and you may require the services of a consultant who specializes in conflict resolution or team-building. In the meantime, keep an eye out for creative ways to build the ties that bind among coworkers.

Engagement Practice # 51: Encourage Fun in the Workplace

"Work should be more fun than fun," said the playwright Noel Coward, a statement that conjures images of the seven dwarfs marching off to the mines singing "hi-ho, hi-ho." Alas, for far too many employees today, the work itself is not fun, and the work environment is even less so.

Generation Xers noticed as children that many of their parents weren't having much fun working long hours and were neglecting their families in the process. Many of them made up their minds early on that when they entered the world of work, they were going to make it more fun and less

---

Reducing Turnover Through Social Bonding

RiverPoint Group, a 70-employee information technology group owned by Jon Schram and his wife, Jill Washington Schram, faced the challenge of a 60 percent turnover rate, made worse by the fact that most of its employees work offsite. The Schrams wanted to create a stronger common culture that would make employees feel more bonded to one another and to the organization. Among other initiatives, they created an associate management program, in which senior-level employees mentor their junior counterparts. Mentors and mentees talk several times a month by telephone and face-to-face at least monthly. Account managers are required to be on job sites once a week to ensure "face time" with associates. When employees start new projects, they are greeted with bagels from the owners and a cake on their birthdays. The owners also schedule quarterly staff meetings and social outings every three months so employees can get better acquainted. Everyone stays connected through a corporate Web site

Result: RiverPoint's turnover rate fell to 25 percent, well below the industry average. This has been critical to the retention of important clients.[32]

---

formal. In the late 1990s, when the war for talent was most intense, Silicon Valley companies worked hard to create more fun for younger workers—putting in game rooms with foosball and pinball, throwing keg parties on Friday afternoons, creating quiet rooms with recliners for napping, and providing inflatable "stress-relief" punching dummies.

After the dot-com bust, many companies curtailed the "frivolity." Between 2001 and 2003, the American workplace reached unprecedented levels of productivity, but at a price: People weren't having any fun. During this time, some companies felt the need was even greater to reinject some fun into the workplace to relieve the stress from overloaded work schedules.

Not everyone has the same ideas about what is fun, but most of us recognize that whether it is planned or spontaneous, fun activities and celebrations can be highly effective stress-busters. In fact, the more stressful the workplace, and the more employees are vulnerable to burn-out, the more need there is for fun and celebration. Studies have actually shown that workplaces with higher "fun quotients" have lower health-care costs, higher productivity, and improved morale.

Here are some companies who have woven fun into their cultures:

- At *ELetter*, a direct mail company in San Jose, California, the CEO pledged that he would wear high heels to the office every day for a week if they met his ambitious sales goals. They did, and he did.
- To build teamwork and keep his executive team sharp, the CEO of *Demandline.com* of San Francisco told all five of them to meet at the airport with cold-weather gear for a five-day trip to an undisclosed location. They flew to Alaska where they were met by two guides with ice axes and 70-pound backpacks. They then proceeded to climb Matanuska Peak.[32]
- At *Perkins Cole*, a Seattle law firm, "happiness committees" visit employees' offices, leaving baskets of treats.
- *Valassis*, of Livonia, Michigan, publisher of newspaper coupons and inserts, holds limerick contests, and sponsors tail-gating parties at college football games.
- At *Simmons,* the Atlanta mattress manufacturer, employees break the stress by going on ropes-course training once a year. They even get to walk a high wire.
- Employees at *Fannie Mae*, Washington, D.C., complained about too many speeches at the annual holiday party, so the company cut back on the speech-making and created more time for dancing at the next year's party.
- *Republic Bancorp* of Owosso, Michigan, holds an annual Easter egg hunt.
- *Third Federal Savings and Loan* of Cleveland threw a company-wide Mardi Gras party breakfast with Polish doughnuts, magicians, and caricaturists.
- *Duncan Aviation* of Lincoln, Nebraska, announces employees' birthdays over the public address system.
- At *Network Appliance* in Sunnyvale, California, a sign welcomes visitors to "GALACTIC HEADQUARTERS." At a company rally to kick off a new sales campaign, there were life-sized cutouts of executives on the stage in Star Trek costumes.
- Auto lending company *AmeriCredit* in Fort Worth sent each of its branches a "fiesta in a box" with piñata and salsa music to celebrate reaching $15 million in loans.

- At *LensCrafters* in Cincinnati, managers and executives wore white gloves, bow ties, and top hats to welcome employees to the company party. They also opened their doors and parked their cars.
- At *Kimberly-Clark* in Dallas, one unit staged its own version of *Survivor.*
- At *Griffin Hospital* in Derby, Connecticut, musicians and clowns entertain patients and staff, and with each new birth, the Brahms *Lullaby* is played on the sound system. [34]
- *Capital One* provides each employee a "fun budget" of $80 per quarter to spend on such activities as white-water rafting.
- CDW Computer Centers gives employees free Krispy Kreme doughnuts once a month and free Dairy Queen every Wednesday in the summer. If the company meets sales goals, CDW offers an "old-timer" benefit to anyone with three years of service: a free trip for the employee and family anywhere in the continental United States (awarded every other year).
- Southwest Airlines organizes spirit parties, cake-decorating contests, barbecues, and chili cook-offs—all planned by local "culture committees."
- Snapple has "theme Fridays"—tie-dye day, silly-hat day. One year, they built a makeshift miniature golf course inside corporate headquarters. [35]

While most of these examples are planned, some of the best stress reducers are unplanned, such as sharing a cartoon with a coworker, deciding to go out and rent a comedy video to watch over a lunch hour, having an impromptu contest to see who can cheer up the grumpiest person in the office, or buying a beverage on Friday evening for the person with the toughest experience with a customer.

It's worth remembering that not all stress can be relieved by a few moments of fun. More serious and concerted approaches are required to relieve the root source of stress—an individual struggling to perform a job for which she is not suited, a bullying manager taking out frustrations from a dysfunctional home life on his employees, or a management team that has simply pushed its workforce to the brink of burnout and exhaustion. All the fun committees in the world cannot remedy these kinds of problems.

Ultimately, it's a balanced approach combining both serious resolve and spontaneous fun that spells relief for the kinds of stress that is endemic in today's workplaces.

What the Employee Can Do to Relieve Stress and Overwork

Many employers have sponsored stress management training for their employees in recent years, with most getting high marks from those who attend. But because so much of a person's stress is self-imposed, employees must begin to take charge of managing their own stress levels.

Here are a few stress-busters that managers can encourage their employees to start doing, or to set the example, start doing themselves:

- Understand the basic truth that each of us has the freedom to choose how we respond to stressful events. Train yourself to become more conscious of, and accountable for, making those choices.
- Eat breakfast daily, drink less coffee and caffeinated soft drinks, and start eating more healthy foods and, if overweight, in smaller portions.
- Organize the work to be done the day before. Sort your in-basket according to priority and work on high-priority items first.
- Establish set times in the day to review e-mail and voicemail.
- Let go of the need for perfection. Very few things really have to be done perfectly.
- Take all the vacation you have coming. Reserve those days on your calendar as far in advance as possible.
- Don't try to do two or three things at the same time. Chronic multi-tasking takes a toll.
- Don't bring work home with you every night. Instead, stay later or go in earlier occasionally.
- Let voicemail answer when you are extra busy and don't need the distraction. As someone said, "Just because someone throws you the ball doesn't mean you have to catch it."
- Block out your calendar ahead of time to make sure you will have the uninterrupted time you need to finish a large project to complete several smaller tasks.
- If you are annoyed or angry, speak up in a diplomatic way. If you "gunny sack" your frustrations, they will fester and increase your stress levels until they come out in inappropriate ways.
- Don't hesitate to ask coworkers for help when you are trying to handle peak workloads.

- Take breaks to clear your mind and relax for a few minutes at a time. Go outside for fresh air if you can.
- Take lunch out of the office whenever you can, or just go for a lunchtime walk.
- Delegate more.
- Create a morning ritual—either quiet meditation or reading time— that can help set the tome for the entire day.
- Block out your calendar days before it starts to fill up to assure that you have the time needed between appointments or to work on important projects uninterrupted.
- Take a two-day getaway break to do what restores and energizes you—and not just on the weekends.
- Exercise every day, if possible.
- Don't be afraid to ask for flex-time, part-time work, job-sharing, or other family-friendly conditions if it can help to make your life less complicated and stressful.
- Seek more sources of gratification besides your job—pursue a new hobby (or an old one), spend more time with friends and family, take more vacation days, travel more often, treat yourself to a massage, go for a drive to no place in particular—whatever works to give you more balance.
- If you are in the wrong job or working for a manager who cranks up your stress levels, create a plan to change your situation and start working it today.
- Get enough sleep.

Employer-of-Choice Engagement Practices Review and Checklist

Review the engagement practices presented in this chapter and check the ones you believe your organization needs to implement or improve.

To Reduce Stress from Work-Life Imbalance and Overwork:
47. ☐ Initiate a culture of "giving-before-getting."
48. ☐ Tailor the "culture of giving" to the needs of key talent.
49. ☐ Build a culture that values spontaneous acts of caring.
50. ☐ Build social connectedness and harmony among employees.
51. ☐ Encourage fun in the workplace.

Notes:

1. Ellen Galinsky, Stacy S. Kim, and James T. Bond, "Feeling Over-worked: When Work Becomes Too Much," Families and Work Institute, 2002.

2. "Stress at Work," report of The National Institute for Occupational Safety and Health, Cincinnati, 2004, citing survey by Northwestern National Life.

3. Galinsky, Kim, and Bond, op. cit.

4. William Atkinson, "Strategies for Workplace Stress," *Risk & Insurance*, October 15, 2000.

5. "Stress at Work" report.

6. Dori B. Reissman, Peter Orris, Roy Lacey, and David E. Hartman, "Downsizing, Role Demands, and Job Stress," *Journal of Occupational and Environmental Medicine* 41, 4 (1999): 289–293.

7. Galinsky, Kim, and Bond, op. cit.

8. Laura Nash and Howard Stevenson, *Tools for Creating Success in Your Work and Life* (Hoboken, N.J.: John Wiley and Sons, 2004).

9. Galinsky, Kim, and Bond, op. cit.

10. Randstad Workplace Report (Amsterdam, Netherlands, 2002).

11. True Careers Family and Work Survey (Reston, Va., 2002).

12. Radcliffe Public Policy Center research study, 2002.

13. Ibid.

14. Carol Hymowitz, "Bosses Need to Learn Whether They Inspire, or Just Drive, Staffers," *Wall Street Journal*, February 18, 1999.

15. Cited in "Business Briefs," *Wall Street Journal*, April 6, 2000.

16. James L. Heskett, W. Earl Sasser, Jr., and Leonard A. Schlesinger, *The Service-Profit Chain: How Leading Companies Link Profit and Growth to Loyalty, Satisfaction, and Value* (New York: Free Press, 1997).

17. Edward E. Lawler III, *Treat People Right! How Organizations and Individuals Can Propel Each Other into a Virtuous Spiral of Success* (San Francisco: Jossey-Bass, 2003).

18. Julia Boorstin, "The 100 Best Companies to Work For," *Fortune*, January 12, 2004.

19. Ibid.

20. Ibid.

21. Ruth Baum Bigus, "At This Company, It's All About Benefits," *Kansas City Star*, April 20, 2004.

22. ——— "Marketing Firm Tackles Nagging Issue of Burnout," *Kansas City Star*, August 28, 2001.

23. Mary E. Burke, Evren Essen, and Jessica Collison, "2003 Benefits Survey," SHRM/SHRM Foundation, June 2003.

24. Carol Kleiman, "Companies Assess Value of Work-Life Programs," *Omaha World-Herald,* June 24, 2001.

25. Ibid.

26. *Elayne Robertson Demby, "Do Your Family-Friendly Programs Make Cents?" HR* Magazine*, January 2004.*

27. Sue Shellenberger, "This Time, Firms See Work-Life Plans as Aid During the Downturn," *Wall Street Journal*, March 29, 2001.

28. Ruth Baum Bigus, "Firm's Policies Are Aimed at Retaining Workers," *Kansas City Star*, May 15, 2001.

29. Charles Fishman, "Sanity Inc.," *Fast Company*, January 1999.

30. Boorstin, op. cit.

31. Peter Simon, "No Fooling: Fun is Good for Business," reprinted in HRD KC 2000, June 26, 2000.

31. Ruth Baum Bigus, "Creating Bonds Between Far-Flung Workers," *Kansas City Star*, July 17, 2001.

32. Boorstin, op. cit.

33. T. Rotondi, "Organizational Identification and Group Involvement," *Academy of Management Journal* 18, 1975.

34. Matthew Boyle, "Beware the Killjoy," *Fortune,* July 23, 2001.

CHAPTER TEN

Reason #7: Loss of Trust and Confidence in Senior Leaders

> Business begins with trust. . . . As companies abandon bureaucratic mechanisms, their leaders need to understand that trust is as important to management as it is to relationships with customers.
>
> —WARREN BENNIS

Having reviewed so many issues and practices that lie mostly within the sphere of managers to control or influence, we now consider the special challenge facing senior leaders—to create a culture of trust and integrity that strengthens the bonds of employee engagement. While this challenge is shared by all managers and every employee, it is incumbent on senior leaders to set the tone and the example.

The consulting firm, Watson-Wyatt, which evaluates a company's employment brand by its share performance, reports that companies with high trust levels outperform companies with low trust levels by 186 percent.[1] If the bonds of trust are weak, even the best efforts of gifted people managers will not be enough to attract, engage, and keep the people needed for the business to achieve its goals.

Here are the comments from Saratoga's surveys that reveal the issues that workers find most troubling about senior leaders in their organizations:

Basic Lack of Trust and Integrity

- "No follow-up from upper management: Do what you say you'll do and don't make promises you can't keep."
- "The company asks lower-level employees to participate in community service while upper management never does it themselves."
- "Trust is nonexistent within the company. You cannot believe anything that management says. They withhold information from employees."
- "Weak, unapproachable HR department. Most of the staff thinks they are a joke. Nothing is ever kept in confidence. They have betrayed confidence before and the word has gotten out."

Isolated and Out of Touch with Day-to-Day Reality

- "I don't think that upper management truly hears the voices and opinions of the staff. They are definitely not visible. Sometimes the human factor is forgotten, at least with the production staff."
- "Take ideas from field teams who are a great deal closer to customers and know what's going on."
- "I don't feel upper management really knows what is going on in the lower levels when things start getting bad."
- "Upper management is ignorant of our day-to-day processes."

Greed and Self-Interest

- "Top management is nothing but greed personified."
- "High-powered managers were typically uninterested in anyone but themselves."
- "Very poor support of employee morale. They are more worried about making money than anything."
- "Post-merger management is too focused on protecting their own jobs, that they have ceased being both advocates for the employees and the supervisors."

Lack of Concern and Appreciation for Workers

- "Upper management tends not to take employees needs into consideration when deciding changes. They also convey the attitude that if employees don't like what is going on, they can just look elsewhere for employment."

- "Upper management doesn't even know that we are here."
- "Upper management comes into our departments and doesn't even speak to us 'unknown' employees."

Lack of Trust and Respect for Workers

- "Upper management has no respect for the people that do the work. They do not recognize their good employees. ABC Company management is all about the bottom line."
- "XYZ Company has a vicious, cavalier attitude towards its employees that makes it hard for employees to feel important and valued. I felt constantly watched and threatened."
- "Upper management are clearly the ones running the show. No one is allowed to make any decisions except for the upper management."
- "They treat their employees like garbage. They use them up and then throw them out."

Isolated and Unapproachable

- "Completely and utterly unknown, unseen, uncaring, unconcerned and unapproachable upper management."
- "Management needs more individual concern for each employee. They need to be able to talk with each employee and not judge through the eyes of another employee. Get to know the individual yourself!"
- "Upper management never takes the time to communicate with the employees, to say 'hello.'"

Mismanagement of Change

- "Provide consistent direction. In the past eight years, ABC Company has made too many management and corporate philosophy changes. Employees have whiplash!"
- "XYZ Company doesn't initiate change well. They make drastic changes too quickly and do not properly prepare employees to adjust to the changes. But they never tell us why the change is happening."
- "Stay with a plan long enough to see if it works before moving on to the next one."

Poor Communication

- "ABC Company doesn't inform employees about decisions that would directly affect them. For the most part, most of the relocation decisions are not relayed to the departments that they affect. The company keeps too many secrets from employees."
- "Upper management has a clear and direct set of objectives, but that message doesn't seem to filter down to the 'worker bees' that are the most important element of the upper management vision."
- "XYZ Company doesn't communicate changes to the masses. Employees normally have to read about it in the newspaper."

A Crisis of Trust and Confidence

If these comments reflect the way departing employees feel about senior leaders, we can only wonder how the employees who stayed must feel. If we are to believe Gallup's surveys reporting that 75 percent of the American workforce is disengaged, then we can only conclude that the lack of engaging leadership is a major root cause.

The corporate scandals of the early years of this decade only served to deepen the hole of distrust that had already been dug by the downsizings of the 1990's. Recent surveys of the American workforce provide ample evidence:

- 82 percent of Americans believe executives help themselves at the expense of their companies.[2]
- Only 39 percent of workers trust senior leaders.[3]
- Only 40 percent of workers believe their organization as a whole is well managed.[4]
- Only 34 percent of workers agree that "I can trust management in my organization to always communicate honestly."[5]
- Only 50 percent of employees believe that managers in their organization are concerned for the well-being of employees.[6]

All this data points to not just a corrosion of trust, but a crisis of confidence in the ability of senior leaders to lead their organizations to success—a basic requirement for engaging and retaining talented workers.

Reading the Signs of Distrust and Doubt

Watch for these signs in your company of growing distrust, cynicism, or loss of confidence in senior leaders:

- Lack of enthusiasm following announcement of new initiatives by senior leaders
- Increasing complaints and questions by employees about policies and practices controlled by senior leaders
- Managers beginning to question decisions and actions of senior leaders
- Increased grumblings by groups of employees
- Morale problems showing up in employee surveys
- Increased mention of senior leaders in exit interviews or surveys
- Active resistance to leader initiatives and change efforts

The Three Questions Employees Need Answered

In reviewing survey comments, it appears that workers have three fundamental questions on their minds when it comes to senior leaders:

1. *Will these leaders steer the ship to success?* Employees want to know whether their leaders have the right vision, the right strategy, the right people, and the personal character and competence to lead the organization where it needs to go. For some companies, this can mean turning the company around to reverse its declining fortunes, while for others it means building on previous success to take the company to new heights. Regardless of the situation, talented employees want to know whether they have hitched their wagon to a star that is burning brighter or burning out.

2. *Can I trust them to do what they say?* No one wants to work for an organization where leaders are always saying one thing and doing another. This question gets right to the heart of organizational integrity and is directed as much toward direct supervisors as it is to senior leaders. Even if senior executives backs up their words with action, if their actions don't reinforce the organization's professed values, trust is lost.

3. *Do they have trust and confidence in me?* Understandably, we all tend to trust and have confidence in those who have trust and confidence in us. The issue of who initiates the building of trust—employer or employee—can be debated, or you can say it doesn't matter. It seems clear, however, that senior leaders are in enough need of employee commitment that they should be willing, even eager, to initiate the reciprocal commitment process.

Criteria for Evaluating Whether to Trust and Have Confidence

As I conduct postexit interviews, former employees increasingly mention disappointment with senior leaders among their primary reasons for leaving. As consumers of a potential employer's work experience, job seekers seem more interested in checking out the reputation of senior leaders before accepting an offer. Because they have been sensitized by the spectacle of corporate CEOs betraying the trust of their constituents on a large scale, employees now view their leaders through different lenses. Here are three criteria by which employees now judge senior leaders:

1. *Servant Mentality vs. Selfish Greed.* As we have seen in the survey comments, there is a deep suspicion among employees that leaders have mainly their own interests in mind as they go about their daily business. Workers increasingly see business leaders as interested mainly in maximizing their stock options and building their personal wealth, not in pursuing what's best for the long-term interests of shareholders, customers, and employees.

   As evidence supporting this belief, they cite the disproportionate rise in executive compensation. In 2003, the ratio of average CEO pay to average worker pay stood at 281 to 1. In 1983, the ratio had been 42 to 1. During the 1990s, executive pay rose by 570 percent while profits rose by 114 percent. If workers wages had risen since 1990 at the same rate as CEO pay, the average U.S. production worker in 2002 would have earned $68,057 instead of $26,267.[7]

   Yet, there are also plenty of leaders who see their calling to leadership as one in which they will serve those they are called to lead. They do all they can to serve the needs of employees so the employees, in turn, will better serve the customer. Such leaders are interested in building an organization that serves the business community, makes lives better, and makes a profit—not in exploiting others for personal gain. These "servant leaders" (see Robert Greenleaf's classic book, *Servant Leadership*) are striking a chord that resonates among today's workers.

2. *Shareholder Value vs. Employee Value.* Employees have heard the mantra about maximizing shareholder value for so long, and seen so many corporate mission statements that speak almost exclusively about it, their eyes have glossed over. When employees hear and read this, they get the message that the CEOs only real responsibility is to serve the interests of the shareholders. Who *are* these shareholders? They are mostly anonymous mutual fund managers and day traders who never get to know the company, its products or services, employees, or customers. Shareholders interests are important certainly, but employees know when they are being given comparative short shrift.

Companies which, perversely, don't put shareholders first, do better for their shareholders than organizations that only put shareholders first.

—Robert Waterman in *The Frontiers of Excellence*

Contrast this obsession with shareholders against a new attitude that is emerging among a new breed of CEOs. One of these is Dick Kovacevich, CEO and chairman of Wells-Fargo Bank. When Wells-Fargo acquired Utah-based First Security in 2000, Kovacevich chose to fly to Utah and meet directly with First Security employees rather than check in with Wall Street analysts, as many bankers might have under the same circumstances "The way I see it," explained Kovacevich, "when you take care of your employees, they take care of your customers. And your shareholders wind up winning anyway."[8]

In the business press, we read more and more reports of CEOs with similar employee-first attitudes and approaches. Interestingly, most of their companies seem to be building strong reputations for excellent customer service provided by committed front-line employees.

3. *Lean and Mean vs. Nice Workers Giving Great Service.* With the recession of 2001, "lean and mean" came back in style, as businesses

looked for new ways to cut costs. Companies cut to the bone, laying off thousands of workers. Many of these downsizing companies gave little thought to how they might redeploy or retrain these workers before cutting them loose. Remaining workers felt lucky to still have their jobs, but quickly realized they were doing the jobs of two or three people. Before long, employees (and managers) were starting to feel abused and burned out—not exactly the best formula for putting them in the mood to provide world-class customer service. As Sam Walton, the founder of Wal-Mart said years ago, "It takes a week to two weeks for employees to start treating customers the same way the employer is treating the employee."

Smart CEOs intuitively know what Sam Walton knew. One of those CEOs is David Neeleman of Jet Blue Airways, the airline he founded in 1999 and which, by May 2004, he had led to twelve consecutive quarters of profitability, with the highest percentage of seats filled of any other airline. From the start, Neeleman has been committed to running lean, but not mean. To conserve costs, Jet Blue's reservations agents work from home instead of working from an expensive call center. Yet, Neeleman knows many of his 6,000 employees by name, asks about their personal lives, pitches in to pass out snacks when he flies, and stays behind to help clean the plane.

Neeleman is obsessed with reliability and customer service, but says the real secret weapon is the employees, or "crew members," as he calls them. Whenever Neeleman and his senior executives consider making a major change, they first ask, "how will this affect crew members' morale?" If they conclude it would hurt morale, they elect not to make the change, because it would not be worth it—"employees treat customers the way they are treated themselves," he says.

When a company survey revealed that one third of the crew members were unhappy with the abrasiveness and favoritism of their supervisors, Neeleman and his COO realized that they were promoting people without teaching them how to manage. That's when Neeleman decided to create a five-day training program called "Principles of Leadership," taught by senior executives. One of the five key principles is "treat your people right."

Neeleman's decision to make an up-front commitment to his employees has been returned in kind. Says one of his pilots, "I would walk through a burning building for him."[9]

How many "lean and mean" companies have created this kind of loyalty? Mean leaders make for mean employees who are often mean to customers. It is a formula that is destined to fail in the long term.

Engagement Practice # 52: Inspire Confidence in a Clear Vision, a Workable Plan, and the Competence to Achieve It

One of the first requirements of trust is competence. We will follow only those leaders we judge to be capable. Traditionally, leaders were selected from among the most skilled functional specialists, but that is certainly not the case today. Leaders are more like orchestra conductors, blending the efforts of the most skilled musicians.

So what kind of competence do employees expect from leaders today? At the most basic level, they simply want to know that the organization will be successful, assuring them of a job and a future. Because so many businesses fail, this is unfortunately a promise that many employers cannot deliver. So, as a prerequisite for becoming an employer of choice, an employer must be successful currently and inspire the confidence of workers that it will be successful going forward.

It is natural that we look to the leaders for this assurance. We want our leaders to have a clear and achievable vision, confidence in their capacity to achieve the vision, the ability to inspire and mobilize followers to achieve the vision, the ability to transform the vision into a workable strategy and plan, the right team of people in place to carry it out, and the ability to follow through with persistence to achieve the plan. And while they are at it, we require complete honesty and integrity, and, yes, please show us you care about us as individuals. This is a tall order, but we demand nothing less.

We may want servant leaders, but we do not want "soft" leaders. In his best-seller, *Good to Great: Why Some Companies Make the Leap and Others Don't,* Jim Collins studies the leaders of companies that achieved and sustained exceptional financial performance over a fifteen-year period. He describes them as "Level 5" leaders—executives who "build enduring greatness through a paradoxical blend of personal humility and professional will."[10]

As an example, Collins profiles Cork Walgreen, CEO of Walgreen Drugs, a man of fierce resolve who saw that the company's future lay in convenient drugstores, not in the food service business it had built. He challenged his executive team to get the company out of the restaurant business within five years. At the time, Walgreens had 500 restaurants, but the CEO was firm and fanatical in his vision, which turned out to be the right one.

Walgreen and all the other CEOs of the good-to-great companies did not fit the mold of the attention-seeking, heroic CEOs who were glorified in the press during the 1980s and 1990s. In fact, all these executives were described by their associates as rather quiet, self-effacing, and humble. "It's not that Level 5 leaders have no ego or self-interest," writes Collins. "Indeed, they are incredibly ambitious—but their ambition is first and foremost for the institution, not themselves."[11]

Collins also profiles George Cain, CEO of Abbott Laboratories, who turned the pharmaceutical company around by courageously attacking its greatest weakness—nepotism. Cain, who had been with the company for eighteen years when he took over as CEO, instituted new standards of excellence for every position and rigorously raised the talent level of the management team by gradually replacing mediocre family members with the best professionals he could find.

While he cares deeply about his people, Jet Blue's David Neeleman appears to be cast in the same mold as other "Level 5" leaders, although only time will tell if he can sustain the financial success he attained in the airline's first five years of operation. He is firm about his "tripod" business model: "low costs, a great product, and capitalization." But Neeleman knows his limitations. Because he had never run a large company before, he surrounded himself with senior executives who had.[12]

Humble, yet passionately determined, Neeleman and the other chief executives briefly profiled here are the kinds of leader that today's workforce seems to find most engaging. Bottom line: it's not about ego, quick results, and personal ambition—it's about patiently, quietly, but tenaciously, executing a shared, compelling vision with a valued and dedicated team.

 ## Engagement Practice #53: Back Up Words with Actions

> Followers are more interested in
> our integrity than in our
> speeches about integrity, and
> their antennae are sensitive and
> efficient to any possible
> incongruities.
>
> —LANCE SECRETAN

One of the greatest sources of employee cynicism and disengagement is the failure of leaders to do as they say. We have grown tired of CEOs who say "people are our most important asset," but cut back training budgets without blinking; or those who survey employees as if they intend to follow through with corrective action, but never do; or leaders who say quality is number one, but push employees to do the work in a third of the time it takes to do it right; or CEOs who say that treating people right is a priority for all managers, but fail to hold managers accountable for abusing employees. It's all just more fodder for Dilbert cartoons. Leaders who can't, or won't, back up their good intentions with actions might as well be deliberately driving people out of their organizations.

Words and Deeds out of Synch

A major international corporation that claimed to be committed to work/life values drew up an excellent plan to help managers incorporate work/life balance into the business. The company gathered its top 80 officers to review the plan—but scheduled the meeting on a weekend.[13]

Someone once compared trust to money in a bank account. If people meet our expectations over time, we put coins in the bank and after a while they have earned our trust. If they don't meet our expectations, we take coins out. When it comes to our employers, the more coins we take out, the closer we come to closing our accounts and walking out the door for good.

Some leaders are so externally focused that they make feel-good statements in speeches and annual reports with no apparent awareness that what they are saying may be inconsistent with internal realities. One company displayed its code of conduct in its lobby, proclaiming that "trust" was a driving principle, yet it searched employees' belongings each time they entered and exited the building.

Everyone has a story to tell about the mixed signals companies send. What can employers do about it? Probably the best insurance is to have a CEO who places a high value on integrity and insists on carefully selecting executives and candidates for all positions based on character first and capabilities second.

Some companies conduct surveys in which employees are asked to rank a variety of cultural factors based on how strongly they desire it versus how much they believe it exists in the organization. The larger the "gap" scores, the greater the discrepancy between the actual and desired culture on those factors. Follow-up employee focus groups conducted by outside consultants can help bring to the surface specific issues that senior leaders need to face and reconcile. While this process may be facilitated by HR staff, it needs to be owned by senior line managers.

Often, the mixed signals may be created by executives espousing one thing and middle managers doing another. Some managers believe that, because of their privileged status, they are exempt from the rules that govern everyday life in the organization, such as having to be at work on time or taking reasonable "lunch hours."

In one company, senior leaders solicited employee feedback and invited "different ideas and perspectives" about how projects should be com-

---

It's Not Just What We Do . . . It's What We *Won't* Do

Companies earn trust points not just for the consistency of their internal behavior, but also for the things they will and won't do in their interactions with the outside world. Employees at CenterBeam, Inc. in Santa Clara, California are proud to tell these stories:

The company was trying to recruit enough talented people to support its rapid start-up and had made an offer to a qualified candidate when the resume of a superstar candidate came across the desk of the hiring manager. Managers asked the CEO, Sheldon Laube, if the offer could be rescinded so the company could hire the superstar. Laube's response: "No way. We made a promise to the first candidate. If we're going to be the kind of company that people trust, we've got to keep our promises."

Shortly after that, the company ordered $500,000 worth of tape drives from a distributor. Before they could unpack them they found out that a rival distributor was offering comparable machines at a price that could save the company almost $100,000 per year. A few engineers wanted to refuse delivery of the more expensive tape drives, but CenterBeam executives treated the shipment as binding.

CEO Laube has seen these decisions pay off by deepening the commitment of CenterBeam employees: "It's amazing how many employees have come up to me and said, 'It's great to work at a company that has integrity.' Many employees tell me that at their old companies, 'people promised things that they just didn't deliver.'"[14]

pleted, but some project managers summarily shot down many of the new ideas employees suggested. In these situations, multi-rater feedback from managers, exit surveying, and regular employee surveys can help uncover these demoralizing situations so they can be corrected.

Engagement Practice # 54: Place Your Trust and Confidence in Your Workforce

To demonstrate trust in people before they have even earned it is a risky proposition. We may find out later that our trust was misplaced or even betrayed. We may risk giving away our own power as leaders. We may trust employees too much to make important decisions before they are ready, thus jeopardizing a customer relationship. And yet, employers of choice routinely take these risks and make a habit of trusting employees before they have earned it.

Nordstrom department stores is famous for trusting its sales people with the power to make on-the-spot decisions that build customer loyalty, even if it means spending the company's money to do it. When Bill Gore left DuPont to start W. L. Gore and Associates in the basement of his house, he recognized the importance of trusting employees with the independence to make decisions that serve the interests of the organization.

To formalize this philosophy, Gore sent out a company memo outlining the concept of "the waterline," likening employees to the crew of a ship. Understandably, no employees would be allowed to drill holes below the waterline, as that would endanger every crew member. They would be allowed to drill holes above the waterline, but not below.

In other words, with every decision they faced, employees would ask themselves, "is this decision above or below the waterline?" If they concluded that the decision might significantly impact other crew members, they would be obligated to consult further with more senior colleagues. If, however, they concluded that the impact on other crew members would be negligible, they were free to make their own judgments without consulting more senior crew members.[15]

In his book *Making the Grass Greener on Your Side: A CEOs Journey to Leading by Serving*, Ken Melrose tells the story of taking over as CEO at Toro Company when the emphasis was on getting bottom-line results at all costs. The company had been pushing so hard to get bigger that, somewhere along the way, its reputation for quality among its distributors and customers eroded so badly that it was on the brink of bankruptcy.

Melrose and his executive team decided to put the emphasis on quality and product excellence and aggressively reduced high field inventories. Customer satisfaction became the new byword. At the same time, Melrose became a convert to a servant leadership philosophy and began "driving power down to the people who do the actual work and make things happen."

He established what he called "four leadership imperatives—building trust through openness; fostering risk-taking, innovation, and creativity; practicing a coaching and serving role; and creating win-win situations." He also installed an Employee Stock Ownership Plan so that the title of "owner" became more than symbolic.

Melrose credits the servant leader approach for the company's revival, pointing out that it runs against the grain of traditional corporate leadership, which concentrates power and control at the top. "Ego addiction is the main cause of management failure because it causes people in management positions to suppose they know all, to hoard power, and to destroy trust."[16]

Sometimes managers learn by trial and error. When Gerald Chamales founded Rhinotek Computer Products in Carson, California, he admits he was "completely green" as a manager and found himself behaving in a dictatorial way with his employees. He screamed at employees who didn't follow orders precisely and threw temper tantrums when employees failed to measure up to his standards. As a result, he alienated his workforce. Then he began to notice the company's high turnover and began asking himself if it might be connected to his own management style.

Chamales decided to change his approach—he learned to control his temper, and started walking around his office and plant floor soliciting feedback from his 200 employees. Turnover declined dramatically thereafter. "I've done everything in this company from sweeping floors to typing invoices, yet it is important to have humility and realize that the people doing the jobs have the solutions."[17]

Ultimately, it boils down to simple human respect. In her book with a one-word title—*Respect*—Sara Lawrence-Lightfoot describes her father's secret: "He gained respect by giving it. He talked to the fourth-grade kid in Spring Valley who shined shoes the same way he talked and listened to a bishop or a college president. He was seriously interested in who you were and what you had to say."[18]

When senior leaders invest so much energy in their own self-importance that they cannot adopt this humbler attitude, they lose the opportunity to engage and inspire. Many will never change their authoritarian, micromanaging styles because they are not comfortable with the idea of giving away power. The irony is, when leaders give power away, they increase the collective power of the organization to innovate and meet new challenges, thus enhancing their own power in the long run.

What the Employee Can Do to Build Reciprocal Trust and Confidence

What could a lowly employee possibly do that would cause a senior leader to inspire more trust and confidence? At first, we might respond "not much." But, while employees may not have much control, all employees have some degree of influence.

Here are some actions they can take to exercise the influence they do have:

- Respond honestly on employee surveys—point out how the actions of senior leaders do not match their words and professed values. Describe specific instances of management behavior that have created distrust or caused you to lose confidence.
- Speak up in meetings and express your convictions firmly.
- If you are asked to take part in something unethical or dishonest, refuse to go along, report it to a superior, or be prepared to resign.
- Be willing to take the risk of counseling your manager against taking an action that is unethical and will damage the company's reputation.
- When a leader or manager puts trust and confidence in you by giving you the freedom to do the job without constant oversight, be prepared to take the initiative.
- Show that you are interested in having an "ownership mentality." Learn how the business makes money and what you can do to make it more profitable and perhaps share more in that profitability.
- Earn your manager's trust by constantly looking for ways to take the initiative to meet customers' needs or by improving your own skills so that managers will trust you to handle new challenges.
- Give new leaders the benefit of the doubt. Give them time to communicate and begin to execute their new vision before judging it to be unworthy of following.
- If you feel called to become a leader yourself, resolve to do everything in your power to gain and keep the trust and confidence of your employees.

Employer-of-Choice Engagement Practices Review and Checklist

Do senior leaders in your organization do what it takes to build trust and confidence among employees? Review the engagement practices presented in this chapter and check the ones you believe your organization needs to implement or improve.

To Inspire Trust and Confidence in Senior Leaders:

52. ☐ Inspire confidence in a clear vision, a workable plan, and the competence to achieve it.
53. ☐ Back up words with actions.
54. ☐ Demonstrate trust and confidence in your workforce.

Notes

1. Research study cited by Rachel King, in "Great Things Are Starting at Yum," *Workforce Management*, November 2003.
2. The Gallup Organization, 2002.
3. *"CEO Compensation Practices in the S&P,"* Watson Wyatt survey, 2002.
4. Mercer Consulting, "2002 People at Work Survey," 2002.
5. Ibid.
6. Ibid.
7. "Executive Excess 2003: CEOs Win; Workers and Taxpayers Lose," a report by the Institute for Policy Studies and United for a Fair Economy, 2003.
8. Amy Kover, "Dick Kovacevich Does It His Way," *Fortune*, May 15, 2000.
9. Chuck Salter, "And Now the Hard Part," *Fast Company*, May 2004.
10. Jim Collins, *Good to Great: Why Some Companies Make the Leap and Others Don't* (New York: Harper Business, 2001).
11. Ibid.
12. Salter, "And Now the Hard Part."
13. Pamela Babcock, "Is Your Company Two-Faced," *HR* Magazine, January 2004.

14. George Anders, "Honesty Is the Best Policy—Trust Us," *Fast Company*, August 2000.

15. Lance H. Secretan, *Reclaiming Higher Ground: Building Organizations That Inspire Excellence*" (New York: McGraw-Hill, 1997).

16. Chuck Hutchcraft, "Toro Chairman Sows Seeds of Restructuring," *The Chicago Tribune*, November 21, 1995.

17. Carol Hymowitz, "Bosses Need to Learn Whether They Inspire, or Just Drive, Staffers," *Wall Street Journal*, February 18, 1999.

18. Sara Lawrence-Lightfoot, *Respect: An Explanation* (New York: Perseus Books, 1999).

CHAPTER ELEVEN

Planning to Become an Employer of Choice

> The great French Marshall
> Lyautey once asked his
> gardener to plant a tree.
> The gardener objected that
> the tree was slow-growing
> and would not reach
> maturity for 100 years. The
> Marshall replied, "In that
> case, there is no time to
> lose; plant it this
> afternoon."
>
> —JOHN F. KENNEDY

In February 2004, senior executives polled by McKinsey Consulting reported that their "most pressing concern," other than the overall economic climate, was "hiring and retaining talent."[1] Even after several years of slow labor-market activity, it seems that most company leaders still appreciated the need to focus on talent acquisition and retention as a key imperative.

When the competition for talent gets heated, many companies begin to scramble and cast about for ideas on how to stop the bleeding. Some just put more time and money into their recruiting efforts, which has been likened to speeding up the pace of the blood transfusion while the patient is bleeding to death.

Many companies know they need to stop the bleeding first, but in their search for answers, it seems not to have occurred to them to look for the root causes. Instead, in many cases the CEO asks the HR department to do something about the turnover problem, and the search begins for "what other companies are doing." The only problem with that approach is that the practices that fit the business strategies of other companies may not fit your company.

For example, it may not be appropriate to implement engagement practice # 2—increase hiring from pool of temps, adjunct staff, and part-time workers—if there are already too many of these workers in the company. In such a situation, customer service may begin to suffer because there are too many temps and part-timers, and not enough full-time employees with solid customer service experience. Increasing hiring from within (engagement practice # 6) may not be advisable for companies that are pursuing a business strategy focused on innovation and product development and already know they don't have enough innovators and product developers currently on board.

Yet the instinct to find out what other companies are doing and copy-cat their practices is irresistible to many conscientious professionals. I can even recall seeing several articles in the late 1990s that listed the "top 20 effective retention strategies" in broad terms, like this:

1. Training
2. Flexible work arrangements
3. Tuition reimbursement
4. Sabbaticals
5. Extended parent leave

and so on through all twenty items on the list.

First of all, these are not strategies. Second, they may not be the right practices for your company. And third, these lists are usually dominated by pay-and-benefit practices and typically feature very few intangibles—cultural or management practices, which, as we know, may have a much bigger impact.

Part of the problem is that it is more tempting to select short-term, tangible practices over long-term, intangible ones (see Figure 11-1). Being only human, we prefer short-term solutions to long-term ones. Besides, we are impatient to get results and believe we need to score a quick success. Likewise, the intangible stuff seems just too soft, too squishy, too hard to implement, and too difficult to change in a reasonable time frame. Or so the thinking goes.

Actually, there is plenty of evidence now, such as Gallup's study of 80,000 managers,[2] to support the conclusion that the greatest drivers of employee engagement and retention *are* intangible—mostly related to the

Figure 11-1.

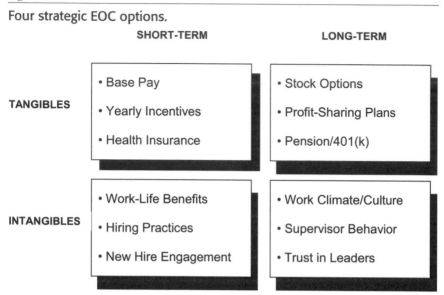

Four strategic EOC options.

	SHORT-TERM	LONG-TERM
TANGIBLES	• Base Pay • Yearly Incentives • Health Insurance	• Stock Options • Profit-Sharing Plans • Pension/401(k)
INTANGIBLES	• Work-Life Benefits • Hiring Practices • New Hire Engagement	• Work Climate/Culture • Supervisor Behavior • Trust in Leaders

way a manager treats employees. In fact, in reviewing the list of 54 engagement practices in Appendix A, you will see that most of them are intangible, and within the power of the manager to implement. In the end, it doesn't matter whether they are short-term, long-term, tangible, or intangible. What matters is whether they are the right practices for your current situation.

So, as you consider the 54 engagement practices in this book, think of them as items in a cafeteria. Some you have already tried and found satisfactory. The ones you have not tried and now choose to put on your tray may be few, but they will be the right ones.

Talent Engagement Strategies in Action

The strategies companies use to engage their workers depend not only on their business strategies, but also on the size and complexity of the organization and its workforce. Here are several examples of companies big and small that are implementing talent selection and engagement strategies differently, but successfully:

United Parcel Service

The Challenge: Engaging and retaining the young, mostly-part-time workers that load, unload, and sort packages in the company's 270,000 square-foot Buffalo, New York distribution center. In 1998, the turnover rate was 50 percent, creating customer service disruptions and proving to be costly in several ways.

Strategic Actions: The new district manager, Jennifer Shroeger, created a five-part strategic plan, as follows:

1. *Meet the expectations of applicants.* Instead of hiring anybody that walked in the door, which it had been doing, UPS started asking applicants if they were hoping for full-time jobs. If the answer was "yes," then they were probably going to be disappointed at some point, because full-time jobs rarely open up. It usually takes six years to work up to a full-time driver's job. "I can't hire workers who want full-time work if there aren't any full-time jobs," Shroeger said. Instead, the company sold part-time work for what it was— short, flexible shifts that could fit the schedules of students from the many colleges in the area.

2. *Communicate differently to different groups of workers.* To better understand the needs of her entire workforce, Shroeger analyzed information that broke down the worker population into five distinctive groups, closely paralleling their age and the stage of their careers. She realized that those older than 35 valued different motivators than their younger coworkers. Understanding these differences, the company tailored its recruiting and re-recruiting messages accordingly.

3. *Take better care of the new hires.* To make the warehouse environment less intimidating to new hires, UPS improved the lighting, upgraded the break rooms, and installed more personal computers on the floor, which provided access to training materials and human resource information on the company's intranet. The best part-time supervisors became trainers, spending a week shadowing new workers. Shroeger initiated an employee-retention committee, composed of both managers and hourly workers, to track new hires through their first few weeks on the job and fix small problems before they become bigger ones. The committee also plans fun social activities, such as after-hours baseball games and floor-wide "super-loader" contests.

4. *Give supervisors the freedom and training to manage people their own way.* The company lets managers figure out their own best way of motivating different workers. Supervisors also complete training in how

to handle difficult situations and respond to different career questions. They also learn how to have more flexibility with students and moms, who have frequent changes in their schedules, and are challenged to find out and remember something about the personal lives of workers.

5. *Let them move on with new skills and good will.* Shroeger realizes that young, part-time workers are going to move on with their lives. But, having given them the opportunity to build their skills via tuition-reimbursement, Saturday computer classes, and career planning discussions, she hopes they will leave with good feelings about UPS and perhaps become customers someday, as many have.

The Results: By the first quarter of 2002, part-time turnover had dropped to 6 percent, which equates to 600 workers staying who otherwise would have left four years earlier. Annual savings due to lowered hiring costs totaled $1 million. Lost work-days due to work-related injuries had dropped by 20 percent, and the percentage of packages delivered on the wrong day or at the wrong time dropped from 4 percent to 1 percent.[3]

Motek Software

The Challenge: This small, privately-held southern California firm customizes industrial computers for use on warehouse forklifts and dominates its market niche. The goal of Motek's founder and CEO, Ann Price, is to attract the very best IT workers and make them want to remain in a work environment that allows them to have a life outside of work.

Strategic Actions: Price expects her twenty employees to keep 9 A.M. to 5 P.M. hours. She also buys lunches for them at the best restaurants, brings in a hairdresser for employees once a week, and gives new employees one month vacation per year. When employees postpone taking their vacation, Price has been known to book it herself and go along with them to make sure they take it. "We're robbing ourselves of the best years of our lives," she says. "I'm living proof that you can achieve the same goals and not give that all up."

The Results: A turnover rate of less than 1 percent and a highly stable workforce, which helps to avoid disruption of service to its clients.[4]

IHS Help Desk

The Challenge: Even though this IT consulting and training company was growing and succeeding, owner Eric Rabinowitz realized that a 113 percent turnover rate was threatening the future of the business. On further inspection of company data, he found that 20 percent of turnovers were happening in the new hires' first month on the job.

Strategic Actions: Rabinowitz began asking employees what he might do differently and he got an ear-full. He had expected that offering full-time work and good benefits would be enough, but his employees saw themselves as temp workers with no career path, and were always looking for their next job. Because most of them worked off-site, they felt like they were working for the client. They also mentioned that they wanted more training and a clearly defined career path.

Rabinowitz realized that most employees would not stay with the company more than two years, but resolved to give them whatever training that would cause them to stay at least that long. He surveyed employees to find out what kind of training they wanted, then set up Web-based training programs that met their needs. He also started a communication program to make workers feel less isolated at remote locations—he created a newsletter and hired an employee advocate to visit work sites once a week and create a stronger bond with the company. The company also improved its benefits plan to include dental and life insurance, and started incentive and employee recognition plans.

The Results: Within a year, the company had lowered its turnover rate to 19 percent.[5]

Meers Marketing Communications, Inc.

The Challenge: This small advertising and marketing communications firm serves large clients by offering superior service and long-term relationships. However, the company began to experience turnover rates as high as 50 percent, compared to an industry average of 30 percent. As a result, they started losing clients as well, some within the first year. Owner and CEO, Sam Meers, knew that keeping clients less than a year meant they were probably losing money on them.

Strategic Actions: After losing a large client and taking another look at the firm's bottom line, Meers started working with a consultant to complete a strategic planning process, with a major emphasis on employee retention. One of the first issues addressed was hiring the right people in the first place, so Meers instituted a more rigorous interviewing process for applicants. Job candidates would be required to be interviewed multiple times by a variety of people before an offer was made.

To create more ownership and give employees more of a stake in the company's success, Meers decided to open the company's financial books to employees. He would go over the financials with employees on a monthly basis and tie their bonuses to the performance of the company and to their own performance on a 50-50 basis. Meers also enlisted the help of all employees to create a procedures manual documenting 150 agency processes so employees would know exactly what was expected and how to do it. Finally, he committed to understand the differing needs of each employee, and decided to give them more flexible work hours, or leaves of absence, or whatever they might need to achieve a better balance between work and home life.

The Results: In the year following implementation of these measures, the firm only lost one person. Said Meers, "People like the culture and because of that, they do good work for our clients. . . . It's a much more consistent experience for our clients and our staff."[6]

Steak and Shake

The Challenge: When Peter Dunn took over as CEO of this fast-casual restaurant chain, earnings had slipped, and crew turnover stood at 200 percent—markedly higher than the 129 percent average reported by other restaurants in its category. At 50 percent, management turnover was also excessive.

If Dunn was going to achieve his goals to turn around the company and fuel an expansion, he knew he was going to have to reduce the high turnover among store employees because it was negatively impacting guest satisfaction scores. The company told investors that it could save $2 million to $4 million per year by increasing the retention of front-line workers. He also estimated that bringing manager turnover under control could save another $1 million to $2 million per year.

Strategic Actions: Dunn hopes to build customer retention based on increased employee retention, an idea known as building a "virtuous cycle," similar to the "service-profit chain" described in Chapter Ten. One of the ways the company planned to do this was by giving store managers more freedom to make decisions about how to increase revenues and efficiency. For the first time ever, Stake and Shake has provided managers with statistics on each store's operations, including turnover rates, customer satisfaction data, drive-through efficiency, and which items produce the most profit. Managers were challenged to create their own business plan for their stores and share them with employees

The company also decided to increase benefits to front-line workers, starting with a 50 percent reduction in their vision and dental expenses, in addition to the health care insurance, and a full range of other benefits it already offers. One of these benefits is life insurance, which the company believes produces the greatest reduction in turnover for the money spent. Stake and Shake has also increased the amount of time new hires spend being oriented, based on industry data showing that restaurants that give four or more hours of orientation enjoy turnover rates 34 percent lower than those who provide only an hour or two.

The Results: In less than a year, manager turnover had dropped to 30 percent and turnover among front-line workers was down 24 points, to 176 percent. Guest satisfaction had improved from 81 percent to 86 percent and same-store sales had increased by 12 percent.[7]

FleetBoston Financial

The Challenge: To reduce annual turnover in the bank's retail operations, which had reached 25 percent overall, with rates as high as 40 percent among tellers and customer service representatives. Such high turnover rates had put the bank's customer-focused strategy at risk. An analysis of the bank's employee survey and exit interview data had suggested that employees were leaving because of low pay and heavy workloads. Despite raising pay rates and installing more flexible pay arrangements, turnover rates continued to rise.

Strategic Actions: The bank suspected that the reasons employees were giving for leaving during their exit interviews were safe and superficial responses, and that they were reluctant to discuss the real reasons. Fleet retained Mercer Consulting to conduct a comprehensive analysis of workforce characteristics and management practices that most directly influenced employees' decisions to stay or leave.

One of the first discoveries was that the bank's active history of mergers, acquisitions, and consolidations had resulted in the closing of some branches, which had raised employees' worries about job insecurity. To counter these concerns, the bank decided to focus on broadening career opportunities within the organization. The idea was that if employees could improve their mobility, they would see that as also enhancing their marketability, making them less vulnerable to possible future layoffs.

By examining the career path history of employees, the bank had learned that those who progressed more rapidly through different jobs were more likely to stay. This finding was surprising to some managers who believed that employees who broaden their experience in the company and become more marketable are more likely to pursue outside opportunities.

Managers began paying more attention to career development needs and encouraging employees to consider a broad range of possible movements within the bank, operating on faith that they would receive their share of mobile new employees to replace those who moved on. The bank also learned that there were two categories of employees at greatest risk of leaving: high-performers who had been in their same position for two or more years, and employees who had just completed their undergraduate or graduate degrees. Managers were encouraged to initiate discussions with these employees in particular to address the sources of their concerns.

Another interesting and valuable finding was that nonexempt employees who had progressed into exempt positions tended to stay longer and earn more frequent promotions than those who entered as exempt employees. As a result, Fleet clarified and publicized its policies outlining how nonexempts can become exempt employees, and began providing career coaching to nonexempt employees to encourage them to pursue new growth opportunities.

Further analysis of employee data revealed that employees whose managers left the bank were themselves more likely to leave. To address this, the bank decided to raise the amount of variable pay that managers can earn in the form of higher performance-based cash bonuses. Fleet also replaced departed supervisors with internal candidates, already known and trusted by current employees.

In exploring the reasons for high first-year turnover, the bank realized it needed to enhance its new-hire orientation process and began giving more frequent feedback and more training during the first year of employment. Recognizing that it may also have been giving new hires more work than they could manage, the bank reduced workloads.

Finally, the bank examined hiring-source patterns and discovered that employees who had been referred by other employees were more likely to stay than employees recruited through agencies or want ads. Fleet decided to lower its investment in recruiters and to increase the bonuses it paid employees for referring new hires who stayed at least six months.

The Results: Within eight months of implementing the new retention initiatives, FleetBoston's turnover rate had decreased by 40 percent among salaried employees and 25 percent among hourly employees. The turnover rate among first-line supervisors declined to 6 percent and first-year turnover dropped by 10 percent. These combined improvements are estimated to have saved the company $50 million.[8]

What Do We Learn from These Success Stories?

There are common threads that run through all these stories and are worth pointing out. Though there were significant differences in company size, industry, circumstances, and range of solutions, all shared a common approach:

1. Resolving to take action without delay as soon as they recognized there could be a serious threat to the fortunes of the business
2. Recognizing key employees on which the business depended and attempting to understand how to better meet their needs
3. Implementing targeted initiatives to meet the needs of those key employees
4. Tracking improvements to demonstrate progress and measure success

In some cases, the approach was straightforward and based on common sense. Others pursued a more sophisticated approach, relying on complex analytical tools that produced some unexpected findings and led to a wide range of solutions. In every instance, the commitment of the CEO was the driving force for the new initiatives.

Linking Talent and Business Objectives

These stories remind us of the business imperative for becoming an employer of choice. In order to reach our business objectives, we must consistently compete for talent and win, not just win in terms of attracting talent, but engaging and retaining it as well, knowing that current employees, especially the best, will always have choices to move elsewhere.

Yet, while 62 percent of corporate officers said that they see the importance of linking business and talent strategies, only 7 percent said their companies were actually doing it. And while 44 percent agreed that line managers should be held accountable for talent objectives, only 10 percent said their companies were doing so.[9]

Part of the problem lies in the fact that in many organizations, senior leaders look to the HR department to focus on increasing efficiencies and reducing costs when they should instead be focused on creating value for the business by linking talent strategies with business objectives. A prime example of focusing on efficiency at the expense of value is when a company measures cost-per-hire, but makes no attempt to measure quality-of-hire.

Linking the Right Measures to Business Results

Instead of simply benchmarking human resource efficiency and cost measures against other companies, many companies are taking a broader business perspective. They are focusing internally, but in a more strategic way, and are measuring the company against itself, not against other companies who may have very different strategies.

The first requirement is for the business to actually have a clear and detailed business strategy. Next, the organization must target the job roles that are most critical to achieving the plan. As we know, as few as 20 percent of the workforce can contribute 80 percent of the value. In the case of a national restaurant chain with a business strategy that depends on improvements in customer service, the front-line workers would have to be considered pivotal to the success of that strategy.

There are many questions to ask: Are there enough of these people on board? Do they have the right competencies and, if not, how will they be developed? How will we attract people with the right talents for these critical roles? Do we have the right human resource systems and practices in place to engage and retain these people? Are they receiving the right rewards? And what about the noncritical employees and "B players" we depend on—are we focused on keeping, re-engaging, and rewarding them as well?

Another important lens to look through is the growth phase of the business. For example, a start-up retail venture would concentrate on selecting and rewarding its top executives, but focus more on middle managers as it begins to expand nationally and open up new stores. Similarly, employers of choice stay attuned to the career phases of their employees. The recruiting pitches, rewards, benefits, and management practices they use to attract, engage, and retain new hires are different from those used with more experienced workers. The same goes for women and other demographically diverse populations of workers.

One definite trend indicating a more proactive approach to talent management is that more companies seem to be conducting comprehensive "talent review" processes, often beginning with in-depth assessments of high potential employees. Senior officers and department heads then review the capabilities of specific individuals deep into the organization, not only to discuss their readiness for promotion, but to assess their strengths against strategic talent needs. Following these sessions, managers are expected to create action plans for employees and talent strategies for their units.

Ultimately, managers and human resource leaders need to be focused on linking talent-related outcomes to customer measures. For example, tracking employee retention as a leading indicator of customer retention and revenues has proved to be particularly compelling. In a recent poll of HR executives, 50 percent of respondents report that their companies are increasing their investments in tracking the impact that metrics such as turnover rates, productivity, and employee morale have on the bottom line.[10]

A Conference Board survey also reported that 76 percent of HR executives say that senior management in their companies will increase their support for "people metric projects" over the next few years. The same report also mentioned that Cisco Systems, one of the most progressive companies when it comes to strategic talent management, has developed "human capital dashboards" to analyze revenue per employee and other such data.[11]

Creating an Employer-of-Choice Scorecard

Rather than try to benchmark themselves against other employers, some companies are creating ways of measuring their own progress toward becoming employers of choice. In other words, they are starting to track year-over-year improvements by creating their own dashboards of talent management indicators. One way of doing this is to track measures of the four things every organization must do with talent: attract, select, engage, and sustain engagement (see Figure 11-2).

Measures of *attraction* could include the following:

- Ratio of employment applicants to open positions
- Percentage of applicants considered "A" candidates
- Average days to fill vacancies
- Ratio of acceptances to offers
- Applicant dropout rate
- Number of recruiting sources used
- Percentile rank of total compensation versus talent competitors
- Percentage of new hire referrals who stay at least six months
- Average monthly percentage of open positions

Employers of choice, for example, typically have ratios of employment applicants to open positions of at least 20 to 1, some as high as 100 to 1.

Figure 11-2.

Four key things we MUST do with talent.

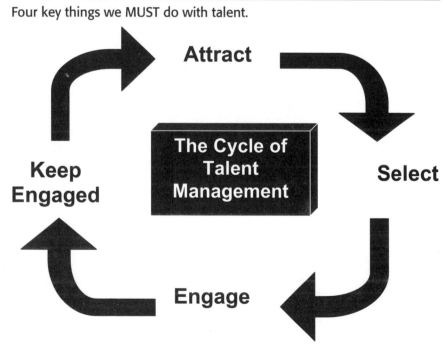

New-hire referral rates of 30 percent are considered healthy, usually indicating that current employees speak well of the company to their friends and feel comfortable recommending the organization as a good place to work.

Measures of *selection* might include:

- First-year voluntary turnover rate
- First-year involuntary turnover rate
- First-year performance results
- First-year performance evaluation by managers
- First-year absenteeism rate
- First-year employee engagement survey scores
- Percentage of candidates hired using behavioral interviewing
- Percentage of selection decisions based on competency analysis

Engagement surveys have become an important tool for many companies, which are using them as a primary indicator of how well talent is being managed. Many see engagement as a much more meaningful measure than employee satisfaction, because it encompasses satisfaction, plus dimensions of performance along with commitment, or intent to stay with the organization. As you would expect, engagement survey scores appear as a key measure in the next two categories.

Measures of *new-hire engagement* might include:

- Percentage completing comprehensive orientation process
- Percentage completing "entrance interview"
- Percentage coached by buddy or mentor
- First-year employee engagement scores
- Percentage of new hires considered "outstanding" performers
- First-year voluntary turnover rates
- Employee survey results of first-year employees
- Percentage whose supervisors leave or are reassigned in first year

Some companies that are especially concerned about quick turnover among new hires might want to track some of these measures during the first 30, 90, or 180 days.

Measures of *sustained employee engagement* could include:

- Voluntary turnover rate
- Top performer voluntary turnover rate
- Performance/quality results
- Absenteeism rates
- Employee engagement scores
- Training hours per employee
- Ratio of internal to external hires
- Percentage of employees completing individual development plans
- Percentage of re-hires among all hires

There are dozens of similar measures that a company might begin to track and report. As shown in Figure 11-3, the scorecard becomes more

Figure 11-3.

Employer-of-choice scorecard.

EOC Indicators	2005	2004
Voluntary Turnover Rate	11.9%	13.2%
Employee Referral Rate	21.2%	17.4%
Ratio of Jobs Filled Internally	39.8%	33.5%
New Hire Retention Rate	76.3%	71.8%
Quit Rate	13.5%	14.4%
Ratio of Acceptances to Offers	64.7%	59.7%
Percentage of Engaged Employees	36.6%	27.9%
Absenteeism Rate	4.0%	5.1%

meaningful in the second and subsequent years as improvements and drop-offs become apparent at a glance. The next logical step would be to begin showing the relationship between some or all of these measures and business results, such as revenue per employee (including outsourced operations) or customer retention rates.

The Plan Works . . . If You Work the Plan

You may have seen the Dilbert cartoon where Catbert asks Dilbert's boss if he has a plan for retaining employees, and the boss responds, "I whittle at their confidence until they believe no one else would ever hire them." The bad news is that there really are such bosses. The good news is that you are now armed with 54 engagement practices from which you can choose to create a better plan for your employees. And the really good news, as we have seen in the success stories presented earlier in this chapter, is that if you work the plan, the plan will work.

When I ask audiences what they hope to get from my presentations, someone often says, "I was hoping for a magic bullet." The urge to slay the two-headed monster of employee disengagement and turnover is primal and hard to resist, but we must. There is only one "magic bullet," and that is the steady commitment to a plan that is made up of several well-targeted practices.

As Jim Collins points out in *Good to Great*, good companies become great not through quick changes, but through patient and determined application: "Sustainable transformations follow a predictable pattern of buildup and breakthrough. Like pushing on a giant, heavy flywheel, it takes a lot of effort to get the thing moving at all, but with persistent pushing in a consistent direction over a long period of time, the flywheel builds momentum, eventually hitting a point of breakthrough."[12]

Partners in Working the Plan

Becoming an employer of choice is a possible dream for every company, no matter how big or how small it may be. But if it were easy, every company would be one. It takes a team effort, with everyone pushing on the flywheel—senior leaders, human resource leaders, managers, and employees.

Senior leaders make the commitment, enlist the support of the board, build the culture of trust, competence, and caring, approve the budgets, and hold all managers accountable for engaging and retaining talent.

Human resource leaders link talent strategies to business objectives, balance value-creating activities with those that cut costs, create the right support systems for managing talent, partner with marketing to build an "employment brand," help the organization understand the true reasons people stay and leave, recommend the right best practices, support line managers in the implementation of those practices, and track the right measures.

Managers bear the greatest responsibility, for they are the main reason most employees decide to stay or to go. The great managers are the ones that make their departments "employers of choice" long before the organization as a whole gains that status. And yet, great managers of people have not been honored as the heroes they are.

Companies need to select more of the right people to become managers in the first place, be more rigorous in the selection process, and take more care not to promote good technical performers above their level of competence. Managers must be challenged to be great managers, given the tools and training they need to become great, and rewarded in meaningful ways for engaging and retaining valued workers. And managers must be relieved of some of the loads they are bearing—doing the work of two or three people in addition to managing their direct reports. Too many managers are simply too busy managing budgets and "getting things done" to spend quality time with their employees.

Finally, many managers have to start taking more responsibility for their role in engaging or disengaging employees. They need to understand that pay is not the reason most employees leave, and accept that their way of managing *is* the number one reason. For many, that means stop blaming senior leaders for not paying more (when low pay is not the culprit), and stop depending on human resources to do all the recruiting and recognizing. In short, managers need to own all four phases of the talent management cycle: attract, select, engage, and sustain engagement.

As for *employees*, they may need to be reminded that no manager has as much power to engage them as they do to engage themselves. Even so, senior leaders in many companies now survey employees to track the percentage that are engaged versus disengaged, then challenge department managers to do whatever it takes to better engage their people and improve their scores in the next survey. While this does engender accountability for managing people with skill and emotional intelligence, there is a potential downside.

It is simply this. The responsibility for being engaged does not just fall on the shoulders of the manager—it is the employee's responsibility as well. One manager asked, "What about the employees? They shouldn't just be waiting around for the manager to engage them. Why don't we just score employees on how well they are keeping themselves engaged?!"

By overemphasizing the manager's role in engaging employees, organizations risk creating an environment where employees may become passive, expecting all motivation and incentive to come from external sources. It is easy enough for many employees to fall into a victim mentality and assume an attitude of entitlement, especially when organizations habitually fail to seek active employee input and put off confronting poor performers.

Maintaining the fine balance between engagement and entitlement is a shared partnership between company leaders and employees. The need for both parties to meet each other halfway in the process makes it all the more important for organizations to spell out exactly how they expect employees to keep themselves engaged, as well as how managers should work to engage their employees.

Notes

1. McKinsey Survey of 7,300 North American Executives, February 2004.

2. Marcus Buckingham and Curt Coffman, *First Break All the Rules: What the World's Great Managers Do Differently* (New York: Simon and Schuster, 1999).

3. Keith Hammonds, "Handle with Care," *Fast Company*, August 2002.

4. Bob Calandra, "Finders Keepers," *Human Resource Executive*, June 2, 2000.

5. Ibid.

6. Ruth Baum Bigus, "Formalizing Policies Helps Firm Retain Employees," *Kansas City Star*, October 9, 2001.

7. Rachael King, "Turnover is the New Enemy at One of America's Oldest Restaurant Chains," *Workforce Management*, April 2004.

8. Haig R. Nalbantian and Anne Szostak, "How Fleet Bank Fought Employee Flight," *Harvard Business Review*, April 2004.

9. Kemba J. Dunham, "Talent Travails," *The Wall Street Journal*, citing McKinsey survey of 3,400 corporate officers and 6,500 middle and senior managers at 56 companies, November 28, 2000.

10. Based on survey conducted by *Workforce Management* Magazine and cited in report, "Spending More Money on Measuring People," March 2004.

11. Ibid.

12. Jim Collins, *Good to Great: Why Some Companies Make the Leap and Others Don't* (New York: Harper Business, 2001).

Summary Checklist of Employer-of-Choice Engagement Practices

The following checklist is provided for readers interested in reviewing all 54 engagement practices presented in Chapters Four through Ten. Because it is difficult to focus on implementing several practices all at once, you may wish to use the checklist to put items in order of importance or urgency as you begin to plan your employer-of-choice strategy.

To Match Candidates' Expectations with Work Realities:

1. ☐ Conduct realistic job previews with every job candidate.
2. ☐ Hire from pool of temp, adjunct staff, interns, and part-time workers.
3. ☐ Hire candidates referred by current employees.
4. ☐ Create a realistic job description with a short list of most critical competencies.
5. ☐ Allow team members to interview candidates.
6. ☐ Hire from pool of current employees.
7. ☐ Create a way for candidates to "sample" the work experience.
8. ☐ Survey or interview new hires to find out how to minimize new hire surprises in the future.

To Match the Person to the Job:

9. ☐ Make a strong commitment to the continuous upgrading of talent.
10. ☐ See that all hiring managers perform talent forecasting and success-factor analysis.
11. ☐ Cast a wide recruiting net to expand the universe of best-fit candidates.
12. ☐ Follow a purposeful and rigorous interview process.
13. ☐ Track measures of hiring success.

215

To Match the Task to the Person:

14. ☐ Conduct "entrance interviews" with all new hires.
15. ☐ Work to enrich the jobs of all employees.
16. ☐ Delegate tasks to challenge employees and enrich jobs.

To Provide Coaching and Feedback:

17. ☐ Provide intensive feedback and coaching to new hires.
18. ☐ Create a culture of continuous feedback and coaching.
19. ☐ Train managers in performance coaching.
20. ☐ Make performance management process less controlling and more of a partnership.
21. ☐ Terminate nonperformers when best efforts to coach or reassign don't pay off.
22. ☐ Hold managers accountable for coaching and giving feedback.

To Provide Career Advancement and Growth Opportunities:

23. ☐ Provide self-assessment tools and career self-management training for all employees.
24. ☐ Offer career coaching tools and training for all managers.
25. ☐ Provide readily accessible information on career paths and competency requirements.
26. ☐ Create alternatives to traditional career ladders.
27. ☐ Keep employees informed about the company's strategy, direction, and talent need forecasts.
28. ☐ Build and maintain a fair and efficient internal job-posting process.
29. ☐ Show clear preference for hiring from within.
30. ☐ Eliminate HR policies and management practices that block internal movement.
31. ☐ Create a strong mentoring culture.
32. ☐ Keep career development and performance appraisal processes separate.
33. ☐ Build an effective talent review and succession management process.
34. ☐ Maintain a strong commitment to employee training.

To Make Employees Feel Valued and Recognized:

35. ☐ Offer competitive base pay linked to value creation.
36. ☐ Reward results with variable pay aligned with business goals.

37. ☐ Reward employees at a high enough level to motivate higher performance.
38. ☐ Use cash payouts for on-the-spot recognition.
39. ☐ Involve employees and encourage two-way communication when designing new pay systems.
40. ☐ Monitor the pay system to ensure fairness, efficiency, consistency, and accuracy.
41. ☐ Create a culture of informal recognition founded on sincere appreciation.
42. ☐ Make new hires feel welcome and important.
43. ☐ Ask for employee input, then listen, and respond.
44. ☐ Keep employees in the loop.
45. ☐ Provide the right tools and resources.
46. ☐ Keep the physical environment fit to work in.

To Reduce Stress from Work-Life Imbalance and Overwork:

47. ☐ Initiate a culture of "giving-before-getting."
48. ☐ Tailor the "culture of giving" to the needs of key talent.
49. ☐ Build a culture that values spontaneous acts of caring.
50. ☐ Build social connectedness and cohesion among employees.
51. ☐ Encourage fun in the workplace.

To Inspire Trust and Confidence in Senior Leaders:

52. ☐ Inspire confidence in a clear vision, a workable plan, and the competence to achieve it
53. ☐ Back up words with actions.
54. ☐ Place your trust and confidence in your workforce.

Guidelines and Considerations for Exit Interviewing/Surveying and Turnover Analysis

Exit survey and interview data should be seen as a valuable source for the analysis of turnover root causes, but it is too often regarded as superficial and relatively meaningless because of the way it is gathered and who does the gathering. When viewed as a strategically important retention practice, conducted skillfully, and incorporated with other relevant organizational data, exit survey and interview data can help organizations develop effective, on-target solutions to the push factors that too often drive good people out of the organization.

The Traditional Exit Interview

As traditionally practiced in many organizations, the exit interview is a perfunctory, multipurpose exercise, conducted on the employee's last day by an HR staffer. The agenda usually includes collecting the employee's keys, badges, or other equipment, completing forms, discussing separation benefits, and interviewing the employee about his or her feelings about working at the company and reasons for leaving. The employee may also be asked to fill out an exit survey form.

As discussed in Chapter One, the employee is often reluctant to reveal the true reasons for leaving to a company representative, the interviewer may have never been trained in the art of exit interviewing, and the collected data may never be analyzed and made available to management. These are serious limitations that undermine the legitimate purposes of exit interviewing and surveying.

The Best Reasons to Conduct Exit Interviews and Surveys

Many organizations have decided not to conduct the exit interview at the same time as employee's keys are collected and benefits are discussed because these agenda items may set the wrong tone and conditions for an open discussion of the real reasons for leaving. They also muddy and detract from the true purposes of an exit interview, which include:

- Bringing any "push-factor" reasons for leaving to the surface
- Alerting the organization to specific issues to be addressed
- Giving the employee a chance to vent and gain a sense of closure
- Giving the employee the opportunity to provide information that may help colleagues left behind
- Providing information about competitors and their practices
- In some situations, offering a final opportunity to eliminate the "push factor" reason for leaving and convincing the employee to stay

Most Favorable Conditions for Conducting Exit Interviews and Surveys

Whether interviews or surveys are used, there are certain conditions that tend to create optimum results in achieving the above benefits to the individual and the organization:

1. *Trained, Independent Interviewers.* The critical skills needed for successful exit interviewers do not come naturally for many—putting the employee at ease, creating rapport, and asking probing, follow up questions instead of accepting the individual's initial surface response. Interviewers must also understand the distinction between asking employees why they are leaving and asking why they didn't stay. No matter how well a company representative may have been trained, there will always be those departing employees who do not feel comfortable opening up with any representative of the organization.

   This is why more companies have elected to use independent third parties to conduct the interviews by phone, in-person, or through secure Web sites. The downside is that employees become more difficult to reach once they have left the company. Another alternative is to have all employees complete a written survey on their last day, then notify them that they will be receiving a phone call to obtain clarification on some of their responses.

2. *Offered on a Post-Exit Basis.* Because departing individuals may still have unresolved emotions and be preoccupied with other matters on the day of their departure, many employers contact the employee during the evening at home a few weeks after exiting. This allows the employee time to gain perspective and speak with the benefit of time for reflection.

   It is more expensive to have third-party consultants conduct phone interviews than to have departed employees complete a post-exit Web survey. This is why many companies have third parties conduct actual interviews only with those employees the company regretted losing the most and invite all others to complete a confidential password–protected Web survey.

3. *Guaranteed Confidentiality and Anonymity.* Departing employees need to be assured that they can provide frank and candid feedback without fear of retribution by their former manager or a coworker. Many employees are more likely to accept such assurances when they come from a third-party interviewer or surveyor than from a company representative.

   This is a more difficult issue for smaller organizations that conduct interviews with fewer employees and can therefore more easily identify departed employees by their comments and demographic information. CEOs at these smaller companies therefore cannot confront managers with specific information that is critical of them without revealing the identity of the departed employee. Smaller companies typically resolve this problem either by not using the specific information with the manager or by waiting until they have exit data from five or more employees, a number considered sufficient to protect the anonymity of the former employee.

4. *Conducted with All Employees Who Leave.* To have the broadest possible understanding of all reasons for employee turnover among all categories of employees, it is important to survey all departing employees in one form or another. All employees may not complete and return surveys after their departure, or be reachable by telephone, but they should at least have the opportunity to participate.

It is also a good idea to interview or survey employees who leave the company involuntarily because they may have valuable insights to share. However, they may also be more emotional on the day of their separation, so a post-exit survey will usually be more effective. Another category of employee not to be overlooked are those transferring from one location to another within the company. Having them complete exit surveys is another way to capture potentially valuable information about their work experiences and feelings even though they are staying with the organization.

5. *Consistent Survey Questions.* Once the survey has been designed, it is important not to keep changing the questions, at least not the core questions. This will help assure that the data received is reliable. Many organizations also intentionally use the same questions in exit interviews that they use in employee attitude surveys, thus allowing comparisons to be made and patterns to be detected.

6. *Findings Reported to Management.* Because "push-factor" reasons for leaving are within the control of managers and senior leaders, they should have the opportunity to see the findings in both summary form and more detailed reports so they may take corrective action. Senior leaders will certainly need to see this data in order to hold their direct reports accountable for making appropriate corrective changes to prevent future regrettable departures of valued employees. Larger companies that do regular exit surveying typically issue quarterly and annual reports of findings.

7. *Exit Findings Combined with Other Organizational Data.* Exit survey data by itself can be quite revealing, but to assure a more rounded view of organizational issues and trends they are best reviewed in combination with data from surveys of current employees and other organizational trend data. Such data may include the average tenure of employees in various positions, the number of years with the company when various employees are most at risk of leaving, quit rate, average vacancy rate, and other data of this kind. This type of comprehensive analysis can help identify predictors of turnover among various groups of employees so that actions can be taken to keep it from occurring.

8. *Leaders and Managers Taking Action Based on Findings.* As mentioned in Chapter One, 95 percent of companies conduct exit interviews or surveys, but only 30 percent report that they ever take corrective action based on what they learn. There we have one more reason

why most companies are not employers of choice. Employers of choice view every avoidable turnover of a valued employee as a failure to be analyzed and understood in terms of its true causes, in order to prevent such future turnovers.

This means that every piece of data at the disposal of company leaders must be taken seriously. However, if senior leaders and managers do not believe that the information gathered is based on the skilled questioning of candid departing employees, they certainly cannot be expected to trust the findings or take action based on it.

One Last Chance to Reclaim a Valued Employee

There are times during an exit interview when it may become obvious that an employee who has decided to leave is really heartbroken at the prospect of leaving, but feels there is no alternative. For example, an employee may love the job, the work environment, and the colleagues, but has decided to leave because the boss would not grant flexible hours. In these situations, an alert and proactive exit interviewer may be able to intervene to help change the boss's mind or report the situation to higher ups who may be able to assign the individual to a different manager.

In her book, *HR from the Heart*, Libby Sartain, senior vice president of human resources at Yahoo! Inc., recommends always asking departing employees, "Is there anything we could have done to keep you here?"[1] You may discover that there may still be a sliver of a chance to keep valued talent and save the company money in avoided turnover costs.

Sartain also recommends trying to connect with departing employees on a deeper, more human level by asking such questions as:

- If you had the last three months to live over again, what do you think you would do differently?
- What have you learned that you can take with you to your next job?
- What are you proud of from your time here?
- What goals did you meet?
- What accomplishments will you be able to take with you?[2]

Just One More Question

One question that should be on every company's survey is "Would you consider returning to the company, and if so, under what conditions?" Of course, asking this question requires that the company be willing to rehire former employees; as amazing as it may seem, there are still lots of companies who will not. Employers of choice, however, realize that former employees are to be viewed as alumni—to be kept in touch with and considered for rehire when the time is right.

Departing employees who answer this question affirmatively should be listed in a special recruiting database and contacted periodically by e-mail. There are few things more gratifying than welcoming back to the company a former employee who thought the grass might be greener, found out it wasn't, and has come back to tell and retell that story to their colleagues.

Note to Readers

To view our own post-exit survey, visit *www.keepingthepeople.com* and click on "surveys," then on "decision to leave." Visitors to the Web site are encouraged to complete this survey as part of our ongoing research into the root causes of avoidable employee turnover.

Notes

1. Libby Sartain, with Martha I. Finney, *HR from the Heart: Inspiring Stories and Strategies for Building the People Side of Great Business* (New York: AMACOM, 2003).
2. Ibid.

Employer of Choice Strategies and Practices

Ahlrichs, Nancy S. *Competing for Talent: Key Recruitment and Retention Strategies for Becoming and Employer of Choice*. Palo Alto: Davies-Black Publishing, 2000.

Branham, Leigh. *Keeping the People Who Keep You in Business: 24 Ways to Hang On to Your Most Valuable Talent*. New York: AMACOM, 2001.

Davidson, Barbara, and Jac Fitz-enz. *Retention Management*, a study released by The Saratoga Institute, Santa Clara, California. New York: American Management Association, 1997.

Harris, Jim, and Joan Brannick. *Finding and Keeping Great Employees*. New York: AMACOM, 1999.

Kaye, Beverly, and Sharon Jordan-Evans. *Love 'Em or Lose 'Em: Getting Good People to Stay*. San Francisco: Berrett-Koehler Publishers, 1999.

Putzier, John. *Get Weird! 101 Innovative Ways to Make Your Company a Great Place to Work*. New York: AMACOM, 2001.

Talent Management and Business Strategy

Friedman, Brian, James Hatch, and David M. Walker. *Delivering on the Promise: How to Attract, Manage, and Retain Human Capital*. New York, The Free Press, 1998.

Gubman, Edward L. *The Talent Solution: Aligning Strategy and People to Achieve Extraordinary Results*. New York: McGraw-Hill, 1998.

Levin, Robert, and Joseph Rosse. *Talent Flow: A Strategic Approach to Keeping Good Employees, Helping Them Grow, and Letting Them Go*. San Francisco: Jossey-Bass, 2001.

Michaels, Ed, Helen Handfield-Jones, and Beth Axelrod. *The War for Talent*. Boston: Harvard Business School Press, 2001.

Nalbantian, Haig R., Richard A. Guzzo, Dave Kieffer, and Jay Doherty. *Play to Your Strengths: Managing Internal Labor Markets for Lasting Competitive Advantage.* New York: McGraw-Hill, 2004.

Sartain, Libby, with Martha Finney. *HR from the Heart: Inspiring Stories and Strategies for Building the People Side of Great Business.* New York: AMA-COM, 2003.

People Management Best Practices

Ahlrichs, Nancy S. *Manager of Choice: 5 Competencies for Cultivating Top Talent.* Palo Alto: Davies-Black Publishing, 2003.

Buckingham, Marcus, and Curt Coffman, *First, Break All the Rules: What the World's Great Managers Do Differently.* New York: Simon & Schuster, 1999.

Buckingham, Marcus, and Donald O. Clifton. *Now, Discover Your Strengths.* New York: The Free Press, 2001.

Harvard Business Review on Finding and Keeping the Best People. Boston: Harvard Business School Press, 2001.

Harvard Business Review on Managing People. Boston: Harvard Business School Press, 1999.

Lancaster, Lynne C., and David Stillman. *When Generations Collide.* New York: HarperBusiness, 2001.

Noer, David. *Healing the Wounds: Overcoming the Trauma of Layoffs and Revitalizing Downsized Organizations.* San Francisco: Jossey-Bass, 1993.

Tulgan, Bruce. *Winning the Talent Wars.* New York: W.W. Norton, 2001.

Zemke, Ron, Claire Raines, and Bob Filipzak. *Generations at Work: Managing the Clash of Veterans, Boomers, Xers, and Nexters in Your Workplace.* New York: AMACOM, 2000.

Employee Turnover

Ahr, Paul R., and Thomas B. Ahr. *Overturn Turnover: Why Some Employees Leave, Why Some Employees Stay, and Ways to Keep the Ones You Want to Stay.* St. Louis: Causeway Publishing, 2000.

Mobley, William H. *Employee Turnover: Causes, Consequences, and Control.* Reading, Mass.: Addison-Wesley, 1982.

Roseman, Edward. *Managing Employee Turnover: A Positive Approach.* New York: AMACOM, 1981.

Employee Commitment and Engagement

Loehr, Jim, and Tony Schwartz. *The Power of Full Engagement: Managing Energy, Not Time, is the Key to High Performance and Personal Renewal.* New York: Free Press, 2003.

O'Malley, Michael N. *Creating Commitment: How to Attract Employees by Building Relationships That Last.* New York: John Wiley & Sons, 2000.

Human Capital ROI

Becker, Brian E., Mark A. Huselid, and Dave Ulrich. *The HR Scorecard: Linking People, Strategy, and Performance.* Boston: Harvard Business School Press, 2001.

Coffman, Curt, and Gabriel Gonzalez-Molina. *Follow This Path: How the World's Greatest Organizations Drive Growth by Unleashing Human Potential.* New York: Warner Business Books, 2002.

Collins, Jim. *Good to Great: Why Some Companies Make the Leap and Others Don't.* New York: Harper Business, 2001.

Fitz-enz, Jac. *The ROI of Human Capital.* New York: AMACOM, 2000.

Heskett, James L., W. Earl Sasser, Jr., and Leonard A. Schlesinger. *The Service-Profit Chain: How Leading Companies Link Profit and Growth to Loyalty, Satisfaction, and Value.* New York: Free Press, 1997.

Lawler, Edward E., III. *Treat People Right! How Organizations and Individuals Can Propel Each Other into a Virtual Spiral of Success.* San Francisco: Jossey-Bass, 2003.

Pfeffer, Jeffrey. *The Human Equation: Building Profits by Putting People First.* Boston: Harvard Business School Press, 1998.

Reichheld, Frederick F. *Loyalty Rules: How Today's Leaders Build Lasting Relationships.* Boston: Harvard Business School Press, 2001.

Reichheld, Frederick F. *The Loyalty Effect: The Hidden Force Behind Growth, Profits, and Lasting Value.* Boston: Harvard Business School Press, 1996.

Rosenbluth, Hal F., and Diane McFerrin Peters. *The Customer Comes Second: And Other Secrets of Exceptional Service.* New York: Quill Morrow, 1992.

Ulrich, Dave, and Norm Smallwood. *When the Bottom-Line Isn't: How to Build Value Through People and Organization.* Hoboken, N.J.: John Wiley & Sons, 2003.

Work Design and Job Enrichment

Csikszentmihalyi, Mihaly. *Flow: The Psychology of Optimal Experience*. New York: Harper & Row Publishers, 1990.

Hackman, Richard, and Greg R. Oldham. *Work Redesign*. Reading, Mass.: Addison-Wesley, 1980.

Leadership

Abrashoff, Michael (former commander, USS Benfold). *It's Your Ship: Management Techniques from the Best Damn Ship in the Navy*. New York: Warner Books, 2002.

Block, Peter. *Stewardship: Choosing Service Over Self-Interest*. San Francisco: Berrett-Koehler, 1996.

Bossidy, Larry, and Ram Charan. *Execution: The Discipline of Getting Things Done*. New York: Random House, 2002.

DePree, Max. *Leadership Is an Art*. New York: Dell Publishing, 1989.

Downey, Diane, with Tom March and Adena Berkman. *Assimilating New Leaders: The Key to Executive Retention*. New York: AMACOM, 2001.

Farson, Richard. *Management of the Absurd: Paradoxes in Leadership*. New York: Simon & Schuster, 1996.

Goleman, Daniel. *Primal Leadership: Realizing the Power of Emotional Intelligence*. Boston: Harvard Business School Press, 2002.

McCall, Morgan W., Jr. *High Flyers: Developing the Next Generation of Leaders*. Boston: Harvard Business School Press, 1998.

Welch, Jack, and John A. Byrne. *Jack: Straight from the Gut*. New York: Warner Books, 2001.

Servant Leadership

Greenleaf, Robert K. *Servant Leadership: A Journey into the Nature of Legitimate Power and Greatness*. Mahwah, N.J.: Paulist Press, 1977.

Melrose, Ken. *Making the Grass Greener on Your Side: A CEO's Journey to Leading by Serving*. San Francisco: Berrett-Koehler, 1995.

Secretan, Lance H. *Reclaiming Higher Ground: Building Organizations That Inspire Excellence*. New York: McGraw-Hill, 1997.

Performance Management

Coens, Tom, and Mary Jenkins. *Abolishing Performance Appraisals: Why They Backfire and What to Do Instead*. San Francisco: Berrett-Koehler, 2000.

Fournies, Ferdinand. *Coaching for Improved Work Performance.* New York: McGraw-Hill, 2000.

Employee Rewards and Recognition

Kouzes, James M., and Barry Z. Posner. *Encouraging the Heart: A Leader's Guide to Rewarding and Recognizing Others.* San Francisco: Jossey-Bass, 2003.

Lawrence-Lightfoot, Sara. *Respect: An Explanation.* New York: Perseus Books, 1999.

Nelson, Bob. *1001 Ways to Reward Employees.* New York: Workman Publishing, 1994.

Secretan, Lance. *Inspire! What Great Leaders Do.* Hoboken, N.J.: John Wiley & Sons, 2004.

Zingheim, Patricia K., and Jay R. Schuster. *Pay People Right! Breakthrough Reward Strategies to Create Great Companies.* San Francisco: Jossey-Bass, 2000.

Open-Book Management

Case, John. *Open-Book Management.* New York: HarperBusiness, 1995.

Stack, Jack, with Bo Burlingham. *The Great Game of Business: Unlocking the Power and Profitability of Open-Book Management.* New York: Doubleday, 1992.

Organizational Career Management

Bardwick, Judith. *Danger in the Comfort Zone: From Boardroom to Mailroom—How to Break the Entitlement Habit That's Killing American Business.* New York: AMACOM, 1995.

Farren, Caela, Beverly Kaye, and Zandy Liebowitz. *Designing Career Development Systems.* San Francisco: Jossey-Bass, 1988.

Kaye, Beverly. *Up Is Not the Only Way, 2nd Edition.* Palo Alto: Davies-Black Publishing, 2002.

Simonson, Peggy. *Promoting a Developmental Culture in Your Organization.* Palo Alto: Davies-Black Publishing, 1997.

Corporate Culture

Wright, Lesley, and Marti Smye. *Corporate Abuse: How "Lean and Mean" Robs People and Profits.* New York: Macmillan, 1996.

Abrashoff, D. Michael, 139
Addison, Greg, 40
advancement opportunities, *see* career
    opportunities
Agrawal, Vivek, 47
Allstate Insurance Company, psycho-
    logical contract, 35–36
Alston & Bird, 157
Applebees International, 88
appreciation, *see also* recognition
    creating culture of, 134
    employee responsibility for, 144–145
    focus on new hires, 137–138
    forms of expressing, 135
    improving physical environment,
      143–144
    lack of, 118
    "open book management," 141–142
    responding to employee input,
      139–140
Ash, Mary Kay, 118
AT&T, Resource Link program, 108
autonomy, 65

Ball, John, 135
benefit programs
    cost-benefit analyses, 164–165
    1999 *vs.* 2003, 160–164
    recent additions, 164
    strategic options, 198
blocking behavior
    of managers, 107–108
    time-in-grade policies, 108

Boorstin, Daniel J., 1
Bossidy, Larry, 49, 74

Cain, George, 188
Capital One Financial Corporation,
    screening of job applicants, 56
career contract, old *vs.* new, 98
career growth
    employee responsibility for, 99–100,
      114–115
    Lands' End program, 101
    manager responsibility for, 100
    organization responsibility for, 100
    signs of blockage, 99
    tools for, 101–102
    virtual career center, 102
career opportunities
    accessible information for, 103
    alternate career ladders, 103–105
    best practices, 101–113
    checklist, 216
    employee frustration with, 99
    as key to employee satisfaction, 97
    limits of, 93–97
    new realities, 97
    "SWAT Team" concept, 105
    A *vs.* B players, 111
career patterns, types of, 104
CenterBeam, Inc., 190
Cerner Corporation, 107
Chamales, Gerald, 192
Chambers, John, 142

Charles Schwab & Company, 102
chief talent officer, as newly created position, 50
Cisco Systems, 142
  human capital dashboards, 207
civility score, 153
coaching
  checklist, 216
  continuous, 78–80
  critical role in retaining employees, 72–73, 76–77
  five-step process, 82–83
  as key competency, 87
  lack of, 70–72
  management failure to provide, 73–74, 75
  as positive leadership style, 87
  tied to commitment, 73
Collins, Jim, 50, 187, 211
commitment, *vs.* compliance, 63
company loyalty, 158–159
compensation, *see also* pay
  based on job evaluations, 127
  benefit programs, *see* benefit programs
  broadbanding, 128
  competitive pay, 24–26
  executive pay, 184
  fairness of, 26
  less reliance on benchmarking, 128
  ranking systems, 85
  total rewards approach, 132–133
competence
  employees' need for, 20, 23–24
  as key to trust, 187
competencies
  coaching, 87
  employee access to listing of, 103
  feedback, 87
  as job requirements, 41–42
  leadership, 97
  mentoring, 108–109
  used in pay determination, 127
  used in talent review, 110

compliance, *vs.* commitment, 63
Connor, Wilton, 160
Container Store, The, 126, 157–158
Creal, Tom, 158–159
"culture of giving," 165–168

Davison, Barbara, 24
decision to leave, 27–28
deliberation process, 15–16
Deloitte & Touche, 165
DePree, Max, 93
D3 Inc., 161
disengagement, *see also* reasons for leaving
  cost of, 4
  decision to leave, 27–28
  "last straw" events, 13–14
  process, 11–15
  triggering events, 12–13, 75
Disneyland, "Eiffel Tower" organizational structure, 31
Driver, Michael, 104
Dunn, Debra, 86
Dunn, Peter, 202

Eliot, T.S., 31
emotional intelligence
  of managers, 81
  as selection factor, 87
employees
  adapting to company needs, 52
  attraction tracking measures, 208
  cost of replacement, 33
  feeling unappreciated, 118, 123–124
  listening and responding to, 139–141
  mismatched with job, 47–48
  natural talents of, 50
  partnering with company leaders, 83, 212–213
  placing trust in, 191–192
  role in matching process, 67–68
  social connectedness among, 169–171
  training, *see* training

employee selection, tracking measures, 209

employee turnover, *see* turnover

employer-of-choice scorecard, 207–211

employment branding strategies, 159

engagement strategies
  examples, 198–205
  lessons learned, 205
  linked with business objectives, 205–206

engagement-to-departure process, 12
  decision to leave, 27–28
  deliberation, 15–16
  disengagement, *see* disengagement

executive pay, disproportionate, 184

exit interviews
  effective use of findings, 221–222
  favorable conditions for, 219–222
  guaranteed confidentiality of, 220
  HR role in, 8–9
  independent interviewers used for, 219–220
  as last chance to retain talent, 222
  purpose of, 219
  to strengthen realistic job previews, 40–41
  surveys, 20
  traditional, 218

expectations, *see also* psychological contract
  matched against work realities, 215
  matching mutual, 36
  mismatches, 34–35
  unmet, 31 33, 37 38

expert career pattern, 104

Federal Express, management position preview, 43

feedback
  checklist, 216
  continuous, 78–80
  critical role of, 72–73
  360-degree, 80
  importance in employee retention, 73
  importance in job enrichment, 65–66
  as key competency, 87
  lack of, 70–72, 73–74, 75
  management failure to provide, 73–75
  to-do list for employees, 90
  upward evaluation system, 87

feedback culture
  creation of, 79–80
  at General Electric, 79

Financial Associates, "culture of giving," 166–167

First Biomedical, 158–159

First Tennessee National Corporation, 165

Fitz-enz, Jac, 17, 24

FleetBoston Financial, retention strategy, 203–205

Fournies, Ferdinand, 81, 82

fun in the workplace
  encouragement of, 171–174
  examples of, 173–174

General Electric, 88–89
  feedback culture, 79

Gen X and Gen Y workers
  career realities, 97
  customized rewards programs, 130
  lifestyle flexibility needs, 143
  pay options, 130

GeoAccess, realistic job previews, 39–40

Goleman, Daniel, 81, 87

Goodnight, Jim, 28, 160, 167

Gore, Bill, 191

Hackman, Richard, 65

Hartford, The, candidate tracking system, 55

health-care costs, impact on organizations, 154
Heskett, James, 154
hiring
  from within, 107
  criteria for, 57
  priorities, 41–42
  unfair decisions, 94
hiring process, *see also* interview process
  behavioral interviewing, 60
  multiple interviewers used in, 60
  reference checking, 61
Hock, Dee, 57
hope, employees' need for, 19, 23–24
Horn Group, The, 112
human resources
  role in engaging and retaining talent, 212
  role in exit interviews, 8–9
  role in retention strategy, 206–207
100 Best Places to Work in America *(Fortune)*
  Alston & Bird, 157
  applying for selection, 158
  The Container Store, 157–158
  J.M. Smucker Company, 156–157

IHS Help Desk, retention strategy, 201
information sharing, 141–142
integrity, as key hiring criterion, 57
interview process, *see also* hiring process
  establishing trust in, 44–45
  multiple interviewers used in, 60
  team member involved in, 42

Jet Blue Airways, 186
  "Principles of Leadership" program, 186
J.M. Smucker Company, 156–157
job candidates
  checklist for, 44
  hiring priorities, 41–42
  matched against job, 215

on-the-job experience preview, 42–43
  team member interviews of, 42
  tracking system for, 55
job descriptions
  competencies listing, 41–42
  critical success factor listing, 57
  need for realism, 41–42
job enrichment
  contributing factors, 65
  and task delegation, 66–67
job growth, *vs.* workforce growth, 7–8
job-person mismatch
  obstacles to preventing, 53–54
  signs of, 52–53
job-posting process, need for fairness, 106
job previews, *see* realistic job previews (RJPs)
job task assignment, 62–64

Kelleher, Herb, 28, 160
Kelly, W. Michael, 25, 26
Kennedy, John F., 196
Kinko's, 137
Kotter, John Paul, 34
Kovacevich, Dick, 185

labor pool, expansion of, 58
Lands' End, career self-management, 101
Laube, Sheldon, 190
Lawler, Edward, 154
Lawrence-Lightfoot, Sara, 192
leaders, *see* senior leaders
leadership
  competencies, 97
  gaps, 97
  styles, 87
Lee, Thomas, 14
linear career pattern, 104
listening to employees, 139–141

managers, *see also* senior leaders
   accountability for people results,
      87–89
   career coaching tools for, 102
   career growth blocking behavior,
      107–108
   failure to engage talent, 48–50
   failure to provide coaching, 74–75
   failure to provide feedback, 74–75
   failure to recognize employees,
      122–123
   partnering with employees, 83
   performance as reason for leaving, 22
   as performance coaches, 80–81
   role in attracting and retaining talent,
      212
   types of, 88–89
   use of feedback by, 79–80
Meers Marketing Communications,
      Inc., retention strategy, 201–202
Meers, Sam, 201–202
Melrose, Ken, 191–192
mentoring
   as competency, 108
   culture, 108–109
Millennials, 130
Motek Software, retention strategy, 200
motivated abilities, 50, 51

Neeleman, David, 186, 188
Nelson, Bob, 136–137
new hires
   coaching guidelines, 77–78
   entrance interviews, 64
   feedback guidelines, 77–78
   need for surveying, 43
   orientation programs, 138
   tracking measures, 209
   tracking quality, 61–62
   tracking success, 61–62
   welcoming practices, 137–138
Nicholson, Nigel, 70

nonperformers
   forced ranking systems, 86
   termination, 85–86

Oldham, Greg, 65
Organizational Civility Index, 153
organizational cultures
   of caring, 159, 168–169
   of giving, 160–161, 165–168
   people-management, 160
   of recognition, 134
organizations
   civility score, 153
   health-care cost impact, 154
   healthy *vs.* toxic, 152–154

part-time workers, as job candidates, 41
pay, *see also* compensation
   best practices, 126–128
   broad-banding, 128
   criteria for determining, 127
   customized options, 129–130
   as emotional issue, 124–125
   executive, 184
   inadequate, 120
   linked to value creation, 126–127
   monitoring of, 132
   as motivator, 125–128, 130–131
   on-the-spot payouts, 131
   total rewards approach, 132–133
   trends in, 127
   two-way communication about, 131
   variable, 128–130
peer mentoring, 109
people-management
   as corporate culture, 160
   as driver of profits, 154
performance appraisal, distinct from ca-
      reer development, 109
performance coaching, 80–81
performance management
   best practices, 83
   keys to effectiveness, 84–85

performance management (*continued*)
   partnering approach, 83
   traditional approach, 83
Peters, Tom, 140
Pfeffer, Jeffrey, 147
physical environment
   creating suitable, 143–144
   problems with, 121
poach rate, 25
post-exit surveys, 221
Price, Ann, 200
Princely Hotels, 111
"Principles of Leadership" program (Jet
   Blue), 186
promotion, unfair decisions, 94
psychological contract, 34–37
   obstacles to, 38–39
   sample, 35–36
Putzier, John, 25

Qualcomm, 168
quality of work life, links to profitability, 154–155

Rabinowitz, Eric, 201
realistic job previews (RJPs), 39–41
   guidelines, 40
   strengthened by exit interviews,
     40–41
reasons for leaving
   and competitive pay, 24–26
   and individual differences, 27
   initial dissatisfaction, 24
   preventable *vs.* unpreventable, 19
   statistical survey, 20–22
   unmet expectations, 31–33
   voluntary, 17–19
recognition, 136–137, *see also* appreciation
   creating culture of, 134
   employee responsibility for, 144–145
   forms of providing, 135
   lack of, 118

nonpay best practices, 133–135
   outdated programs, 136–137
referrals, as job candidates, 41
resources, providing employees with,
   142–143
retention
   HR role, 206–207
   strategies, 59, 198–205
   tracking of, 207
Rhinotek Computer Products, 192
RiverPoint Group, 172
roamer career pattern, 104
Rosenbluth, Hal, 143, 160

Saratoga Institute survey responses
   on competitive pay, 24–25
   on cost of turnover, 3
   on exit interviews, 8–9
   on lack of feedback, 71
   on reasons for leaving, 17–19
   on senior management, 179–182
   on unmet expectations, 32–33
   on workplace stress, 147–149
Sartain, Libby, 222
SAS Institute, Inc., 167
   "culture of giving," 167
Sasser, Earl, 154
Schlesinger, Leonard, 154
Schmidt, Kevin, 153
Schraad, Mark, 161
Schram, Jill Washington, 172
Schram, Jon, 172
Seagate Technology, 113
Secretan, Lance, 188
Security Benefit Group of Companies,
   The, 87
senior leaders
   actions and statements mismatch,
     189–190
   criteria for judging, 181
   distrust of, 182–183
   employee *vs.* shareholder value, 185
   greed *vs.* servant mentality, 184–185

inspiring trust in, 217
key concerns of workers about, 183–184
lack of integrity and trust, 180
"lean and mean" *vs.* "giving," 185–186
"Level 5," 187
partnership with employees, 212
perceived failures of, 180–182
role in engaging and retaining talent, 211–212
servant leader approach, 192
September 11 events, impact on workers, 97
Shroeger, Jennifer, 199
skill variety, 65
social connectedness, 169–171
and turnover reduction, 171–172
Social Security Administration, New Hire Orientation and Networking program, 138
spiral career pattern, 104
Springfield Remanufacturing Company, "open book management," 141
Stack, Jack, 141
Starbucks, 168
Steak and Shake, retention strategy, 202–203
stress
causes of, 151
survey statistics, 150–151
warning signs of, 151–152
stress relief
checklist, 217
employees' role in, 175–176
fun activities for, 171–174
Studer, Quint, 160
Stumpf, Charles, 166–167
succession management strategies, 110–111
Sullivan, John, 59, 138

sustained employee engagement, tracking measures, 209–210
Svet, David, 161

talent
actions to attract and retain, 207–210
competition for, 196
and "culture of giving," 165–168
expanding pool, 58–59
forecasting needs, 105–106
misconceptions about, 50–52
need for continuous upgrading, 54–55
need for focus on, 49–50
strategies for retaining, 59
success-factor analysis, 55–56
total rewards approach, 132–133
vs. skills and knowledge, 50–51
talent review strategies, 110
task completion, 65
task significance, 65
Tavern on the Green, New York, 140
Taylor, Bob, 102
TD Industries, 168
Tobias, Randall, 147
Toro Company, 191–192
Torre, Joe, 81
total rewards, 132–133
training
cash accounts for, 113
impact on profitability, 111–112
lack of, 95, 96
"soft-skills," 113
trends in, 113–114
Truman Medical Center, Kansas City, 113
trust
competence as key to, 187
employees' role in building, 193
established during interview process, 44–45
key role in company performance, 179

trust (*continued*)
  need for, 19, 23–24
  placed in the workforce, 191–192
turnover
  as "acceptable cost of doing busi-
    ness," 6
  cost of, 3–4
  as "disappointing loss," 6
  identifying root causes of, 5
  management attitudes toward, 5–6
  managers' beliefs *vs.* reality, 3
  reasons for leaving, *see* reasons for
    leaving
  reduced though social bonding,
    171–172
  turning points for, 13–14
  "unfolding model" (Lee), 14–15
  voluntary, 14

United Parcel Service, 113
  retention strategy, 198–200
USA 800 Inc., 201
USS Benfold, 139

variable pay
  attraction of, 129–130
  types of, 129
Vaughn, Laura, 140–141

Walgreen, Cork, 187–188
Walton, Sam, 186
war for talent, 6–7
  in Silicon Valley, 6
Waterman, Robert, 185
Welch, Jack, 78–79, 86, 88
Wells-Fargo Bank, 185
  on-the-job experience preview, 43
Whole Foods Markets, team approach
  to hiring, 61
W.L. Gore, 168
W. L. Gore and Associates, 191
worker shortage, and Baby Boomer retirement, 7
workforce (U.S.), *see also* employees
  disengagement of, 4
  generational differences, 97
  growth *vs.* job growth, 7–8
workplace
  encouraging fun in, 172–174
  stress in, *see* stress
workspace, *see* physical environment
worth, employees' need for, 19–20,
  23–24
Wynn, Steve, 143

Yum Brands, 136